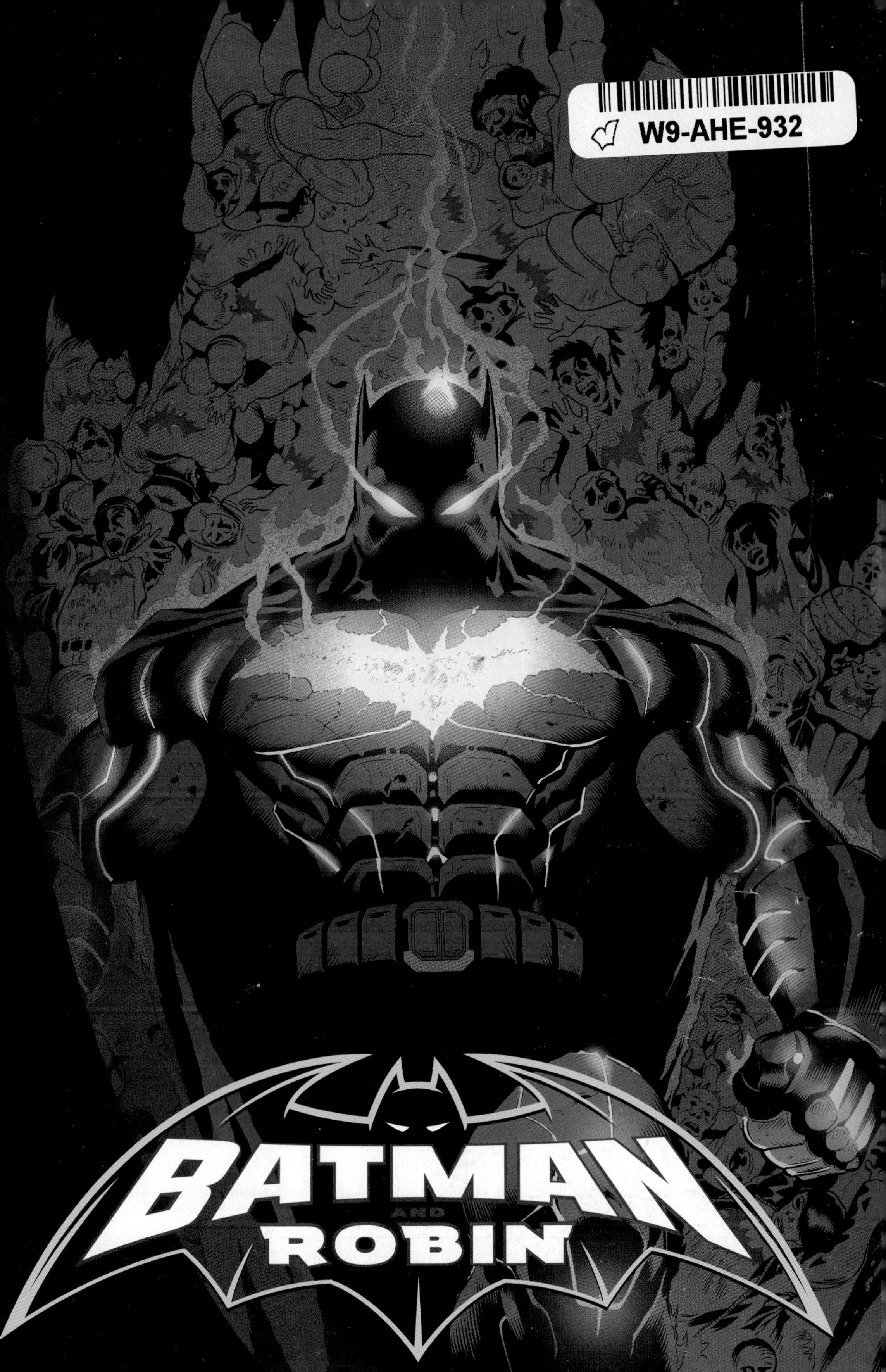
PAT MICK 2012

# BATMAN AND ROBIN

VOLUME 2 **PEARL**

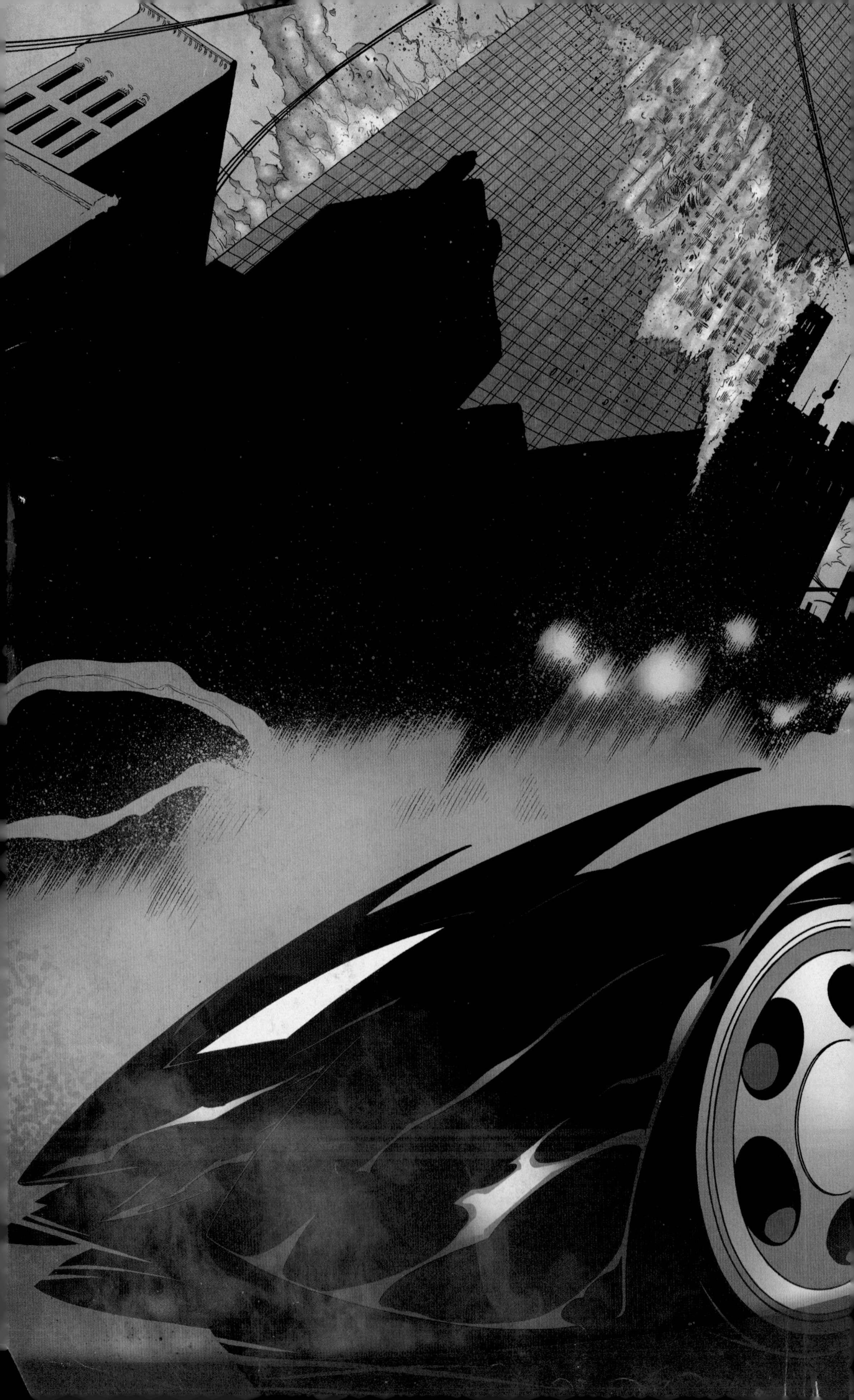

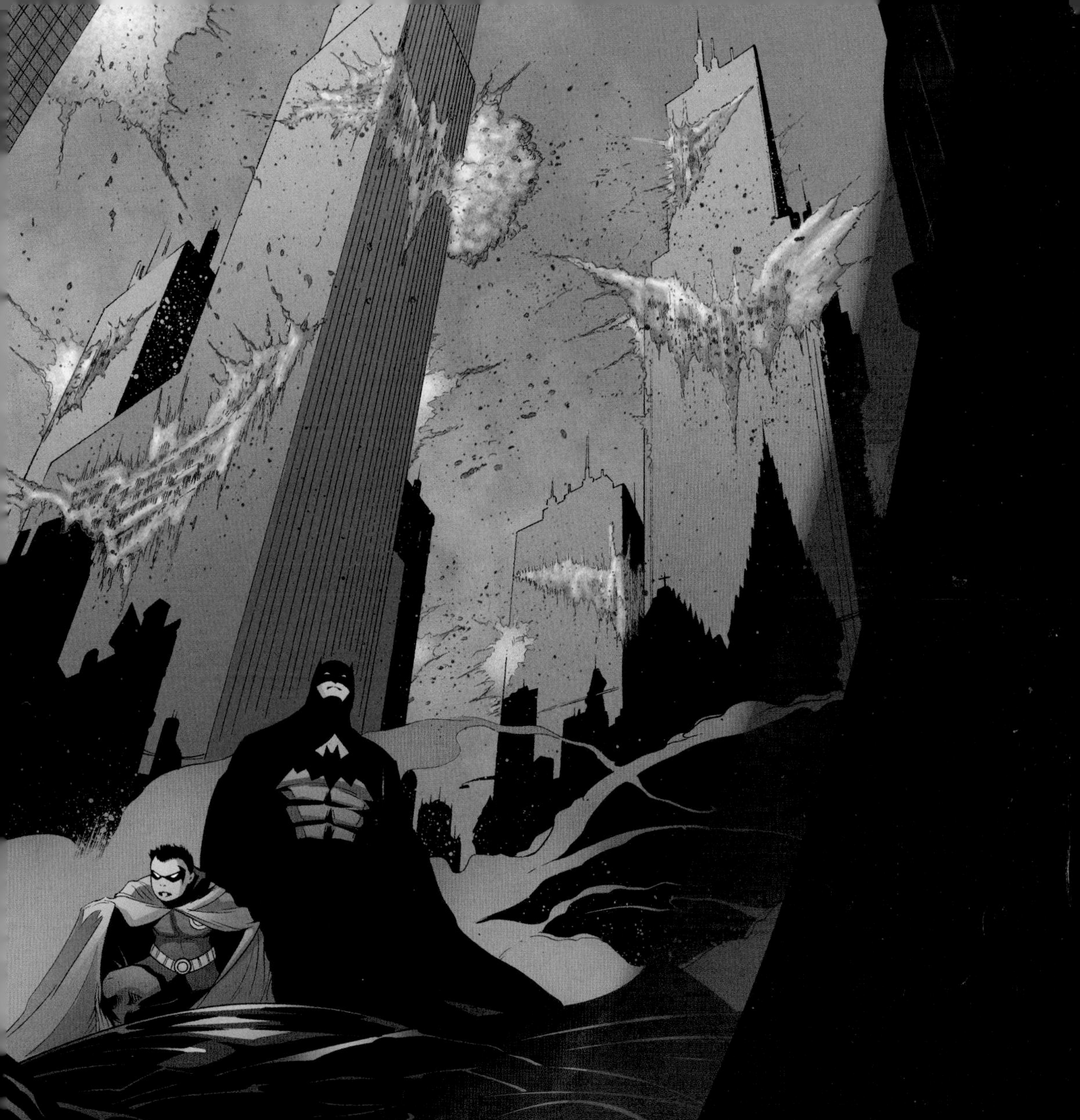

# BATMAN AND ROBIN

## VOLUME 2
## PEARL

PETER J. **TOMASI** writer

PATRICK **GLEASON** LEE **GARBETT**
ANDY **CLARKE** TOMAS **GIORELLO** pencillers

MICK **GRAY** RAY **MCCARTHY** KEITH **CHAMPAGNE**
TOM **NGUYEN** TOMAS **GIORELLO** inkers

JOHN **KALISZ** ALLEN **PASSALAQUA** **HI-FI** colorists

CARLOS M. **MANGUAL** DEZI **SIENTY** letterers

PATRICK **GLEASON**, MICK **GRAY** & JOHN **KALISZ**
collection & original series cover artists

**BATMAN** created by BOB **KANE**

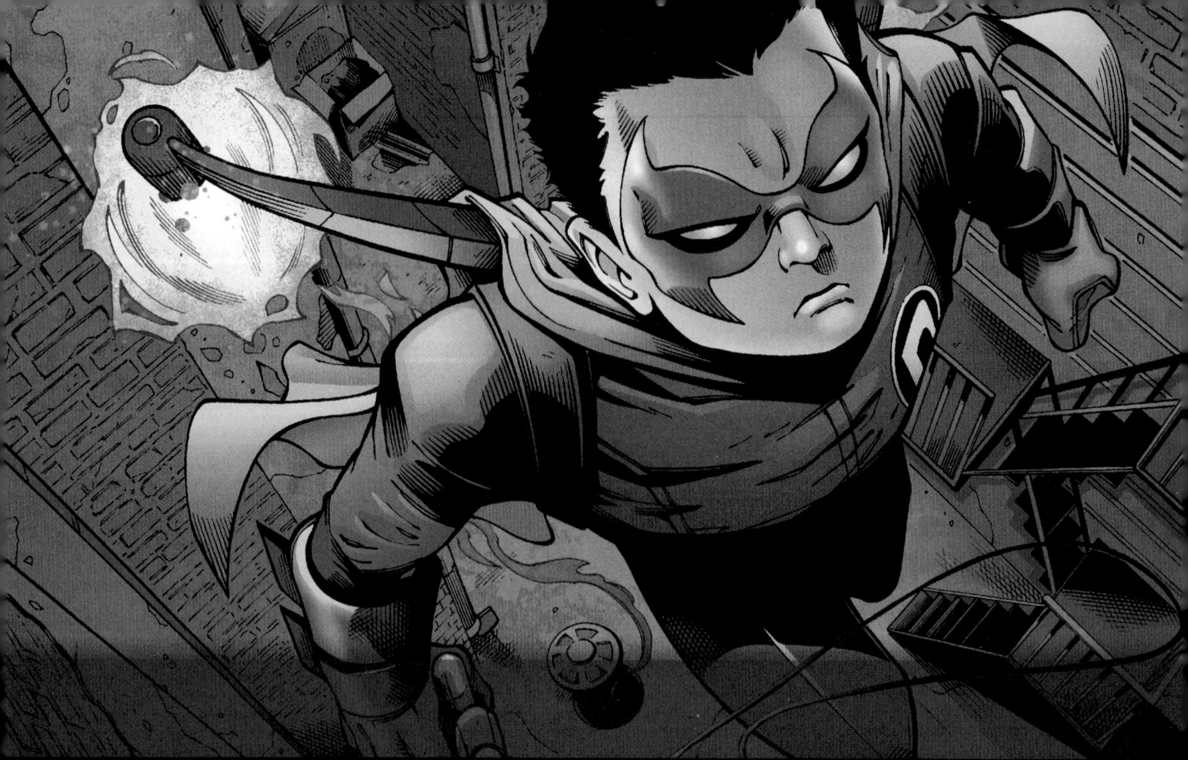

RACHEL GLUCKSTERN MIKE MARTS Editors - Original Series HARVEY RICHARDS Associate Editor - Original Series
RICKEY PURDIN KATIE KUBERT Assistant Editors - Original Series RACHEL PINNELAS Editor
ROBBIN BROSTERMAN Design Director - Books ROBBIE BIEDERMAN Publication Design

BOB HARRAS Senior VP - Editor-in-Chief, DC Comics

DIANE NELSON President DAN DIDIO and JIM LEE Co-Publishers
GEOFF JOHNS Chief Creative Officer
JOHN ROOD Executive VP - Sales, Marketing and Business Development
AMY GENKINS Senior VP - Business and Legal Affairs NAIRI GARDINER Senior VP - Finance
JEFF BOISON VP - Publishing Planning MARK CHIARELLO VP - Art Direction and Design
JOHN CUNNINGHAM VP - Marketing TERRI CUNNINGHAM VP - Editorial Administration
ALISON GILL Senior VP - Manufacturing and Operations HANK KANALZ Senior VP - Vertigo and Integrated Publishing
JAY KOGAN VP - Business and Legal Affairs, Publishing JACK MAHAN VP - Business Affairs, Talent
NICK NAPOLITANO VP - Manufacturing Administration SUE POHJA VP - Book Sales
COURTNEY SIMMONS Senior VP - Publicity BOB WAYNE Senior VP - Sales

BATMAN AND ROBIN VOLUME 2: PEARL


DC Comics, 1700 Broadway, New York, NY 10019
A Warner Bros. Entertainment Company.
Printed by RR Donnelley, Salem, VA, USA. 10/25/13. First Printing.

ISBN: 978-1-4012-4267-1

SUSTAINABLE FORESTRY INITIATIVE Certified Chain of Custody
At Least 20% Certified Forest Content
www.sfiprogram.org
SFI-01042
APPLIES TO TEXT STOCK ONLY

Library of Congress Cataloging-in-Publication Data

Tomasi, Peter, author.
Batman and Robin. Volume 2, Pearl / Peter J. Tomasi, Patrick Gleason.
pages cm
"Originally published in single magazine form in Batman and Robin 9-14, 0."
ISBN 978-1-4012-4089-9
1. Graphic novels. I. Gleason, Patrick, illustrator. II. Title. III. Title: Pearl.
PN6728.B36T644 2013
741.5'973—dc23
2012050765

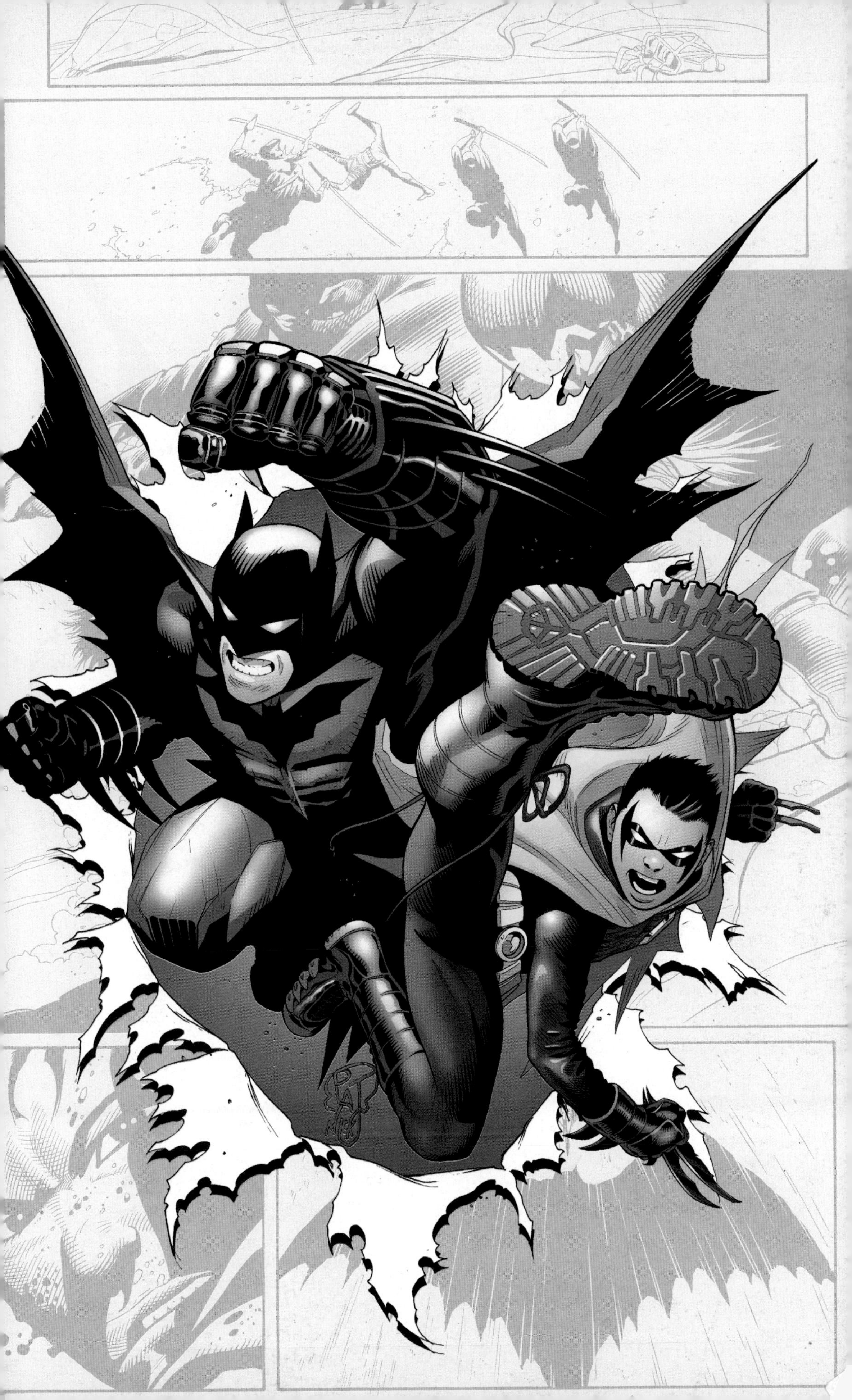

## SOMEDAY NEVER COMES

**PETER J. TOMASI** writer **PATRICK GLEASON** penciller **MICK GRAY** inker
cover by **GLEASON, GRAY & KALISZ**

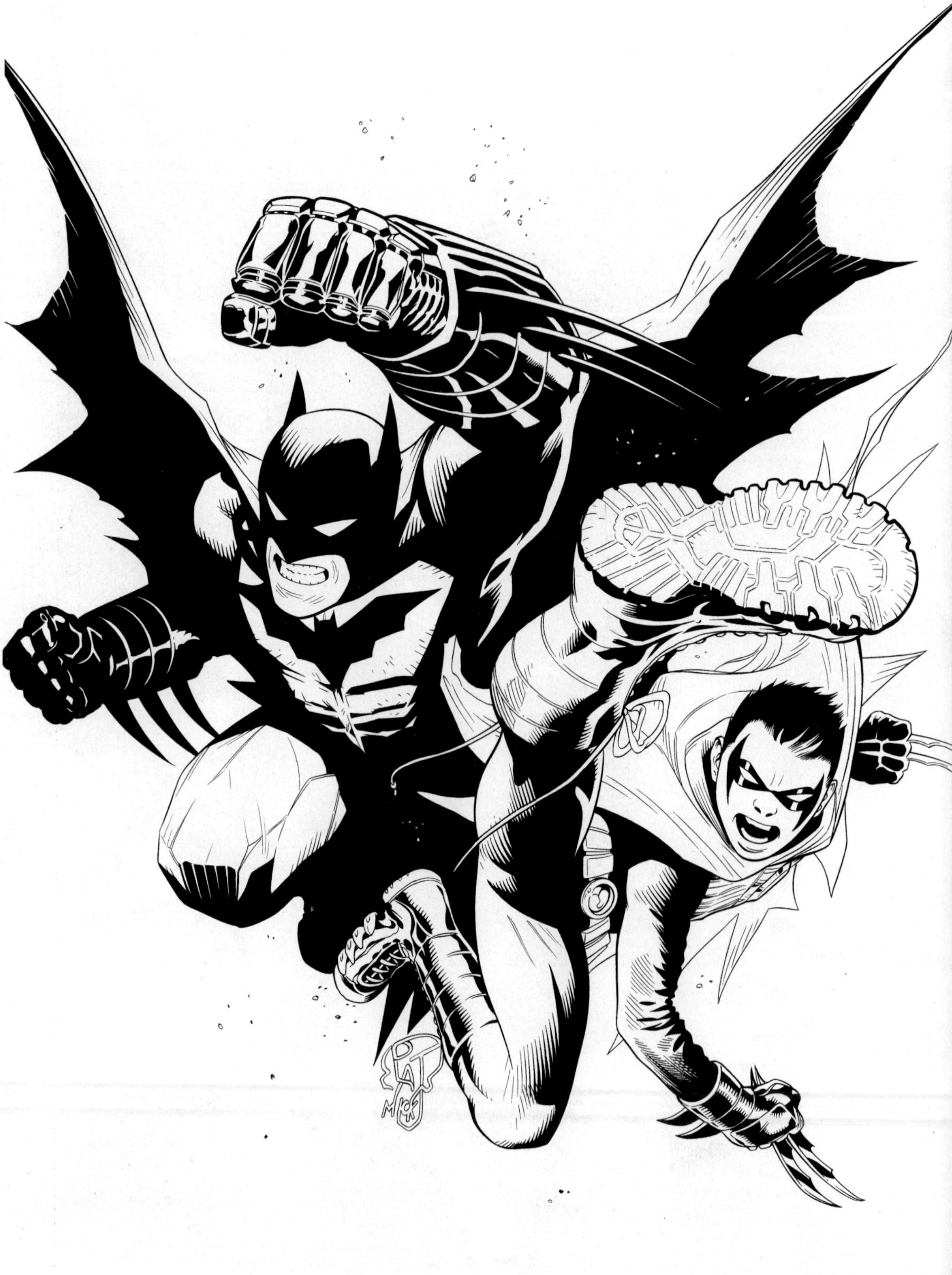

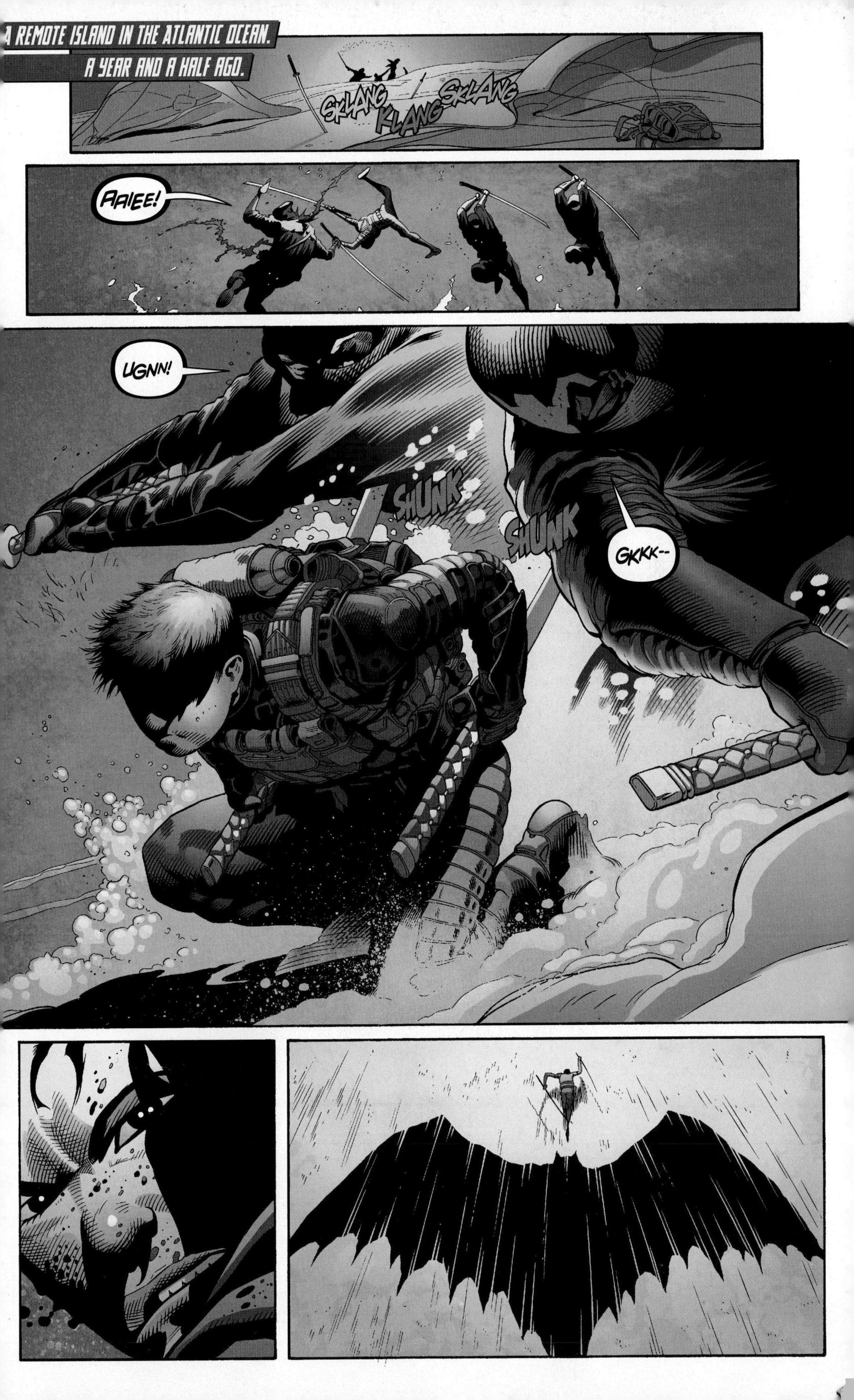
A REMOTE ISLAND IN THE ATLANTIC OCEAN.
A YEAR AND A HALF AGO.
SKLANG
KLANG
SKLANG
AAIEE!
UGNN!
SHUNK
SHUNK
GKKK--

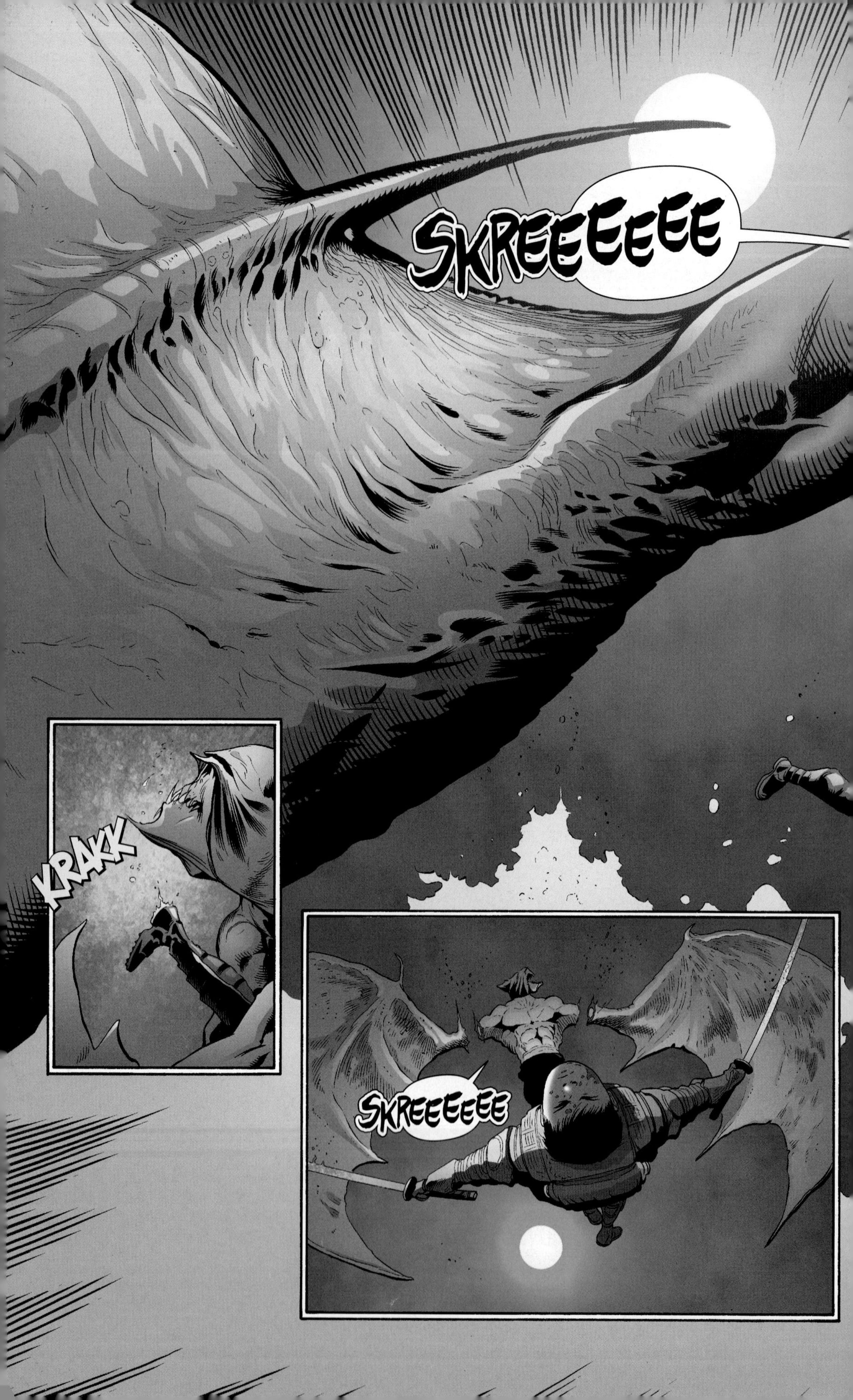
SKREEEEEEE
KRAKK
SKREEEEEEE

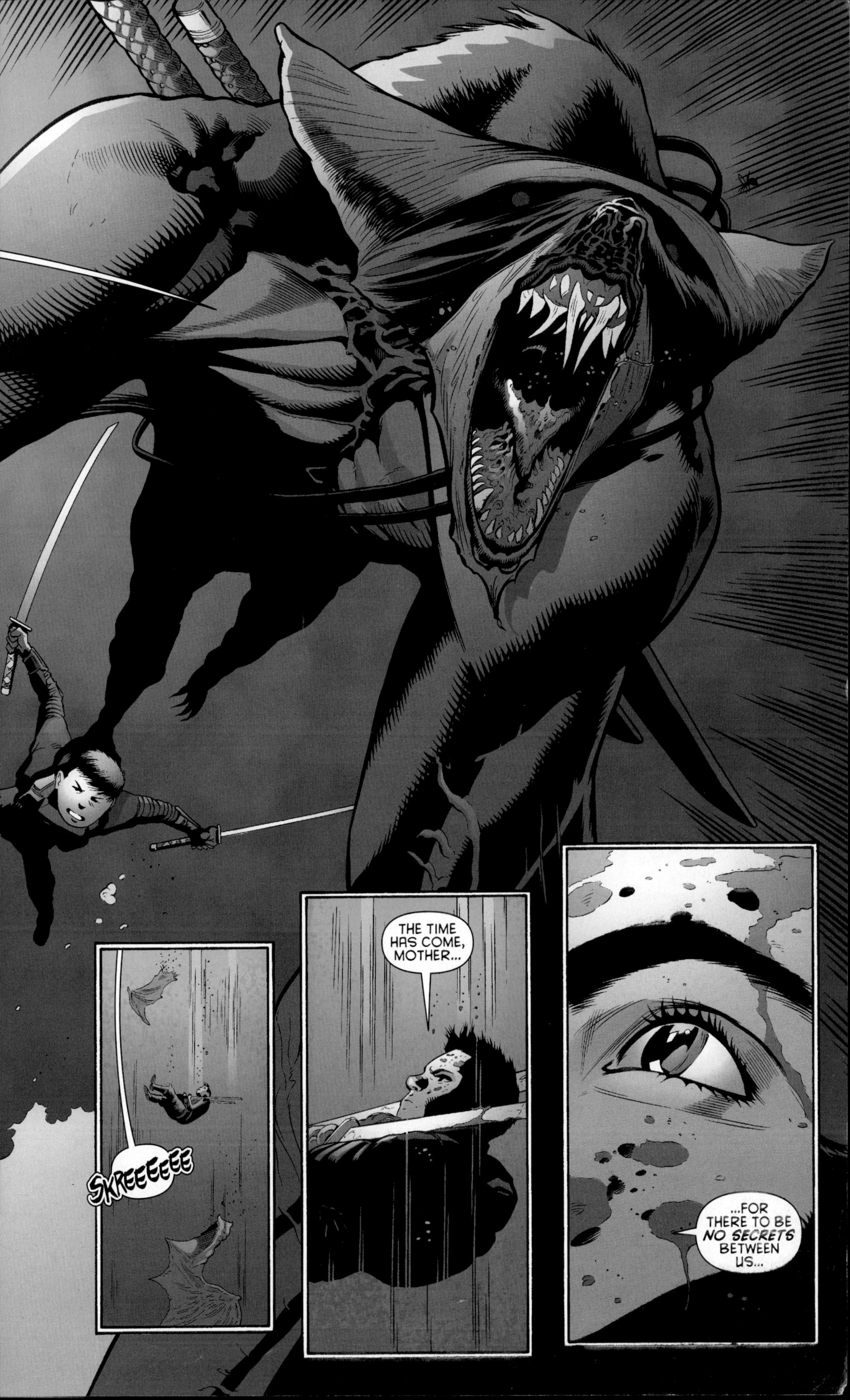
SKREEEEEE
THE TIME HAS COME, MOTHER...
...FOR THERE TO BE NO SECRETS BETWEEN US...

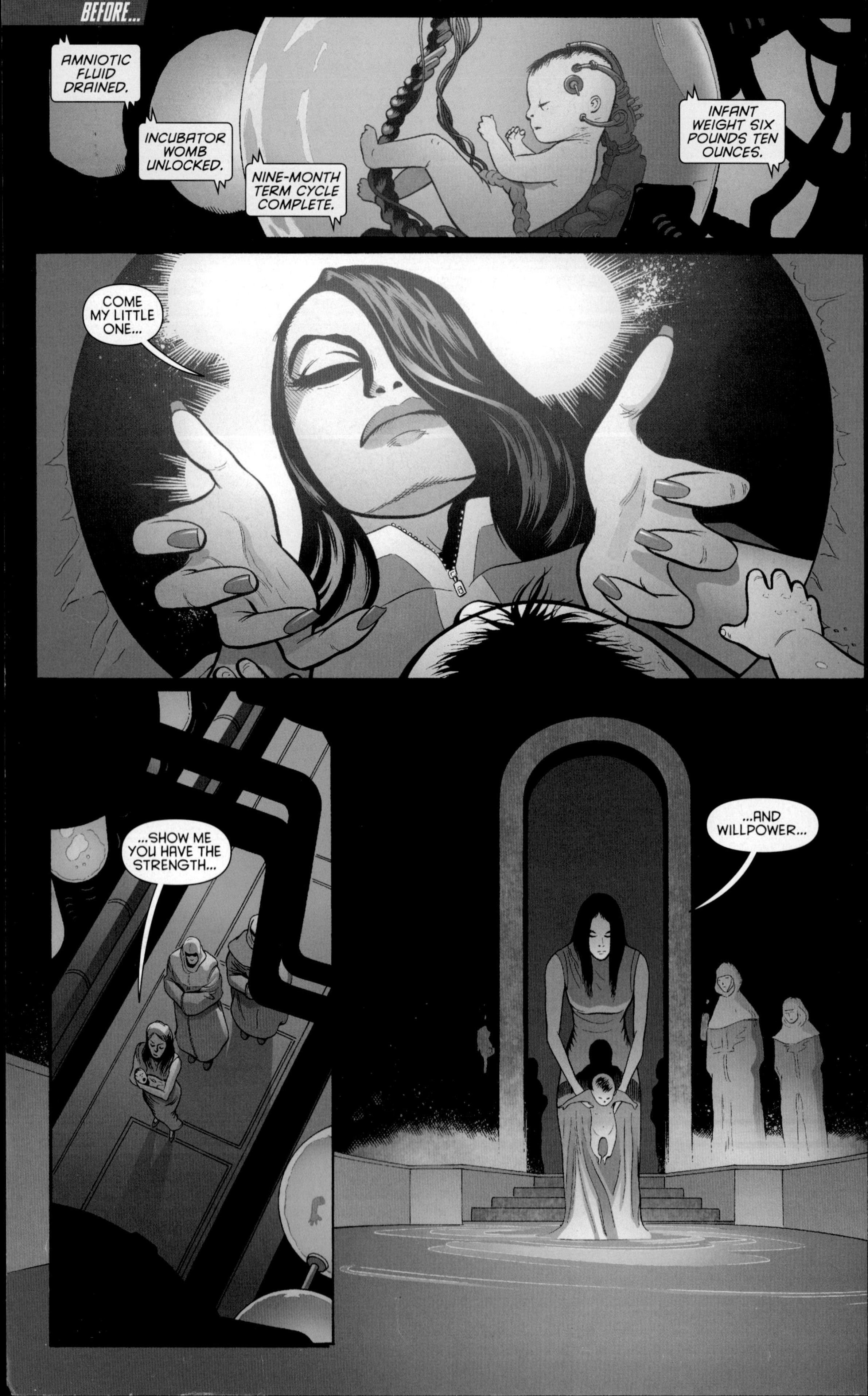
BEFORE...
AMNIOTIC FLUID DRAINED.
INCUBATOR WOMB UNLOCKED.
NINE-MONTH TERM CYCLE COMPLETE.
INFANT WEIGHT SIX POUNDS TEN OUNCES.
COME MY LITTLE ONE...
...SHOW ME YOU HAVE THE STRENGTH...
...AND WILLPOWER...

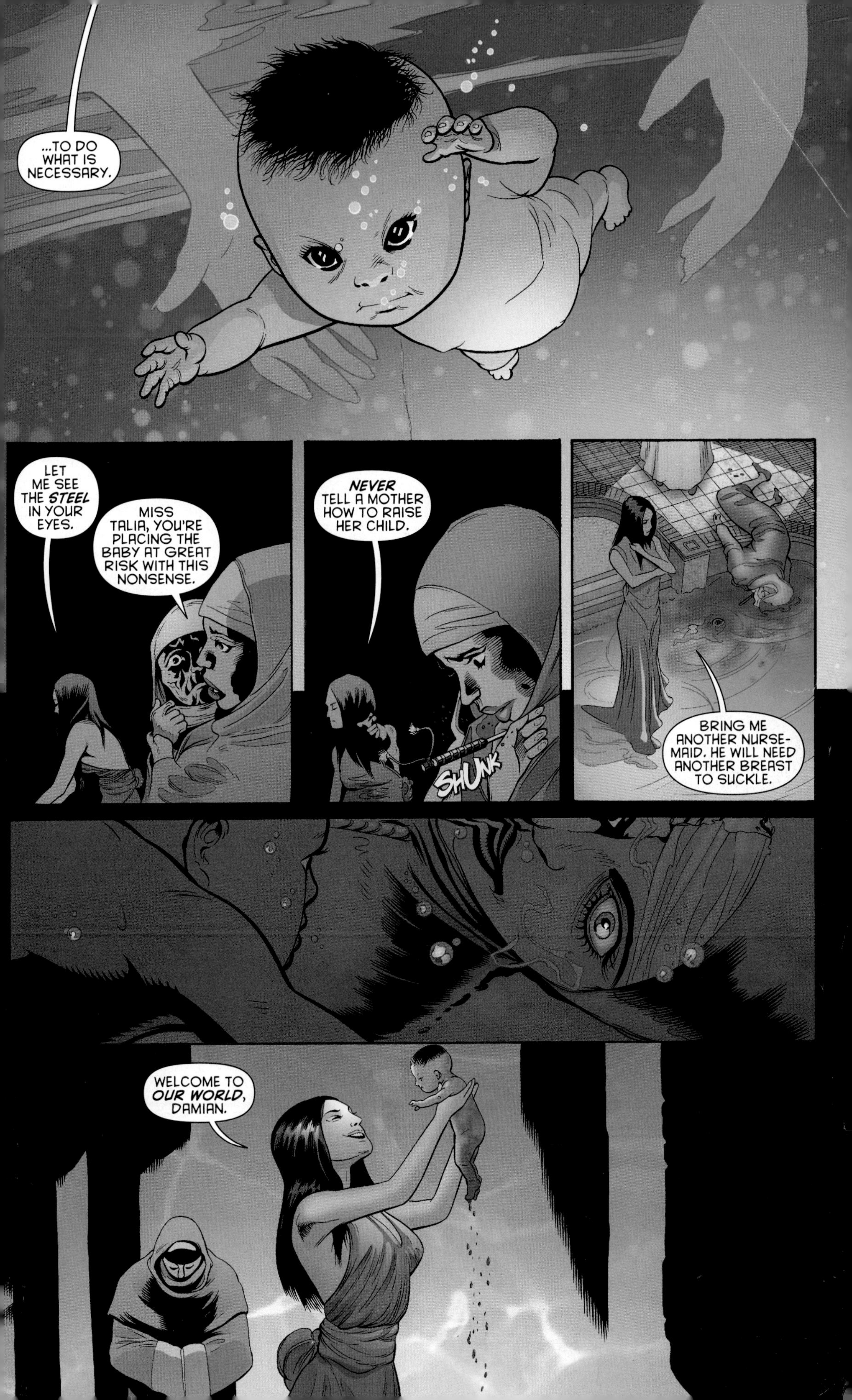
...TO DO WHAT IS NECESSARY.
LET ME SEE THE STEEL IN YOUR EYES.
MISS TALIA, YOU'RE PLACING THE BABY AT GREAT RISK WITH THIS NONSENSE.
NEVER TELL A MOTHER HOW TO RAISE HER CHILD.
SHUNK
BRING ME ANOTHER NURSE-MAID. HE WILL NEED ANOTHER BREAST TO SUCKLE.
WELCOME TO OUR WORLD, DAMIAN.

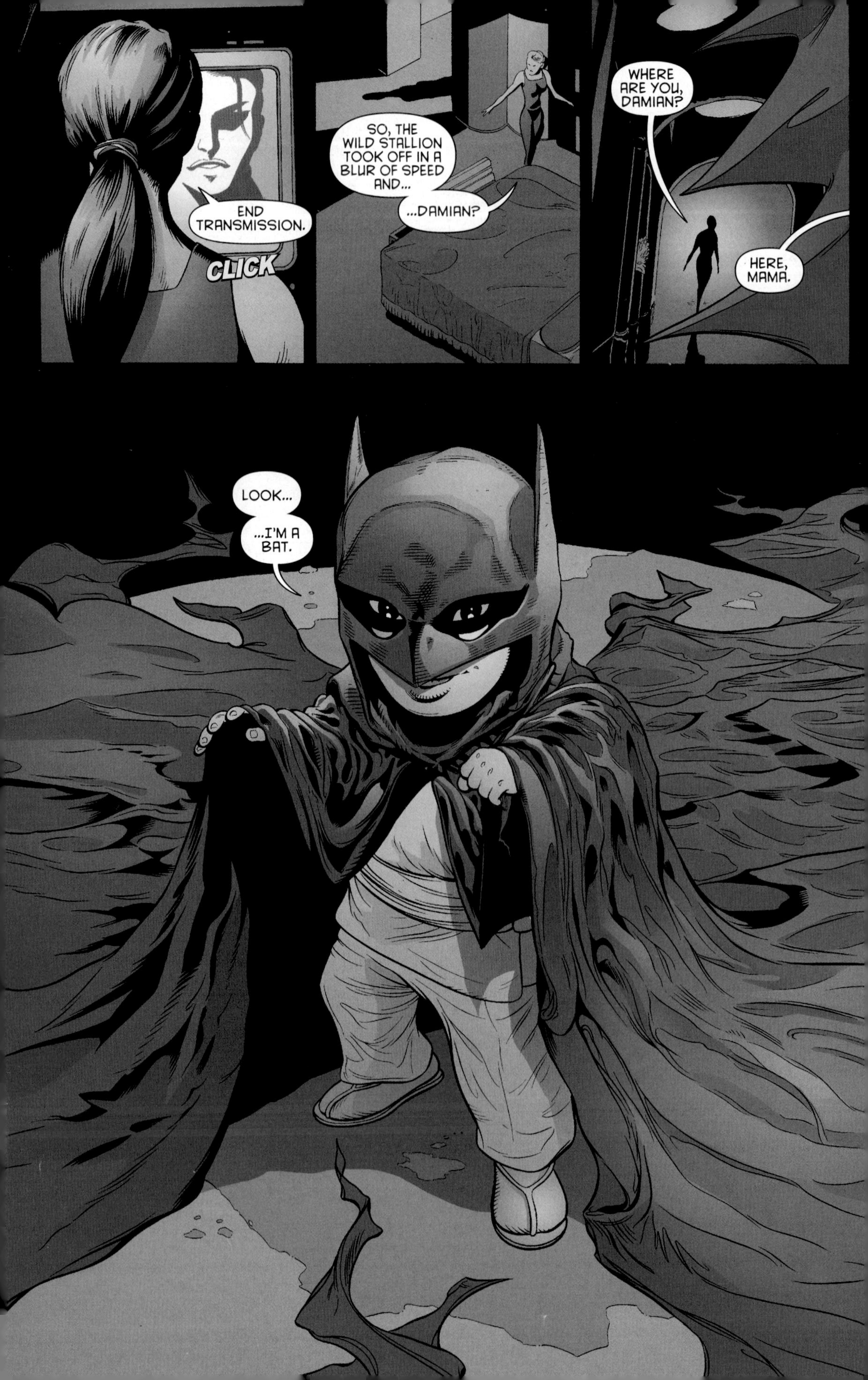
END TRANSMISSION.
CLICK
SO, THE WILD STALLION TOOK OFF IN A BLUR OF SPEED AND...
...DAMIAN?
WHERE ARE YOU, DAMIAN?
HERE, MAMA.
LOOK...
...I'M A BAT.

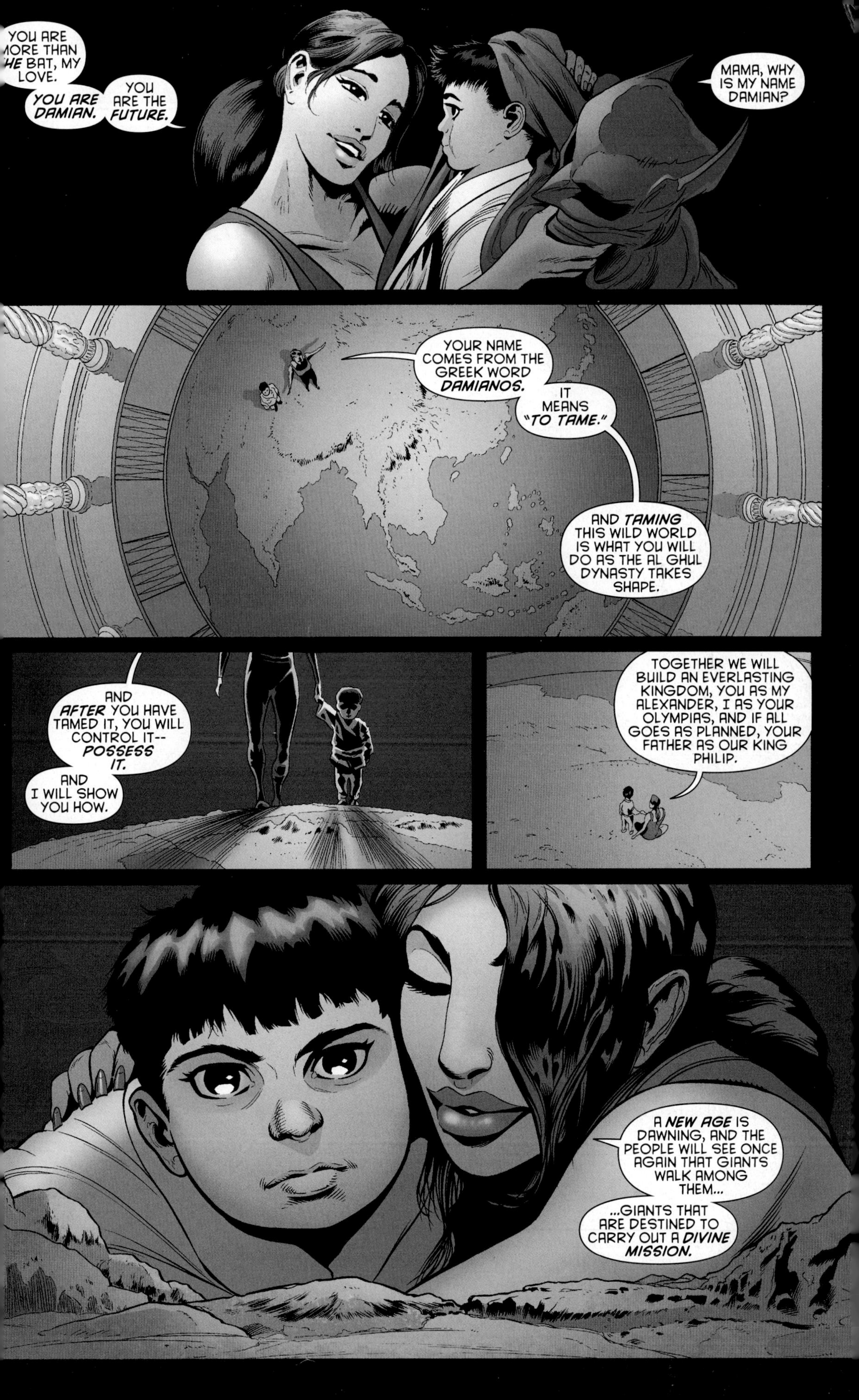

YOU ARE MORE THAN THE BAT, MY LOVE.
YOU ARE DAMIAN.
YOU ARE THE FUTURE.
MAMA, WHY IS MY NAME DAMIAN?
YOUR NAME COMES FROM THE GREEK WORD DAMIANOS.
IT MEANS "TO TAME."
AND TAMING THIS WILD WORLD IS WHAT YOU WILL DO AS THE AL GHUL DYNASTY TAKES SHAPE.
AND AFTER YOU HAVE TAMED IT, YOU WILL CONTROL IT-- POSSESS IT.
AND I WILL SHOW YOU HOW.
TOGETHER WE WILL BUILD AN EVERLASTING KINGDOM, YOU AS MY ALEXANDER, I AS YOUR OLYMPIAS, AND IF ALL GOES AS PLANNED, YOUR FATHER AS OUR KING PHILIP.
A NEW AGE IS DAWNING, AND THE PEOPLE WILL SEE ONCE AGAIN THAT GIANTS WALK AMONG THEM...
...GIANTS THAT ARE DESTINED TO CARRY OUT A DIVINE MISSION.

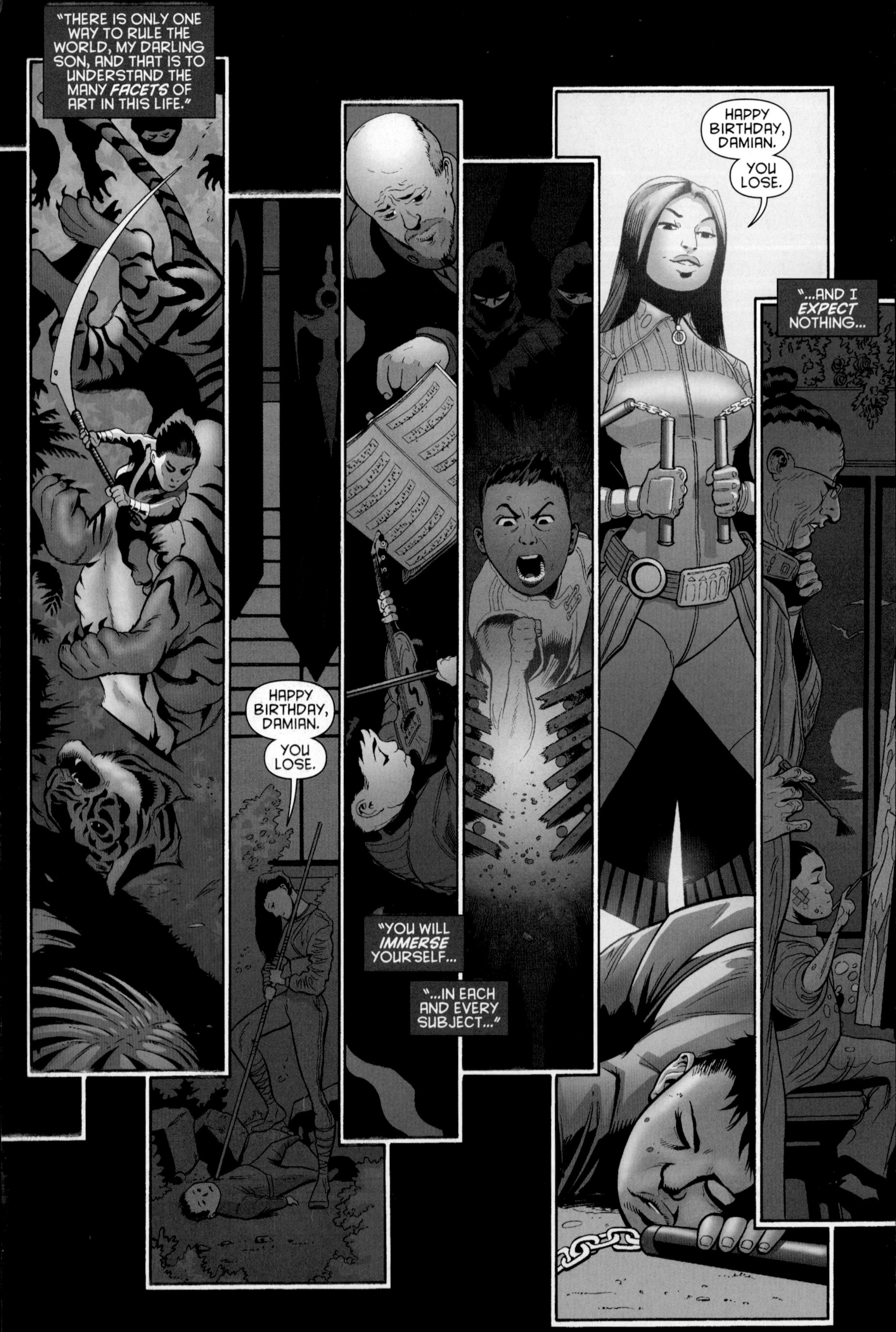
"THERE IS ONLY ONE WAY TO RULE THE WORLD, MY DARLING SON, AND THAT IS TO UNDERSTAND THE MANY FACETS OF ART IN THIS LIFE."
HAPPY BIRTHDAY, DAMIAN.
YOU LOSE.
"YOU WILL IMMERSE YOURSELF...
"...IN EACH AND EVERY SUBJECT..."
HAPPY BIRTHDAY, DAMIAN.
YOU LOSE.
"...AND I EXPECT NOTHING...

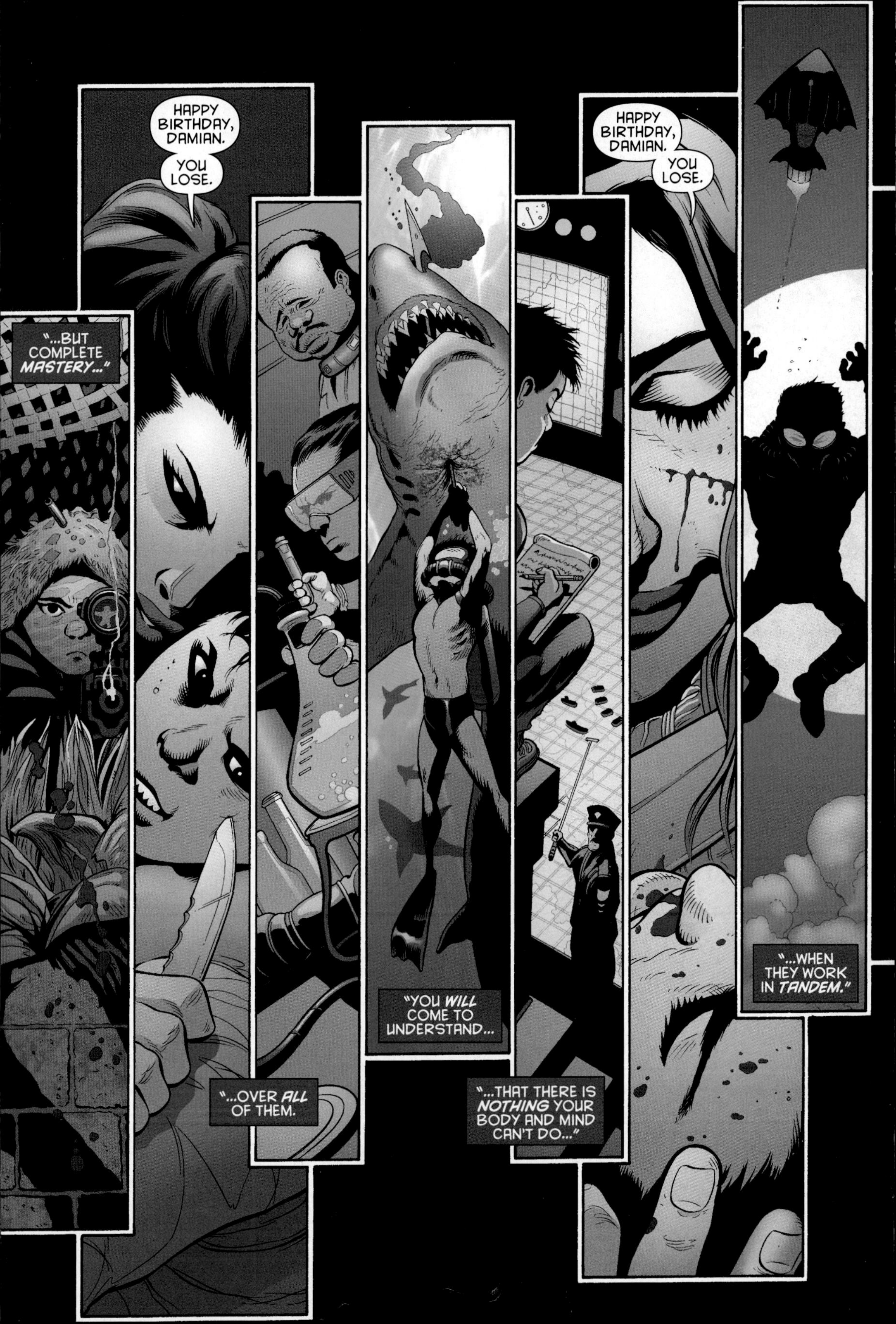
"...BUT COMPLETE MASTERY..."
HAPPY BIRTHDAY, DAMIAN.
YOU LOSE.
"...OVER ALL OF THEM.
"YOU WILL COME TO UNDERSTAND...
"...THAT THERE IS NOTHING YOUR BODY AND MIND CAN'T DO..."
HAPPY BIRTHDAY, DAMIAN.
YOU LOSE.
"...WHEN THEY WORK IN TANDEM."

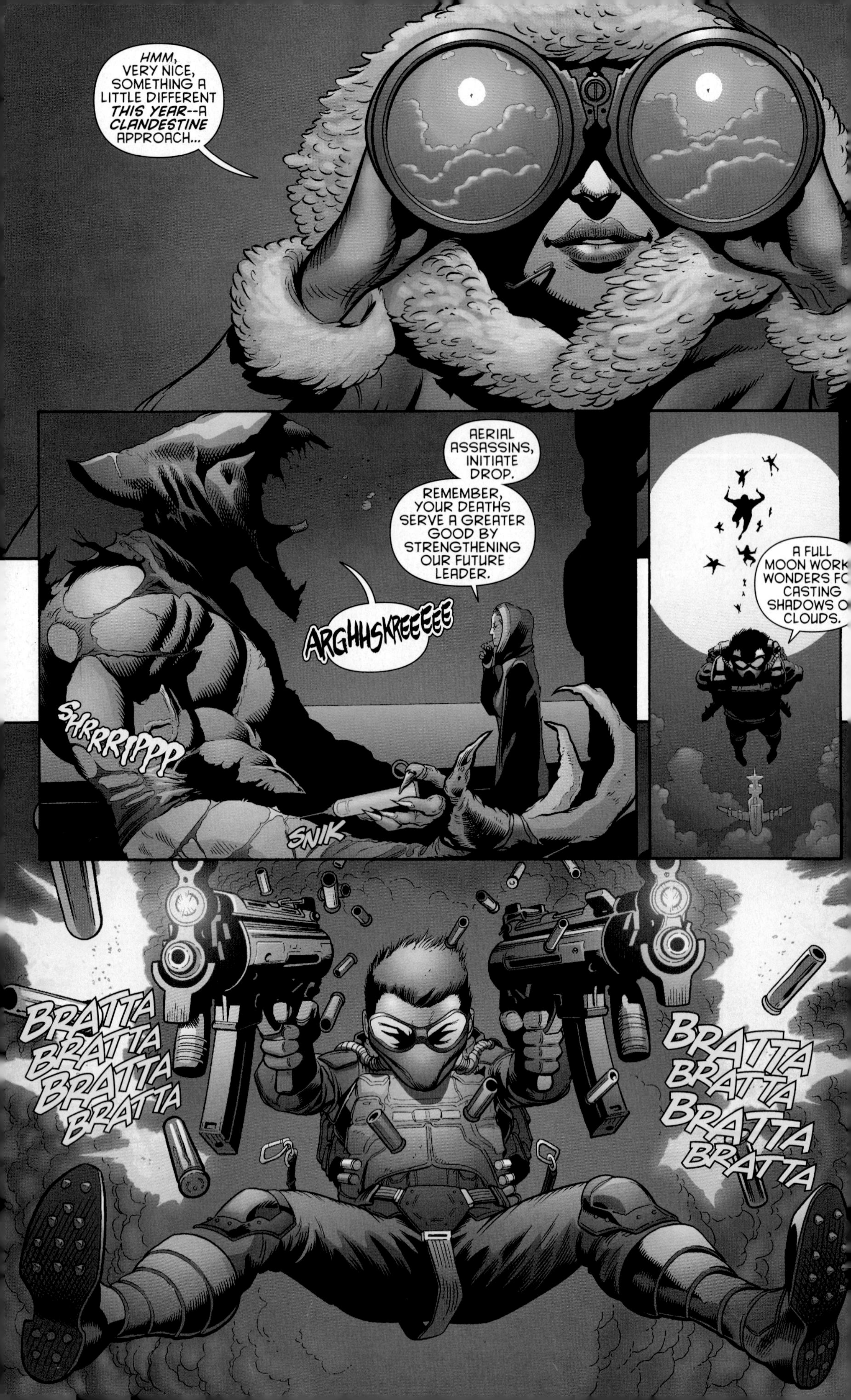
HMM, VERY NICE, SOMETHING A LITTLE DIFFERENT *THIS YEAR*--A *CLANDESTINE* APPROACH...
AERIAL ASSASSINS, INITIATE DROP.
REMEMBER, YOUR DEATHS SERVE A GREATER GOOD BY STRENGTHENING OUR FUTURE LEADER.
ARGHHSKREEEEEE
SHRRRIPPP
SNIK
A FULL MOON WORK WONDERS FC CASTING SHADOWS O CLOUDS.
BRATTA BRATTA BRATTA BRATTA
BRATTA BRATTA BRATTA BRATTA

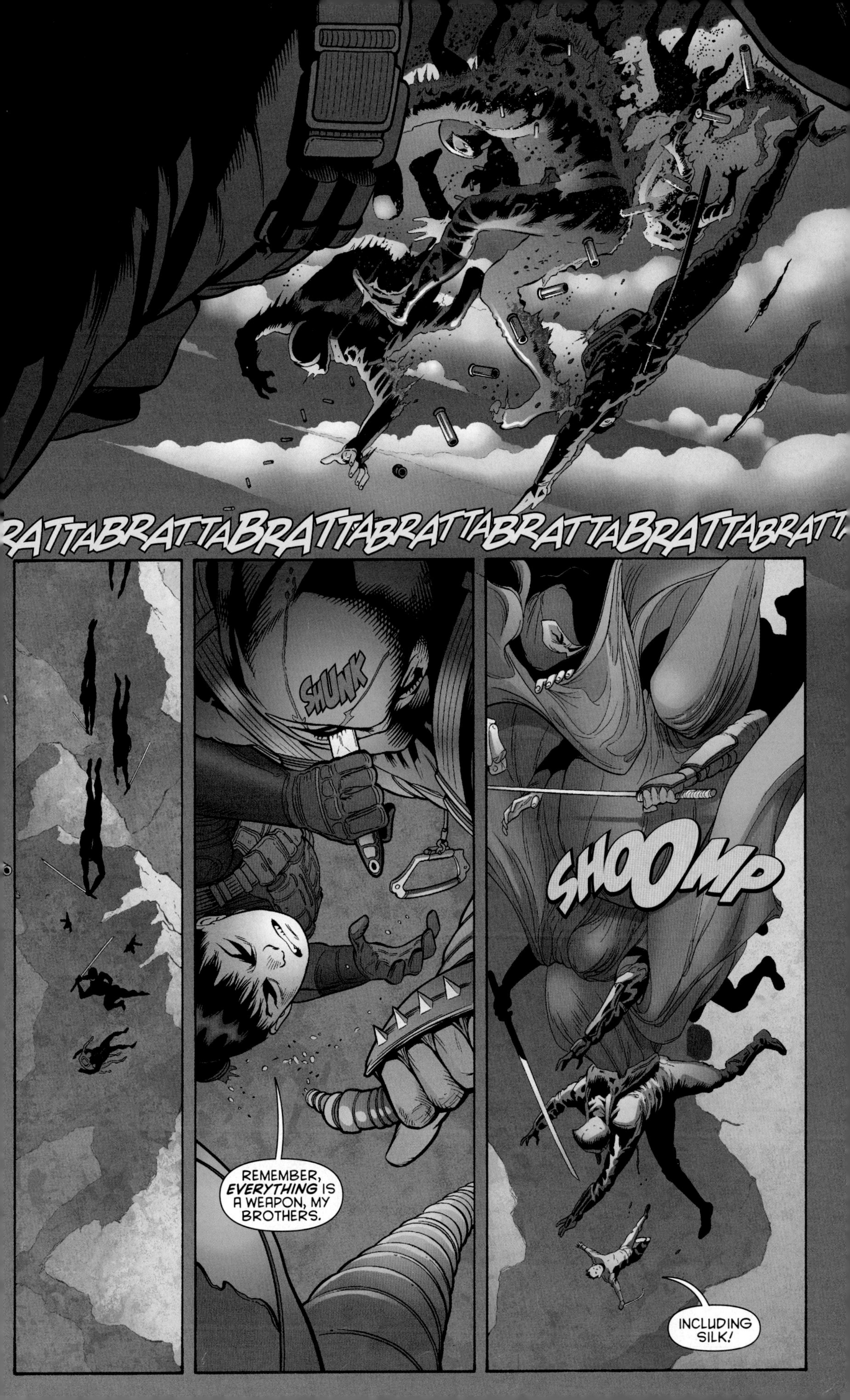
RATTABRATTABRATTABRATTABRATTABRATTABRATT
SHUNK
REMEMBER, EVERYTHING IS A WEAPON, MY BROTHERS.
SHOOOMP
INCLUDING SILK!

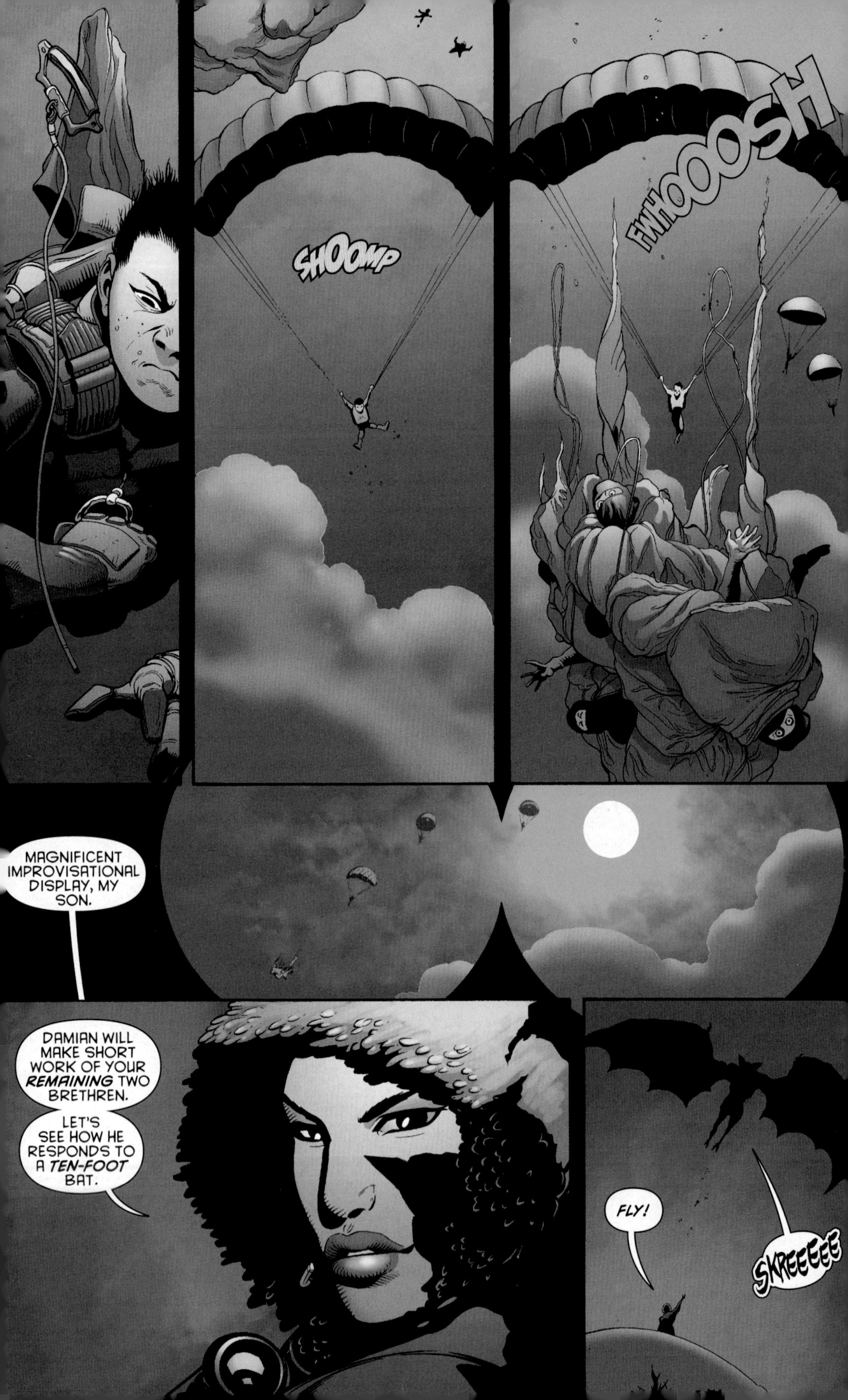
SHOOMP
FWHOOOOSH
MAGNIFICENT IMPROVISATIONAL DISPLAY, MY SON.
DAMIAN WILL MAKE SHORT WORK OF YOUR *REMAINING* TWO BRETHREN.
LET'S SEE HOW HE RESPONDS TO A *TEN-FOOT* BAT.
FLY!
SKREEEEEE

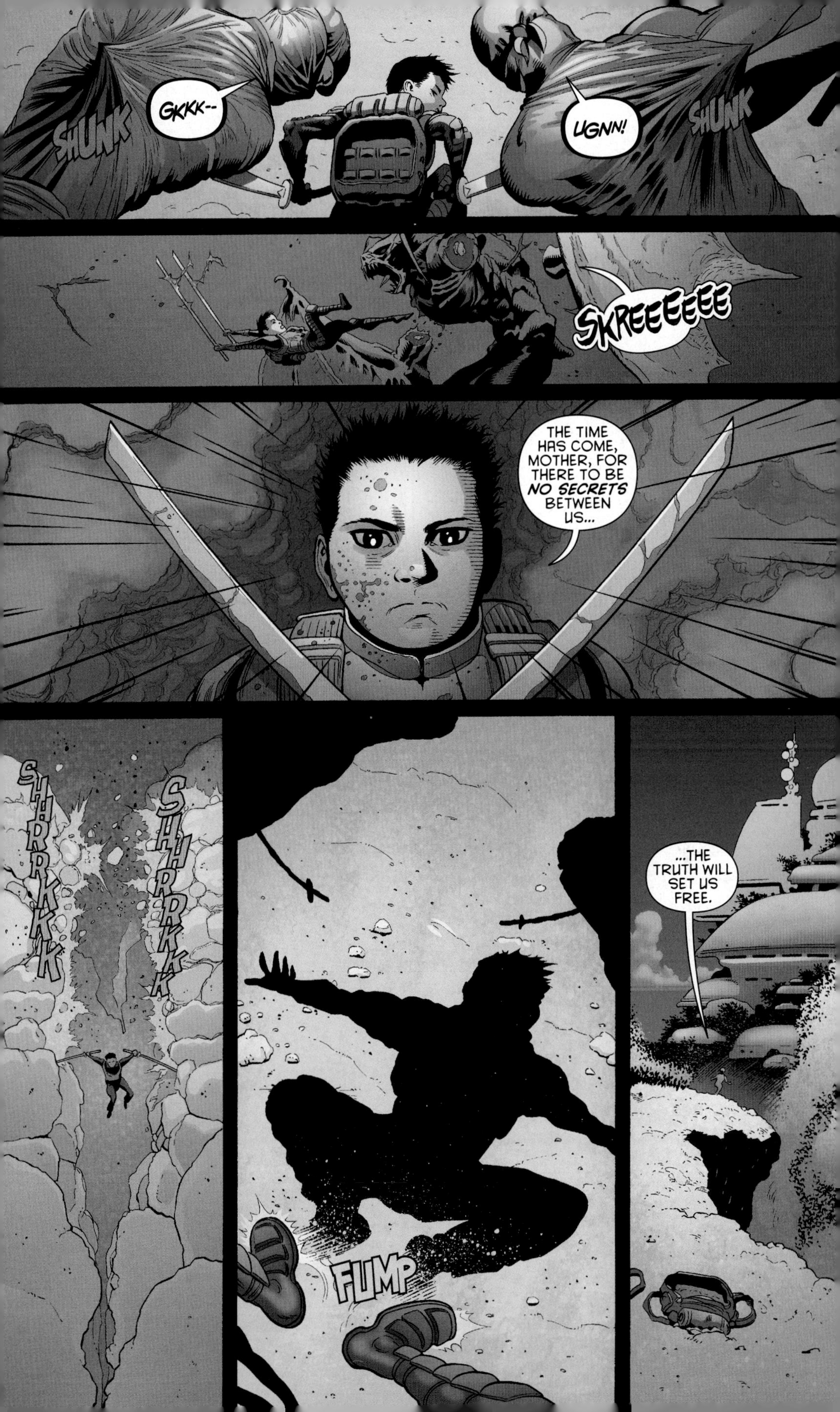
SHUNK
GKKK--
UGNN!
SHUNK
SKREEEEEEE
THE TIME HAS COME, MOTHER, FOR THERE TO BE *NO SECRETS* BETWEEN US...
SHHRRKKK
SHHRRKKK
FLUMP
...THE TRUTH WILL SET US FREE.

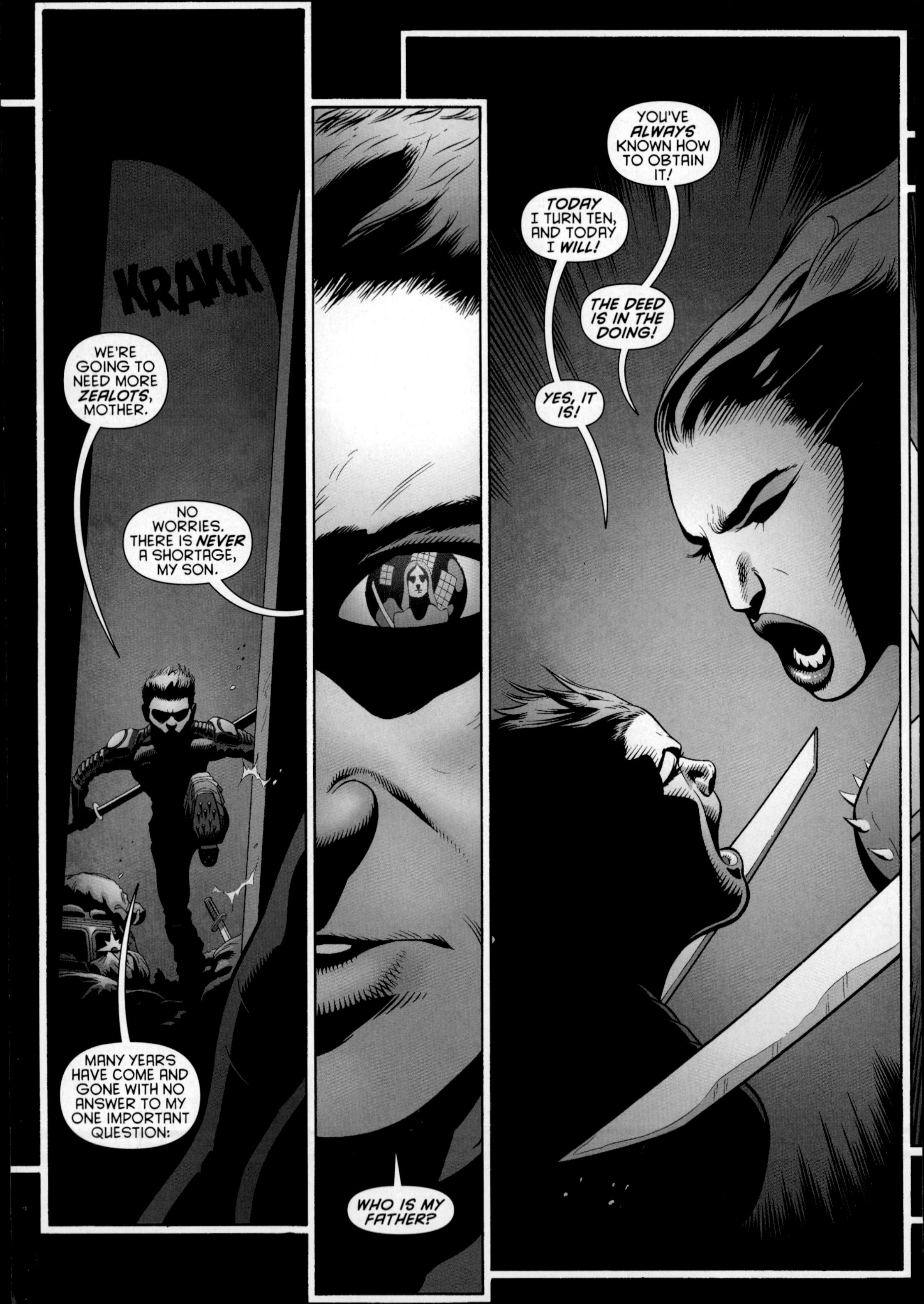
KRAKK
WE'RE GOING TO NEED MORE *ZEALOTS*, MOTHER.
NO WORRIES. THERE IS *NEVER* A SHORTAGE, MY SON.
MANY YEARS HAVE COME AND GONE WITH NO ANSWER TO MY ONE IMPORTANT QUESTION:
*WHO IS MY FATHER?*
YOU'VE *ALWAYS* KNOWN HOW TO OBTAIN IT!
*TODAY* I TURN TEN, AND TODAY I *WILL!*
*THE DEED IS IN THE DOING!*
*YES, IT IS!*

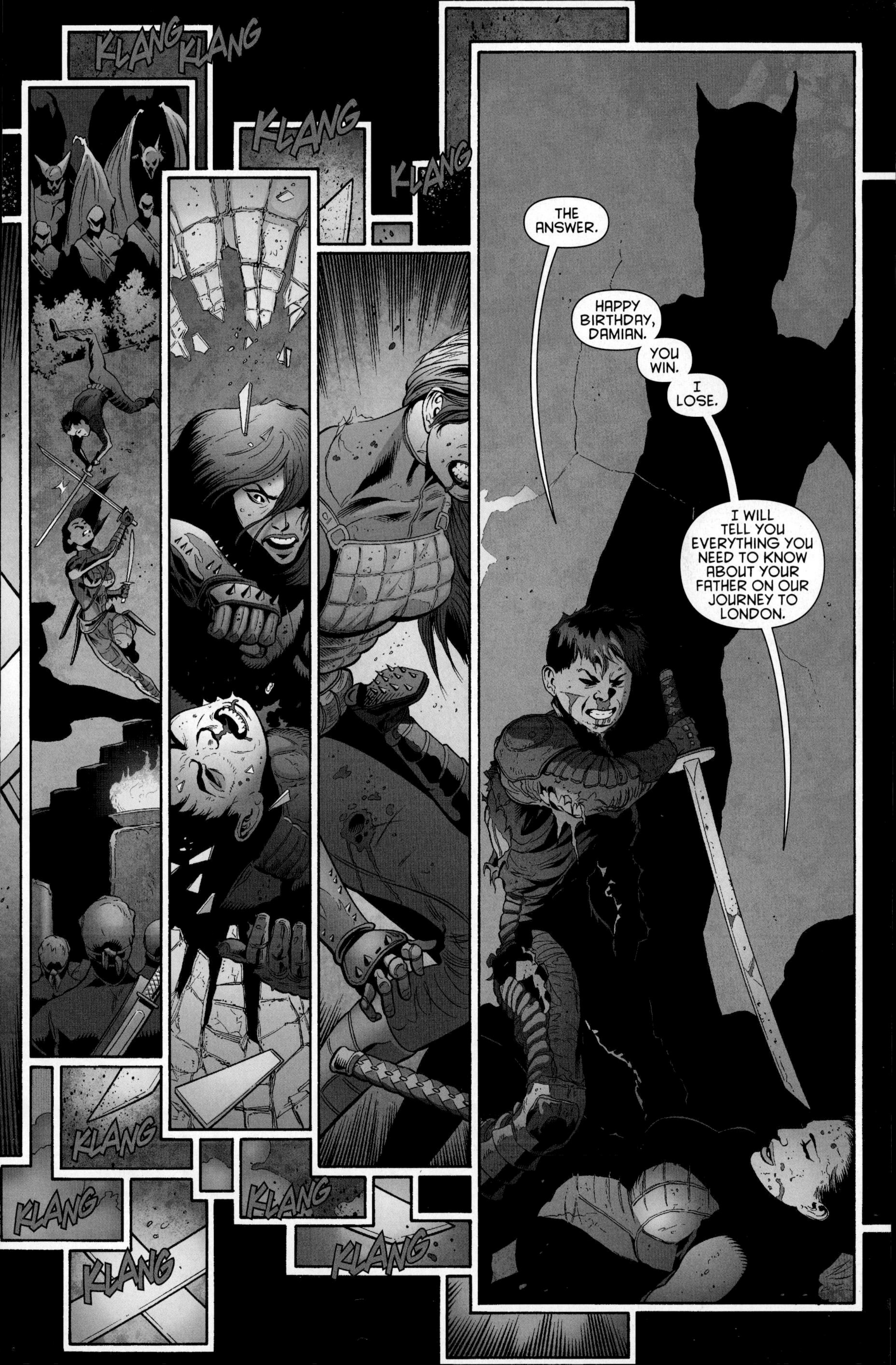
KLANG KLANG
KLANG
KLANG
THE ANSWER.
HAPPY BIRTHDAY, DAMIAN.
YOU WIN.
I LOSE.
I WILL TELL YOU EVERYTHING YOU NEED TO KNOW ABOUT YOUR FATHER ON OUR JOURNEY TO LONDON.
KLANG
KLANG
KLANG
KLANG
KLANG

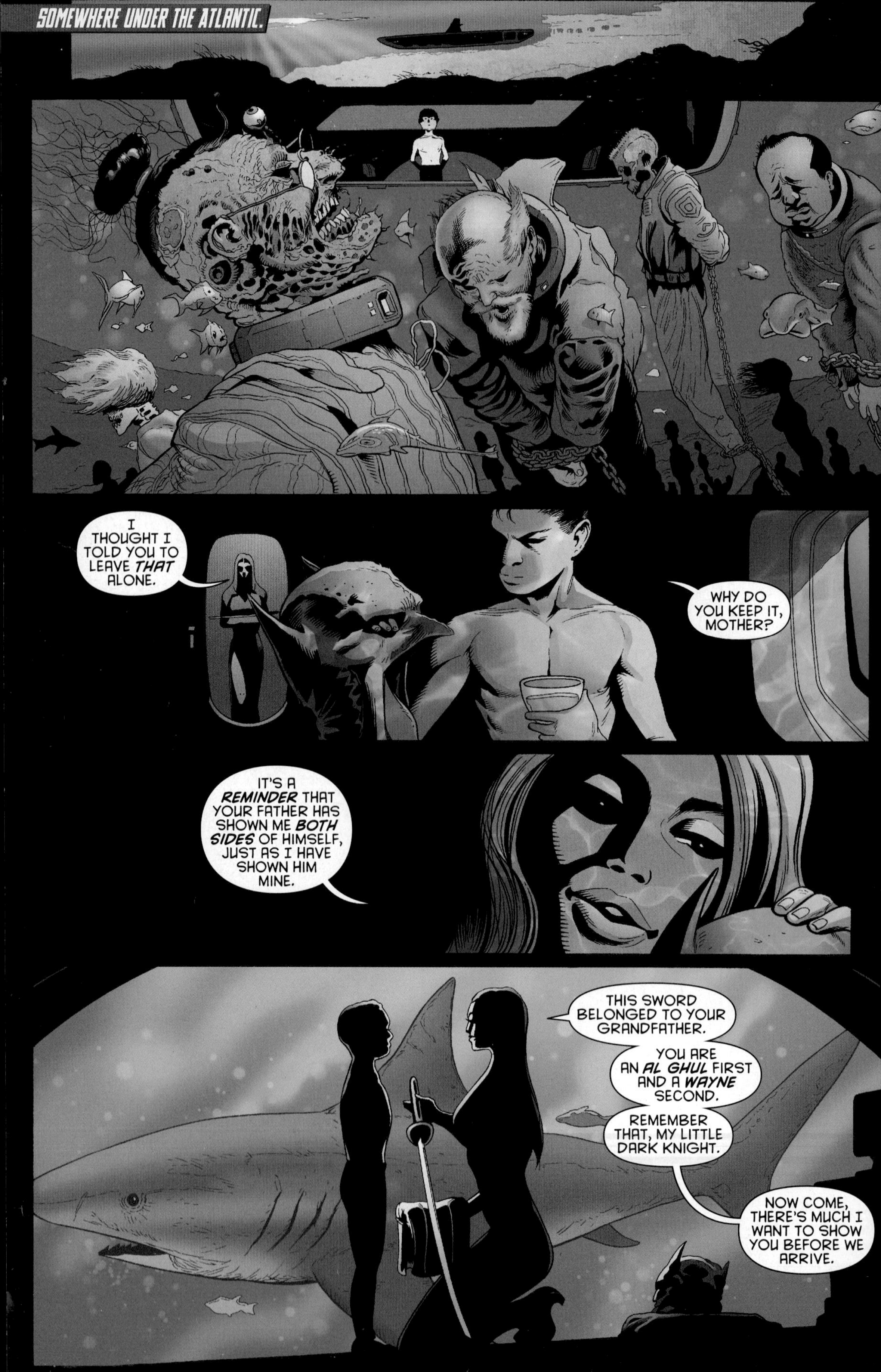
SOMEWHERE UNDER THE ATLANTIC.
I THOUGHT I TOLD YOU TO LEAVE *THAT* ALONE.
WHY DO YOU KEEP IT, MOTHER?
IT'S A ***REMINDER*** THAT YOUR FATHER HAS SHOWN ME ***BOTH SIDES*** OF HIMSELF, JUST AS I HAVE SHOWN HIM MINE.
THIS SWORD BELONGED TO YOUR GRANDFATHER.
YOU ARE AN ***AL GHUL*** FIRST AND A ***WAYNE*** SECOND.
REMEMBER THAT, MY LITTLE DARK KNIGHT.
NOW COME, THERE'S MUCH I WANT TO SHOW YOU BEFORE WE ARRIVE.

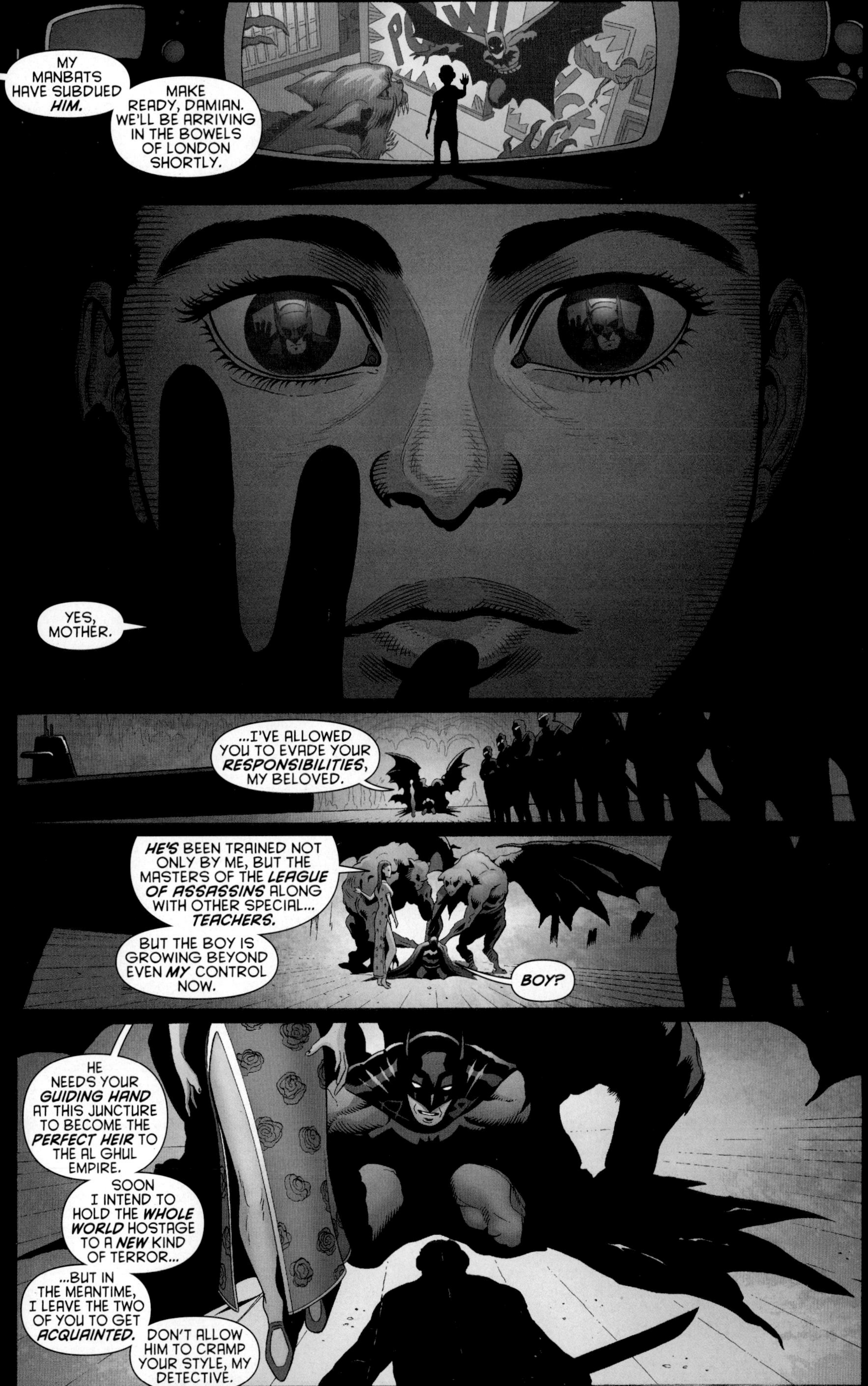
MY MANBATS HAVE SUBDUED HIM.
MAKE READY, DAMIAN. WE'LL BE ARRIVING IN THE BOWELS OF LONDON SHORTLY.
YES, MOTHER.
...I'VE ALLOWED YOU TO EVADE YOUR RESPONSIBILITIES, MY BELOVED.
HE'S BEEN TRAINED NOT ONLY BY ME, BUT THE MASTERS OF THE LEAGUE OF ASSASSINS ALONG WITH OTHER SPECIAL... TEACHERS.
BUT THE BOY IS GROWING BEYOND EVEN MY CONTROL NOW.
BOY?
HE NEEDS YOUR GUIDING HAND AT THIS JUNCTURE TO BECOME THE PERFECT HEIR TO THE AL GHUL EMPIRE.
SOON I INTEND TO HOLD THE WHOLE WORLD HOSTAGE TO A NEW KIND OF TERROR...
...BUT IN THE MEANTIME, I LEAVE THE TWO OF YOU TO GET ACQUAINTED.
DON'T ALLOW HIM TO CRAMP YOUR STYLE, MY DETECTIVE.

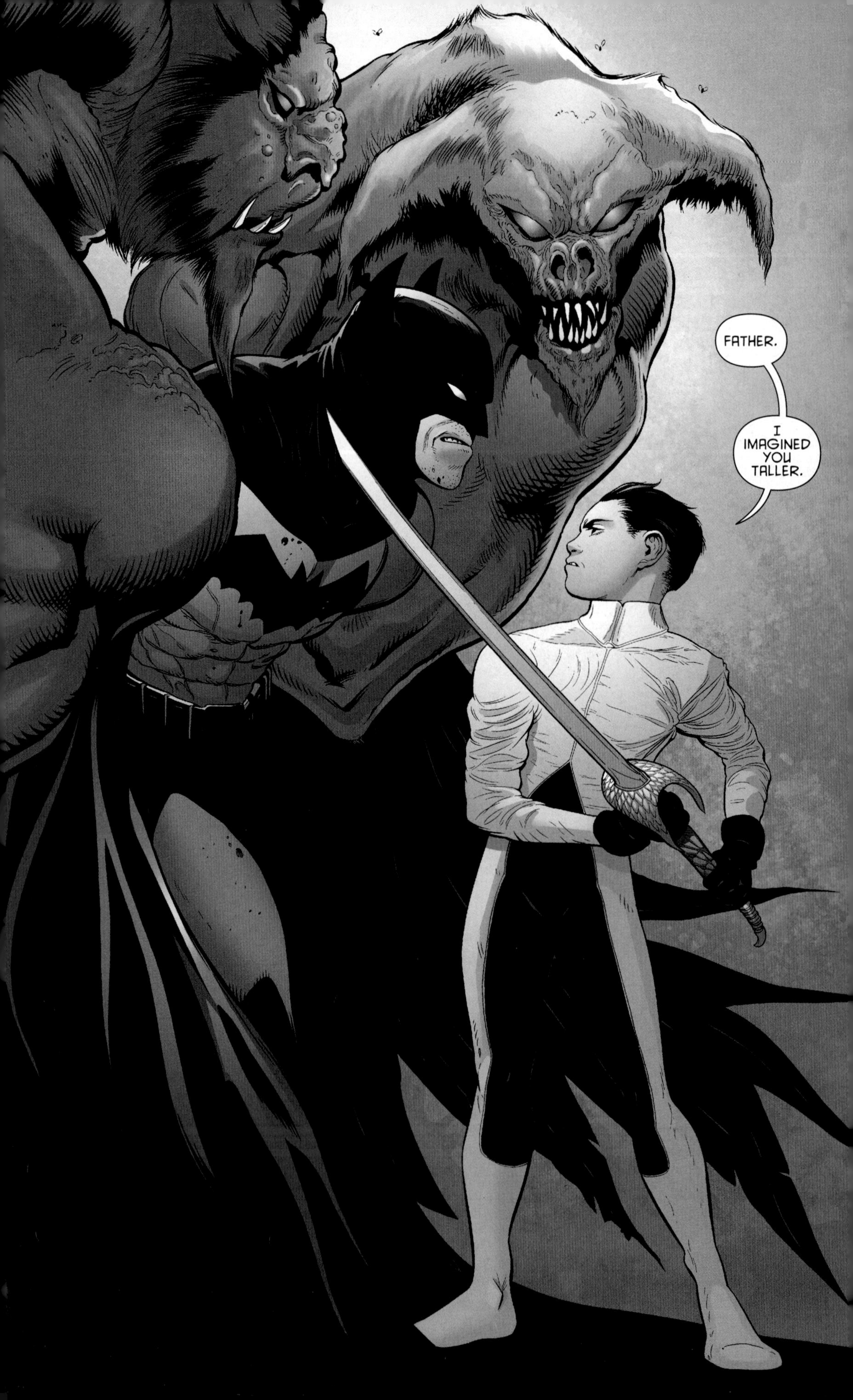
FATHER.
I IMAGINED YOU TALLER.

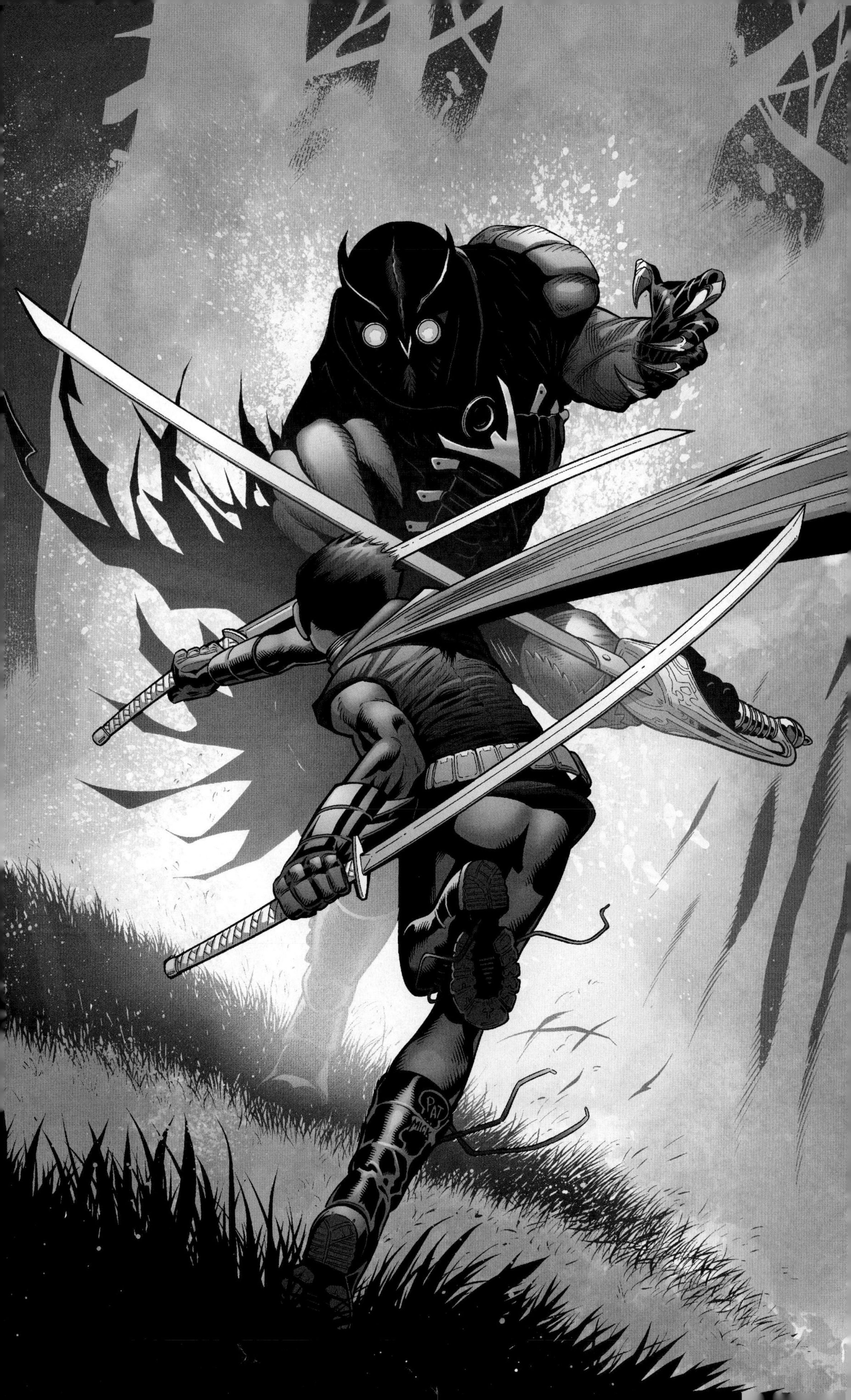
PAT
MICK

## NIGHT OF THE OWLS: ROBIN HEARS A HOO

**PETER J. TOMASI** writer **LEE GARBETT** penciller **ANDY CLARKE** art, pages 16-17 **RAY MCCARTHY & KEITH CHAMPAGNE** inkers
cover by **GLEASON, GRAY & KALISZ**

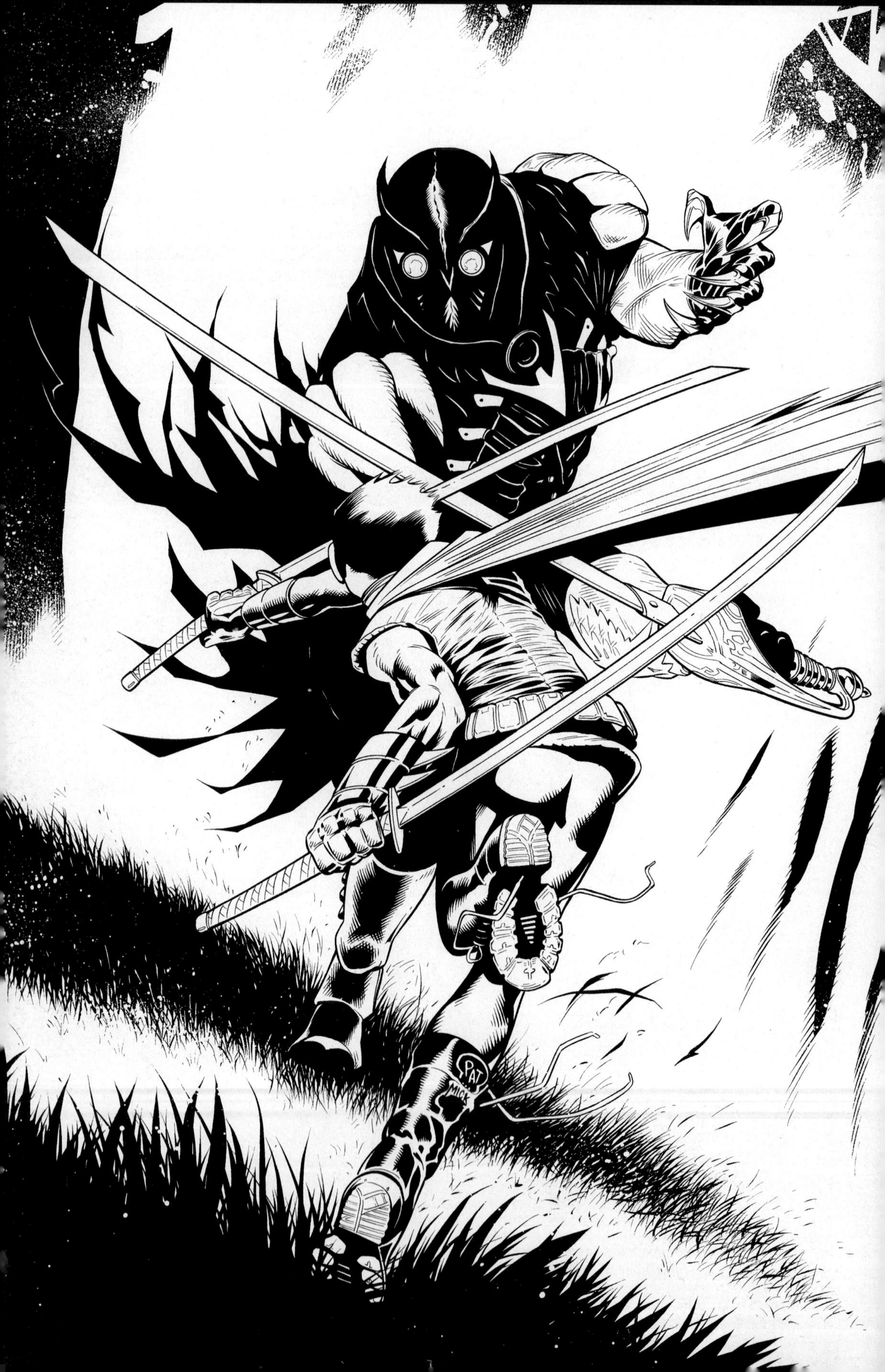
PAT
MICK

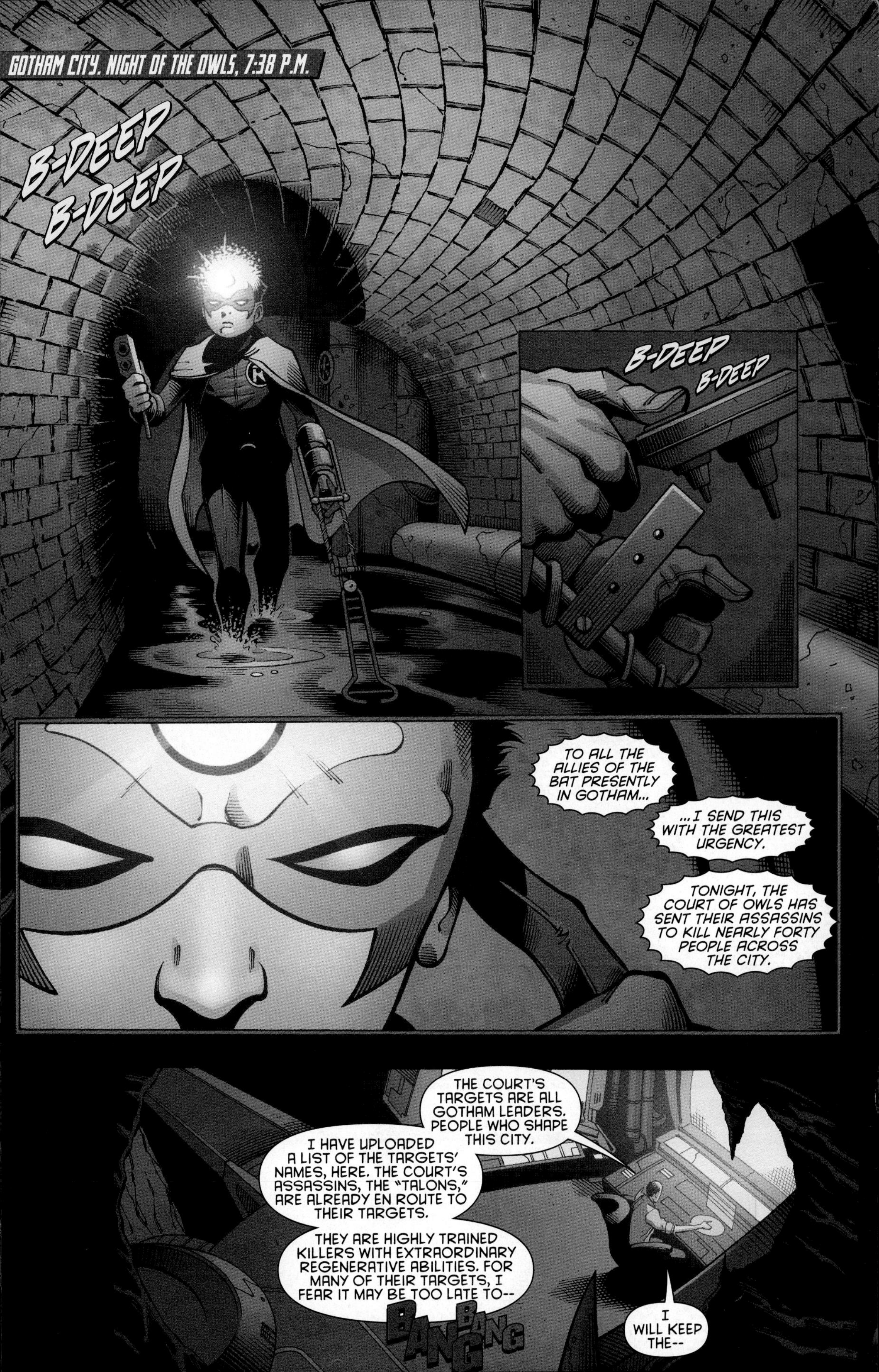
GOTHAM CITY. NIGHT OF THE OWLS, 7:38 P.M.
B-DEEP B-DEEP
B-DEEP B-DEEP
TO ALL THE ALLIES OF THE BAT PRESENTLY IN GOTHAM...
...I SEND THIS WITH THE GREATEST URGENCY.
TONIGHT, THE COURT OF OWLS HAS SENT THEIR ASSASSINS TO KILL NEARLY FORTY PEOPLE ACROSS THE CITY.
THE COURT'S TARGETS ARE ALL GOTHAM LEADERS. PEOPLE WHO SHAPE THIS CITY.
I HAVE UPLOADED A LIST OF THE TARGETS' NAMES, HERE. THE COURT'S ASSASSINS, THE "TALONS," ARE ALREADY EN ROUTE TO THEIR TARGETS.
THEY ARE HIGHLY TRAINED KILLERS WITH EXTRAORDINARY REGENERATIVE ABILITIES. FOR MANY OF THEIR TARGETS, I FEAR IT MAY BE TOO LATE TO--
BANG BANG BANG
I WILL KEEP THE--

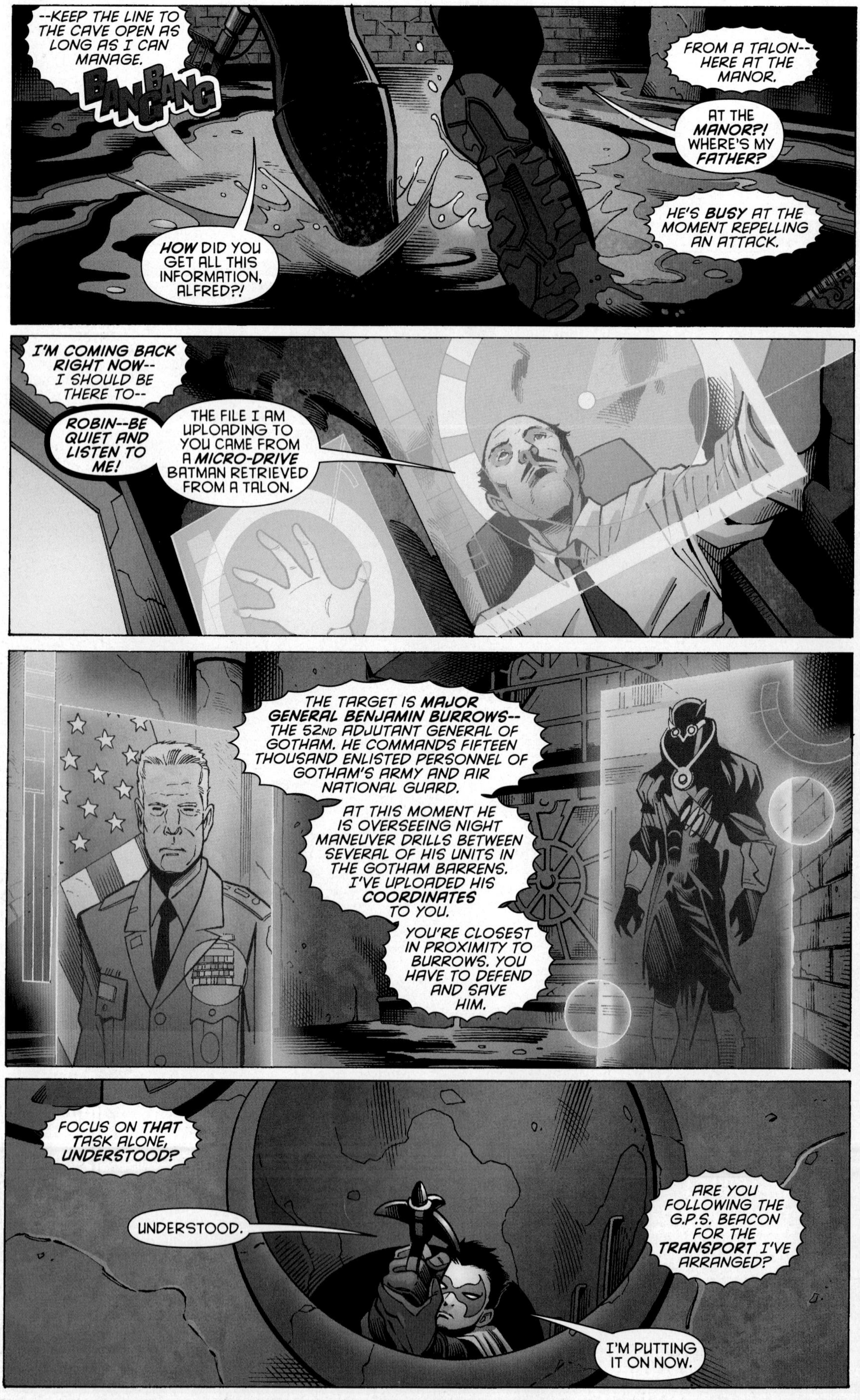
--KEEP THE LINE TO THE CAVE OPEN AS LONG AS I CAN MANAGE.
BANG BANG
HOW DID YOU GET ALL THIS INFORMATION, ALFRED?!
FROM A TALON--HERE AT THE MANOR.
AT THE MANOR?! WHERE'S MY FATHER?
HE'S BUSY AT THE MOMENT REPELLING AN ATTACK.
I'M COMING BACK RIGHT NOW--I SHOULD BE THERE TO--
ROBIN--BE QUIET AND LISTEN TO ME!
THE FILE I AM UPLOADING TO YOU CAME FROM A MICRO-DRIVE BATMAN RETRIEVED FROM A TALON.
THE TARGET IS MAJOR GENERAL BENJAMIN BURROWS--THE 52ND ADJUTANT GENERAL OF GOTHAM. HE COMMANDS FIFTEEN THOUSAND ENLISTED PERSONNEL OF GOTHAM'S ARMY AND AIR NATIONAL GUARD.
AT THIS MOMENT HE IS OVERSEEING NIGHT MANEUVER DRILLS BETWEEN SEVERAL OF HIS UNITS IN THE GOTHAM BARRENS. I'VE UPLOADED HIS COORDINATES TO YOU.
YOU'RE CLOSEST IN PROXIMITY TO BURROWS. YOU HAVE TO DEFEND AND SAVE HIM.
FOCUS ON THAT TASK ALONE, UNDERSTOOD?
UNDERSTOOD.
ARE YOU FOLLOWING THE G.P.S. BEACON FOR THE TRANSPORT I'VE ARRANGED?
I'M PUTTING IT ON NOW.

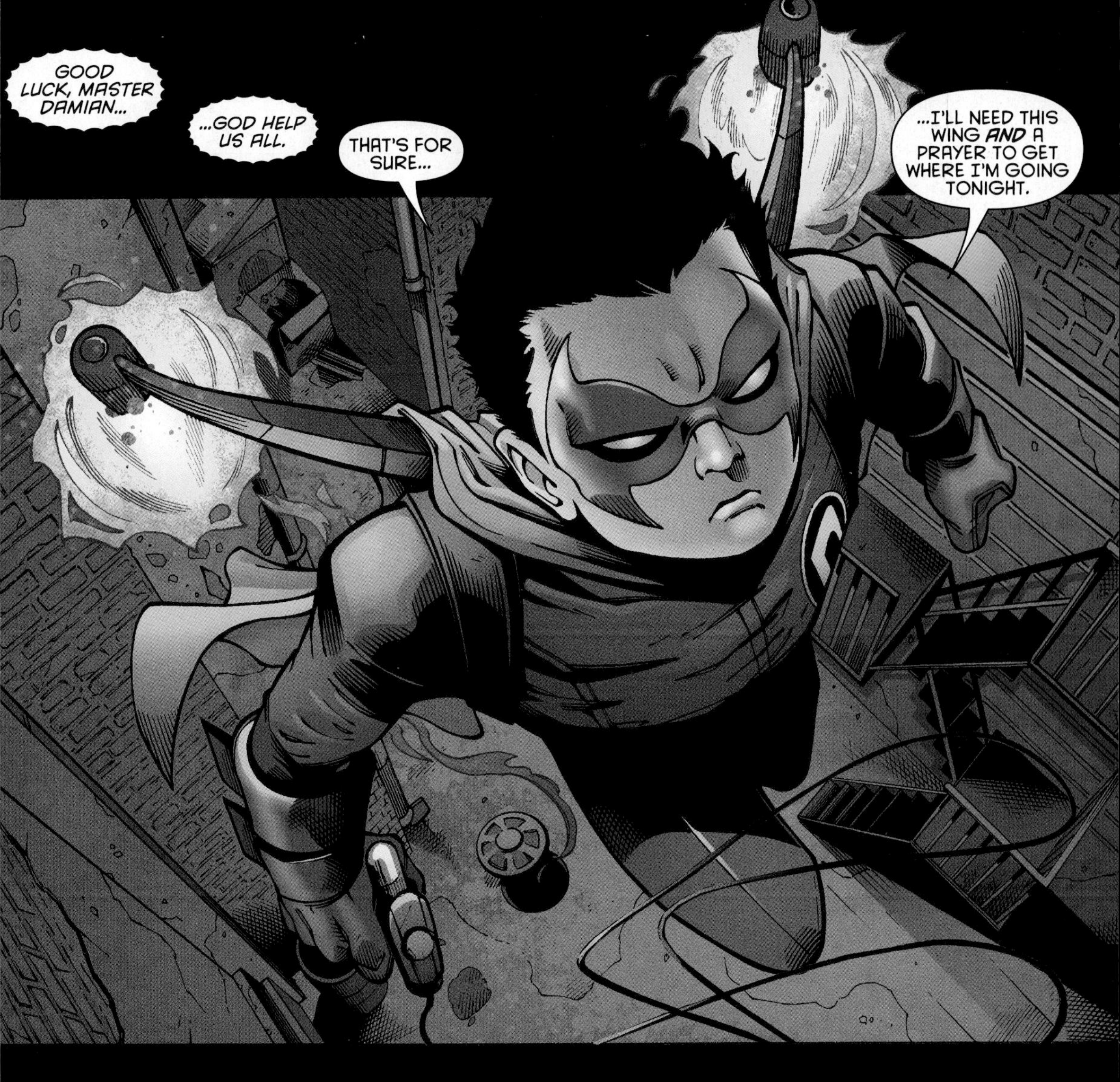
GOOD LUCK, MASTER DAMIAN...
...GOD HELP US ALL.
THAT'S FOR SURE...
...I'LL NEED THIS WING AND A PRAYER TO GET WHERE I'M GOING TONIGHT.

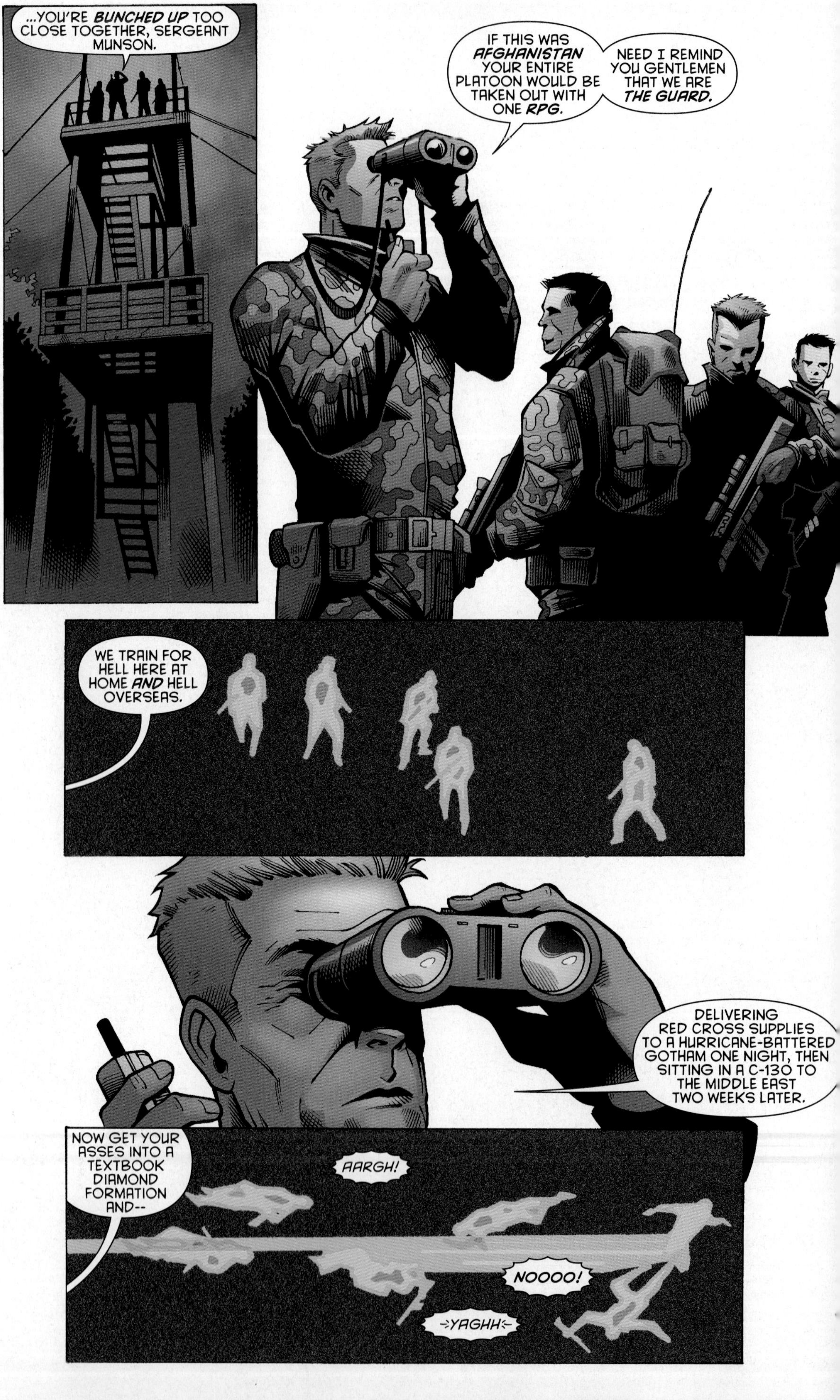
...YOU'RE BUNCHED UP TOO CLOSE TOGETHER, SERGEANT MUNSON.
IF THIS WAS AFGHANISTAN YOUR ENTIRE PLATOON WOULD BE TAKEN OUT WITH ONE RPG.
NEED I REMIND YOU GENTLEMEN THAT WE ARE THE GUARD.
WE TRAIN FOR HELL HERE AT HOME AND HELL OVERSEAS.
DELIVERING RED CROSS SUPPLIES TO A HURRICANE-BATTERED GOTHAM ONE NIGHT, THEN SITTING IN A C-130 TO THE MIDDLE EAST TWO WEEKS LATER.
NOW GET YOUR ASSES INTO A TEXTBOOK DIAMOND FORMATION AND--
AARGH!
NOOOO!
YAGHH

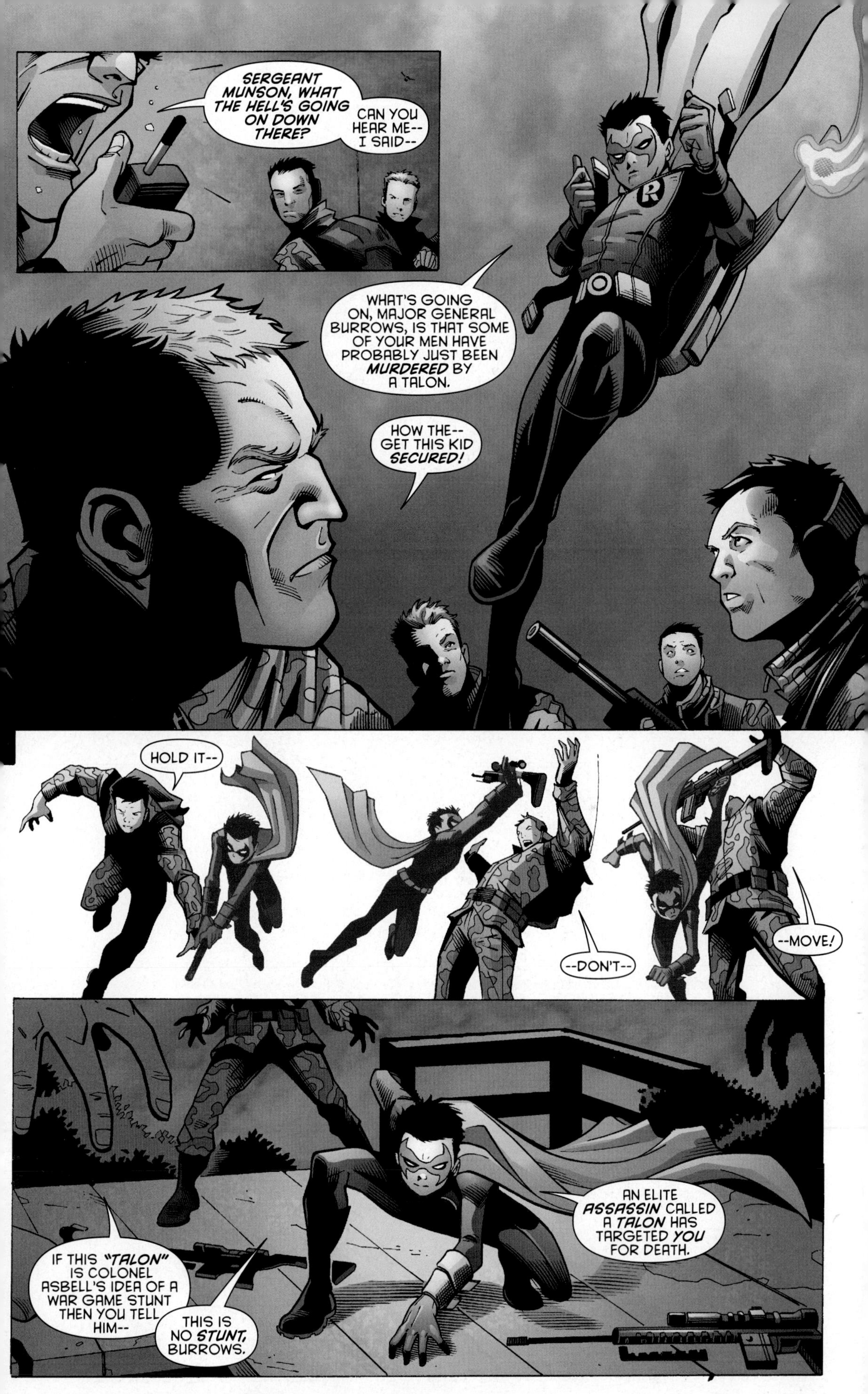
SERGEANT MUNSON, WHAT THE HELL'S GOING ON DOWN THERE?
CAN YOU HEAR ME-- I SAID--
WHAT'S GOING ON, MAJOR GENERAL BURROWS, IS THAT SOME OF YOUR MEN HAVE PROBABLY JUST BEEN MURDERED BY A TALON.
HOW THE-- GET THIS KID SECURED!
HOLD IT--
--DON'T--
--MOVE!
AN ELITE ASSASSIN CALLED A TALON HAS TARGETED YOU FOR DEATH.
IF THIS "TALON" IS COLONEL ASBELL'S IDEA OF A WAR GAME STUNT THEN YOU TELL HIM--
THIS IS NO STUNT, BURROWS.

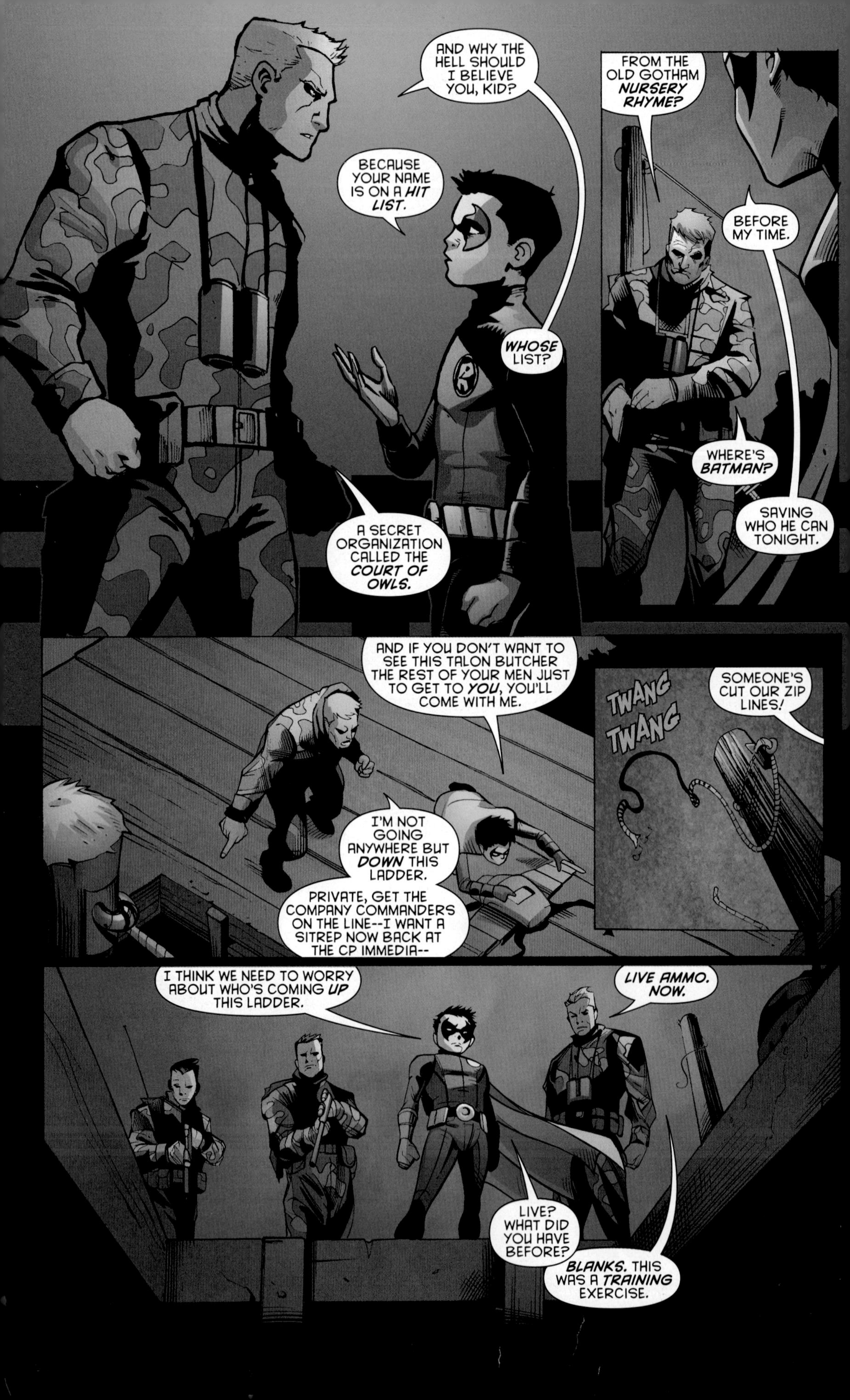
AND WHY THE HELL SHOULD I BELIEVE YOU, KID?
BECAUSE YOUR NAME IS ON A HIT LIST.
WHOSE LIST?
A SECRET ORGANIZATION CALLED THE COURT OF OWLS.
FROM THE OLD GOTHAM NURSERY RHYME?
BEFORE MY TIME.
WHERE'S BATMAN?
SAVING WHO HE CAN TONIGHT.
AND IF YOU DON'T WANT TO SEE THIS TALON BUTCHER THE REST OF YOUR MEN JUST TO GET TO YOU, YOU'LL COME WITH ME.
I'M NOT GOING ANYWHERE BUT DOWN THIS LADDER.
PRIVATE, GET THE COMPANY COMMANDERS ON THE LINE--I WANT A SITREP NOW BACK AT THE CP IMMEDIA--
TWANG
TWANG
SOMEONE'S CUT OUR ZIP LINES!
I THINK WE NEED TO WORRY ABOUT WHO'S COMING UP THIS LADDER.
LIVE AMMO. NOW.
LIVE? WHAT DID YOU HAVE BEFORE?
BLANKS. THIS WAS A TRAINING EXERCISE.

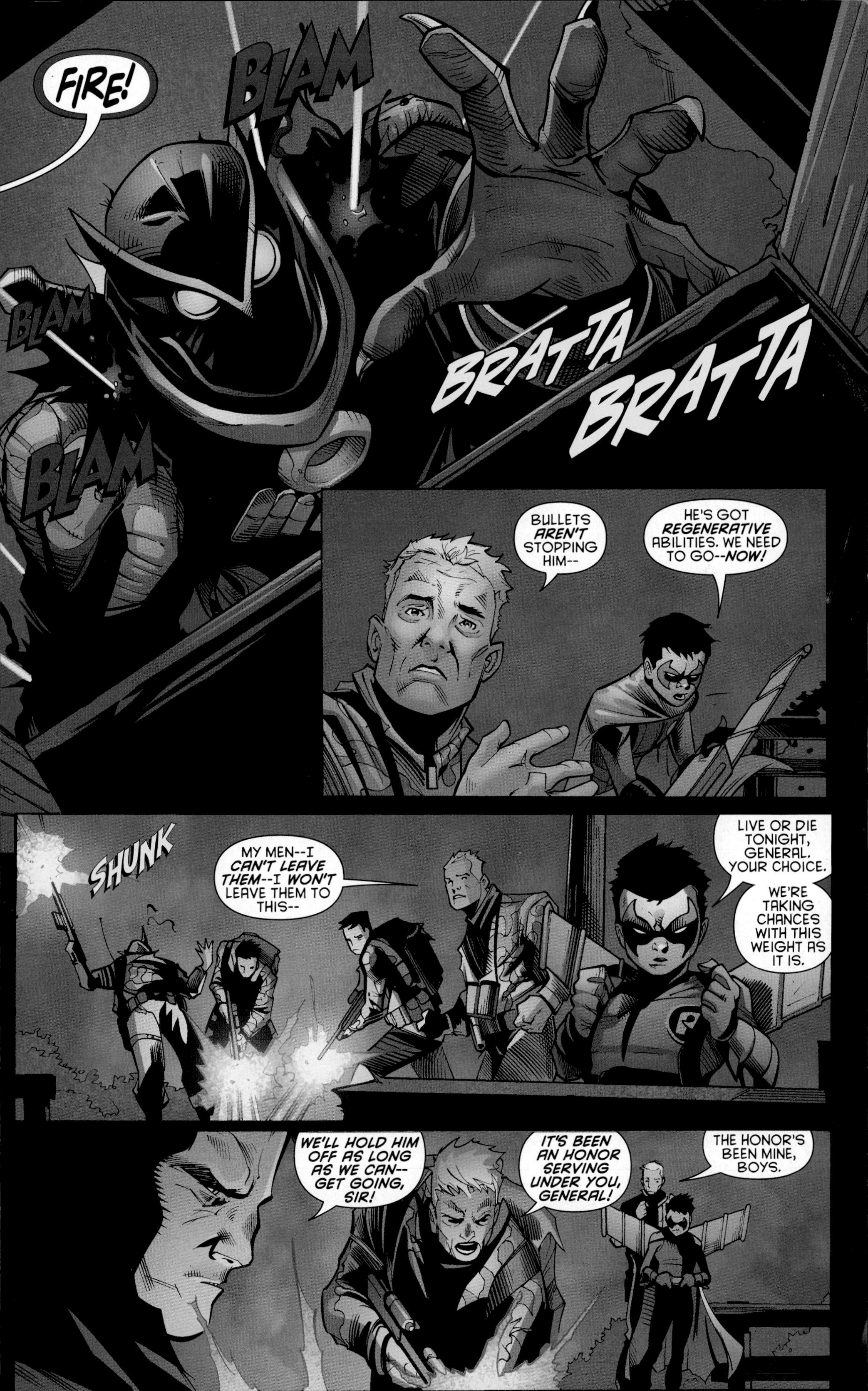
FIRE!
BLAM
BLAM
BLAM
BRATTA
BRATTA
BULLETS AREN'T STOPPING HIM--
HE'S GOT REGENERATIVE ABILITIES. WE NEED TO GO--NOW!
SHUNK
MY MEN--I CAN'T LEAVE THEM--I WON'T LEAVE THEM TO THIS--
LIVE OR DIE TONIGHT, GENERAL. YOUR CHOICE.
WE'RE TAKING CHANCES WITH THIS WEIGHT AS IT IS.
WE'LL HOLD HIM OFF AS LONG AS WE CAN--GET GOING, SIR!
IT'S BEEN AN HONOR SERVING UNDER YOU, GENERAL!
THE HONOR'S BEEN MINE, BOYS.

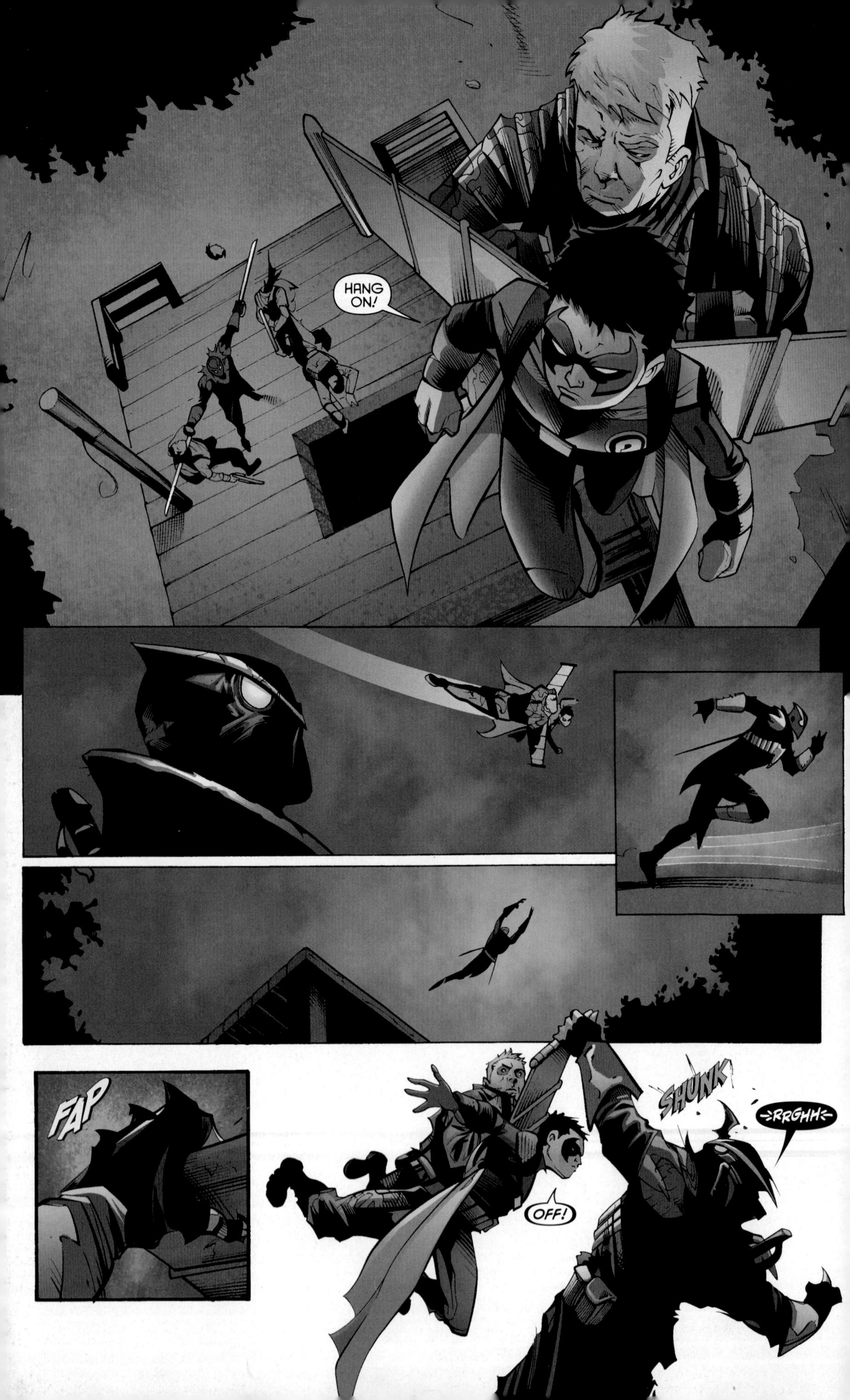
HANG ON!
FAP
SHUNK
RRGHH
OFF!

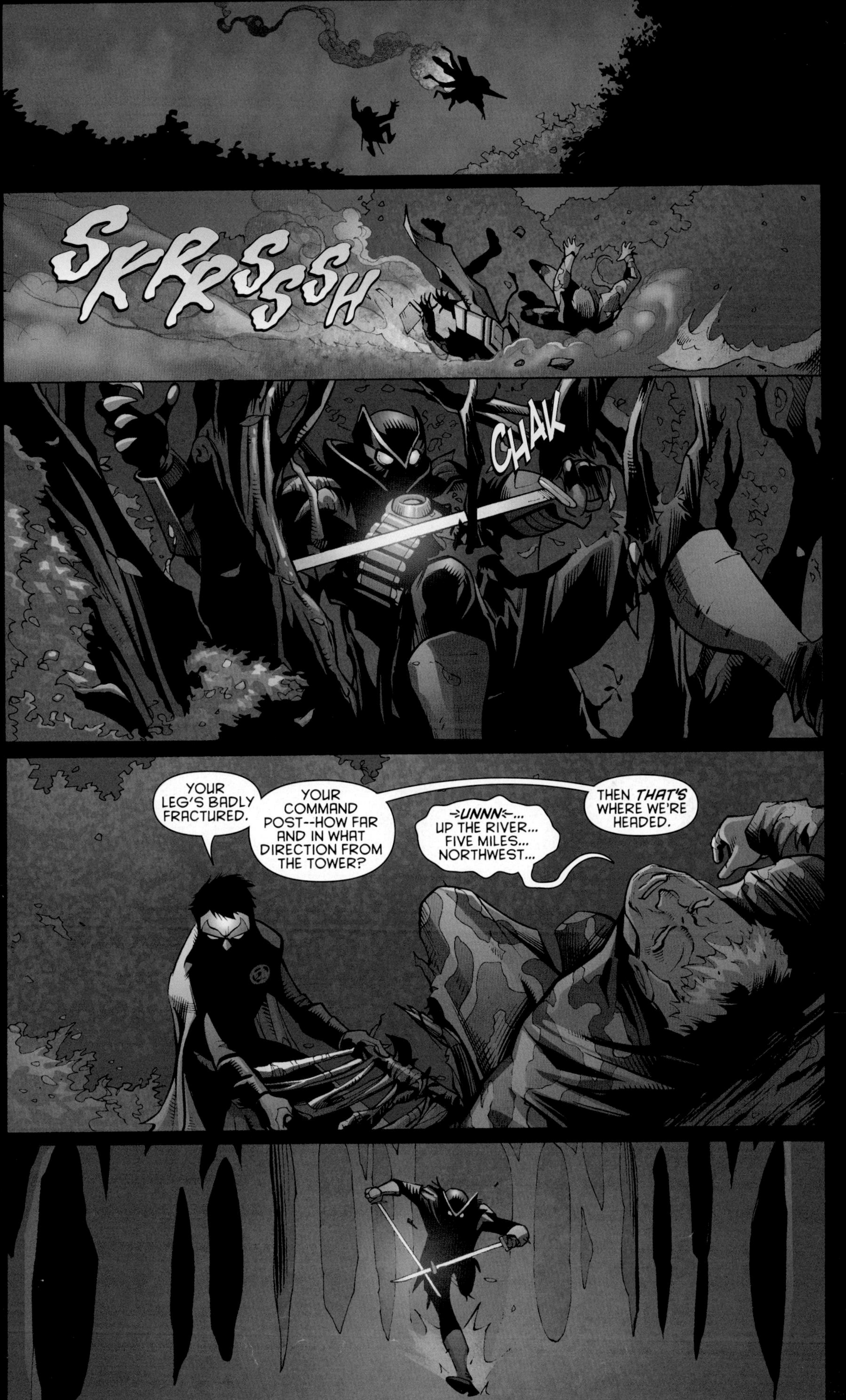
SKRSSSH
CHAK
YOUR LEG'S BADLY FRACTURED.
YOUR COMMAND POST--HOW FAR AND IN WHAT DIRECTION FROM THE TOWER?
UNNN... UP THE RIVER... FIVE MILES... NORTHWEST...
THEN THAT'S WHERE WE'RE HEADED.

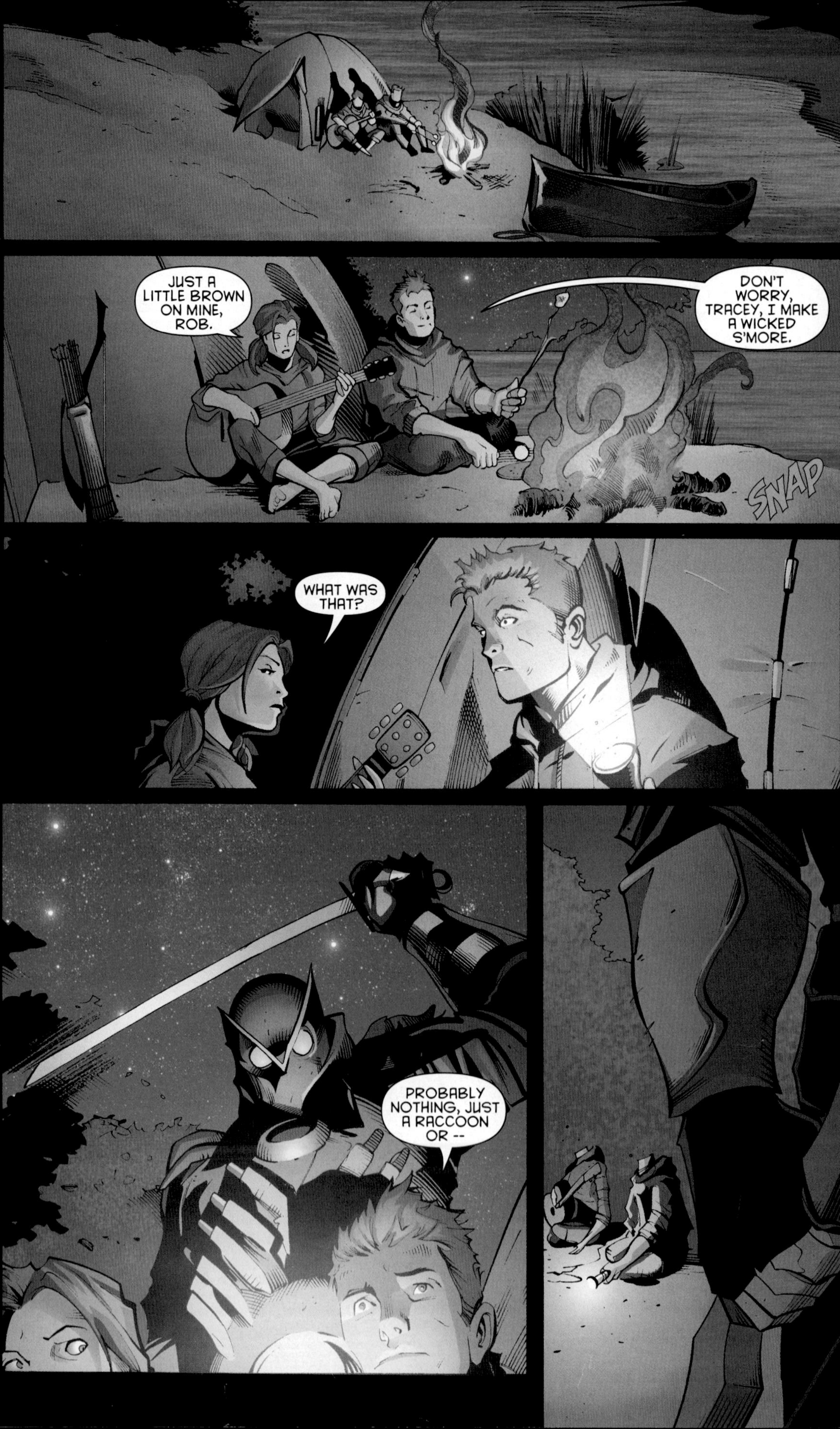
JUST A LITTLE BROWN ON MINE, ROB.
DON'T WORRY, TRACEY, I MAKE A WICKED S'MORE.
SNAP
WHAT WAS THAT?
PROBABLY NOTHING, JUST A RACCOON OR --

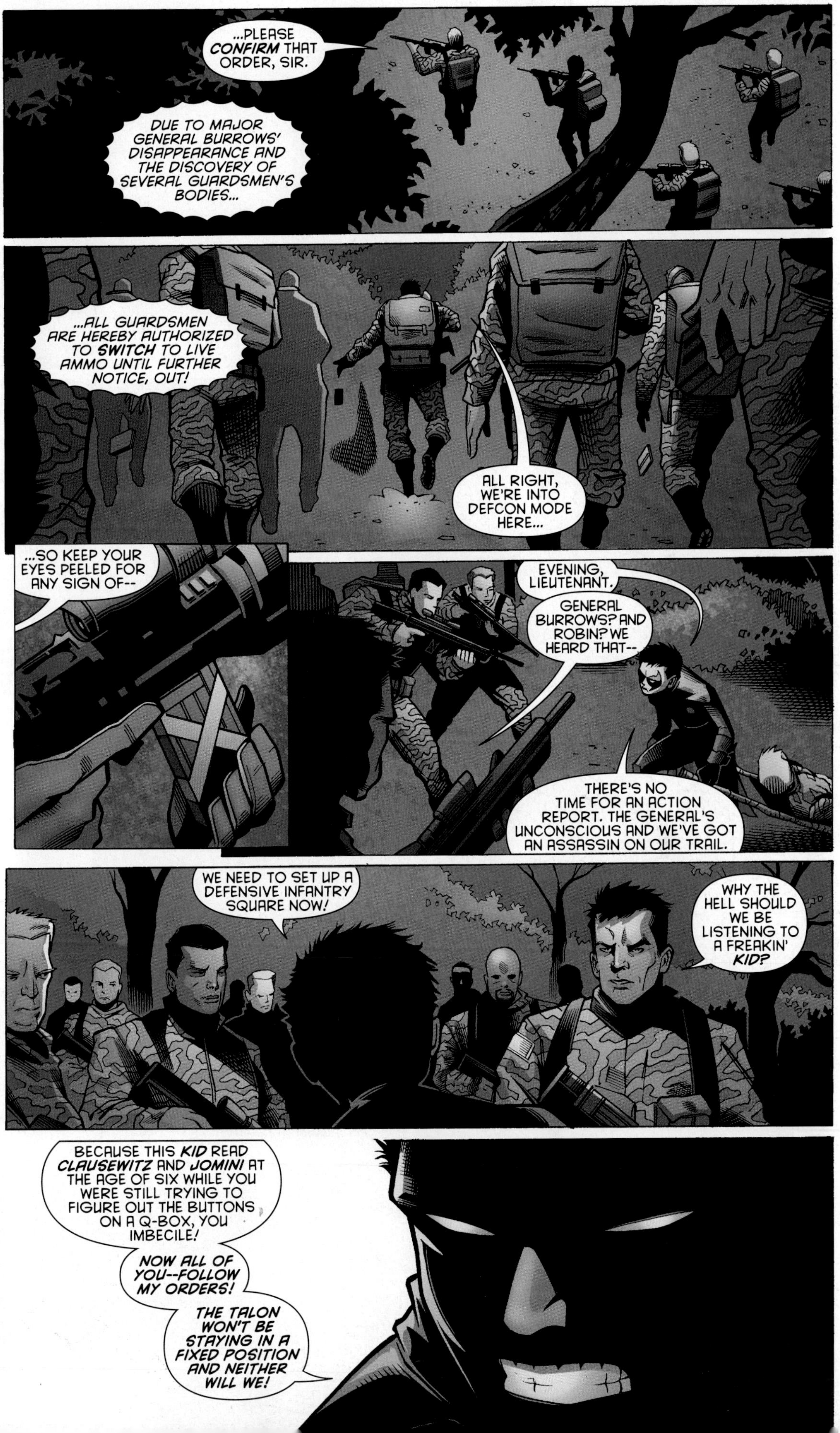
...PLEASE CONFIRM THAT ORDER, SIR.
DUE TO MAJOR GENERAL BURROWS' DISAPPEARANCE AND THE DISCOVERY OF SEVERAL GUARDSMEN'S BODIES...
...ALL GUARDSMEN ARE HEREBY AUTHORIZED TO SWITCH TO LIVE AMMO UNTIL FURTHER NOTICE, OUT!
ALL RIGHT, WE'RE INTO DEFCON MODE HERE...
...SO KEEP YOUR EYES PEELED FOR ANY SIGN OF--
EVENING, LIEUTENANT.
GENERAL BURROWS? AND ROBIN? WE HEARD THAT--
THERE'S NO TIME FOR AN ACTION REPORT. THE GENERAL'S UNCONSCIOUS AND WE'VE GOT AN ASSASSIN ON OUR TRAIL.
WE NEED TO SET UP A DEFENSIVE INFANTRY SQUARE NOW!
WHY THE HELL SHOULD WE BE LISTENING TO A FREAKIN' KID?
BECAUSE THIS KID READ CLAUSEWITZ AND JOMINI AT THE AGE OF SIX WHILE YOU WERE STILL TRYING TO FIGURE OUT THE BUTTONS ON A Q-BOX, YOU IMBECILE!
NOW ALL OF YOU--FOLLOW MY ORDERS!
THE TALON WON'T BE STAYING IN A FIXED POSITION AND NEITHER WILL WE!

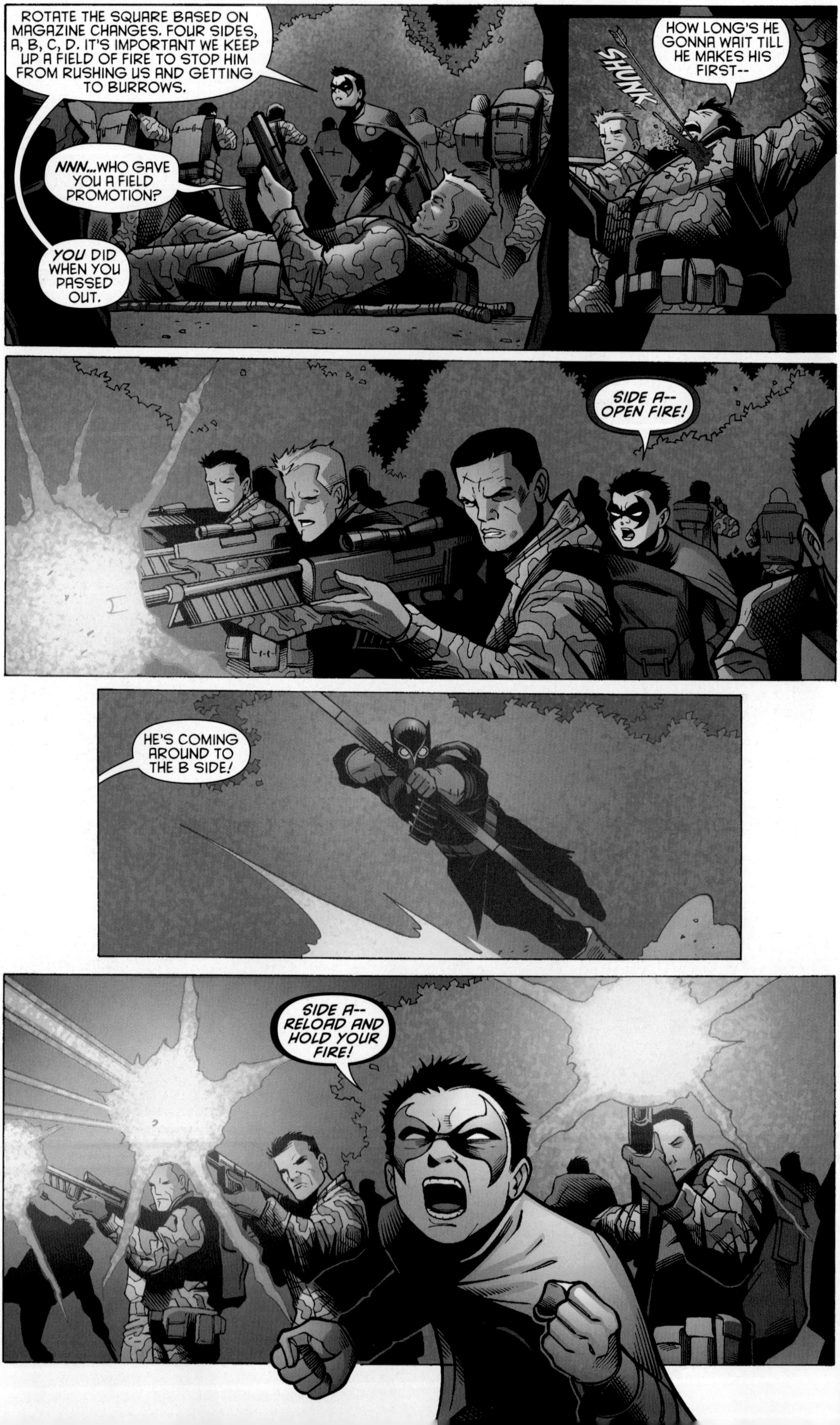
ROTATE THE SQUARE BASED ON MAGAZINE CHANGES. FOUR SIDES, A, B, C, D. IT'S IMPORTANT WE KEEP UP A FIELD OF FIRE TO STOP HIM FROM RUSHING US AND GETTING TO BURROWS.
NNN...WHO GAVE YOU A FIELD PROMOTION?
YOU DID WHEN YOU PASSED OUT.
HOW LONG'S HE GONNA WAIT TILL HE MAKES HIS FIRST--
SHUNK
SIDE A-- OPEN FIRE!
HE'S COMING AROUND TO THE B SIDE!
SIDE A-- RELOAD AND HOLD YOUR FIRE!

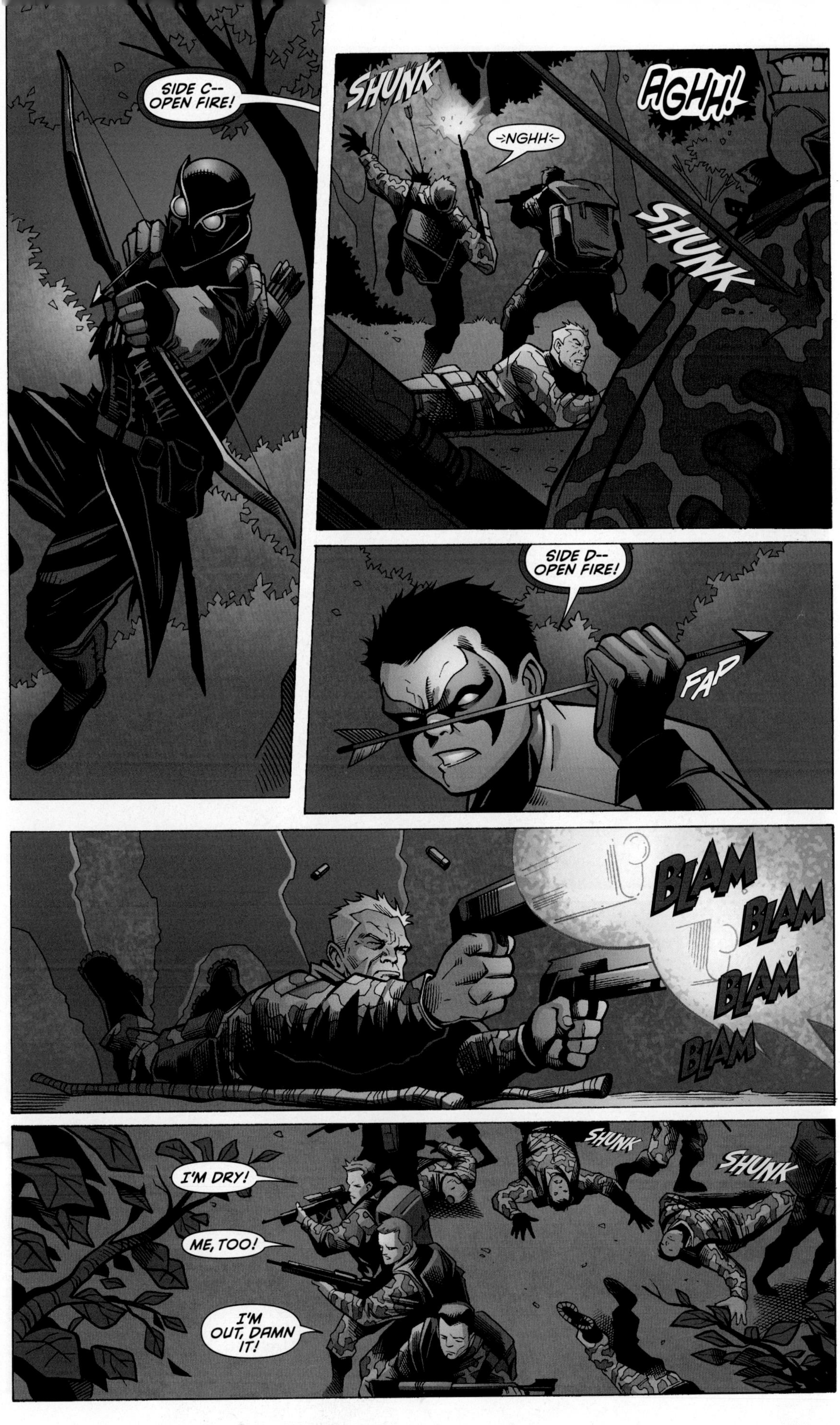
SIDE C--
OPEN FIRE!
SHUNK
-NGHH-
AGHH!
SHUNK
SIDE D--
OPEN FIRE!
FAP
BLAM
BLAM
BLAM
BLAM
SHUNK
SHUNK
I'M DRY!
ME, TOO!
I'M
OUT, DAMN
IT!

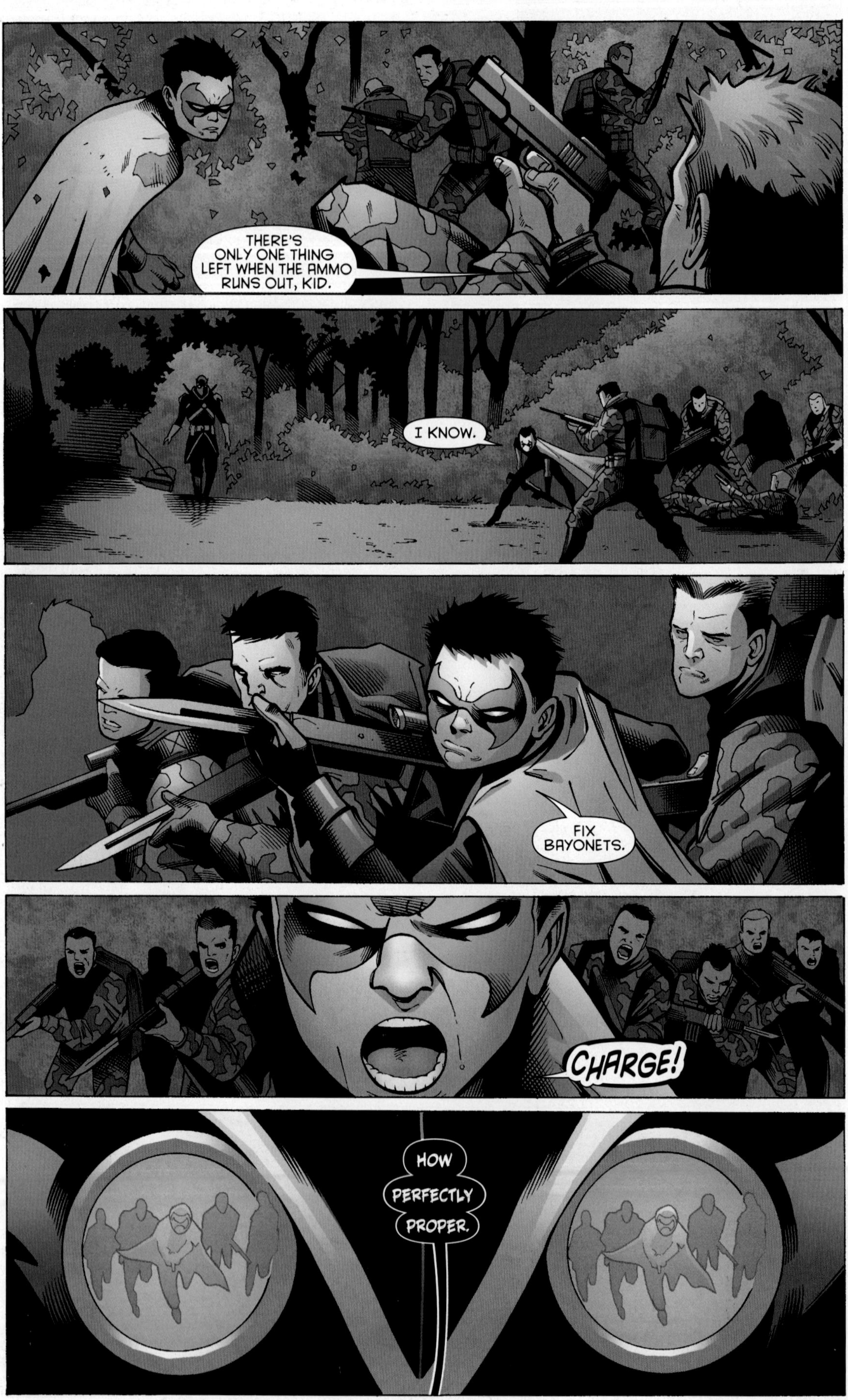
THERE'S ONLY ONE THING LEFT WHEN THE AMMO RUNS OUT, KID.
I KNOW.
FIX BAYONETS.
CHARGE!
HOW PERFECTLY PROPER.

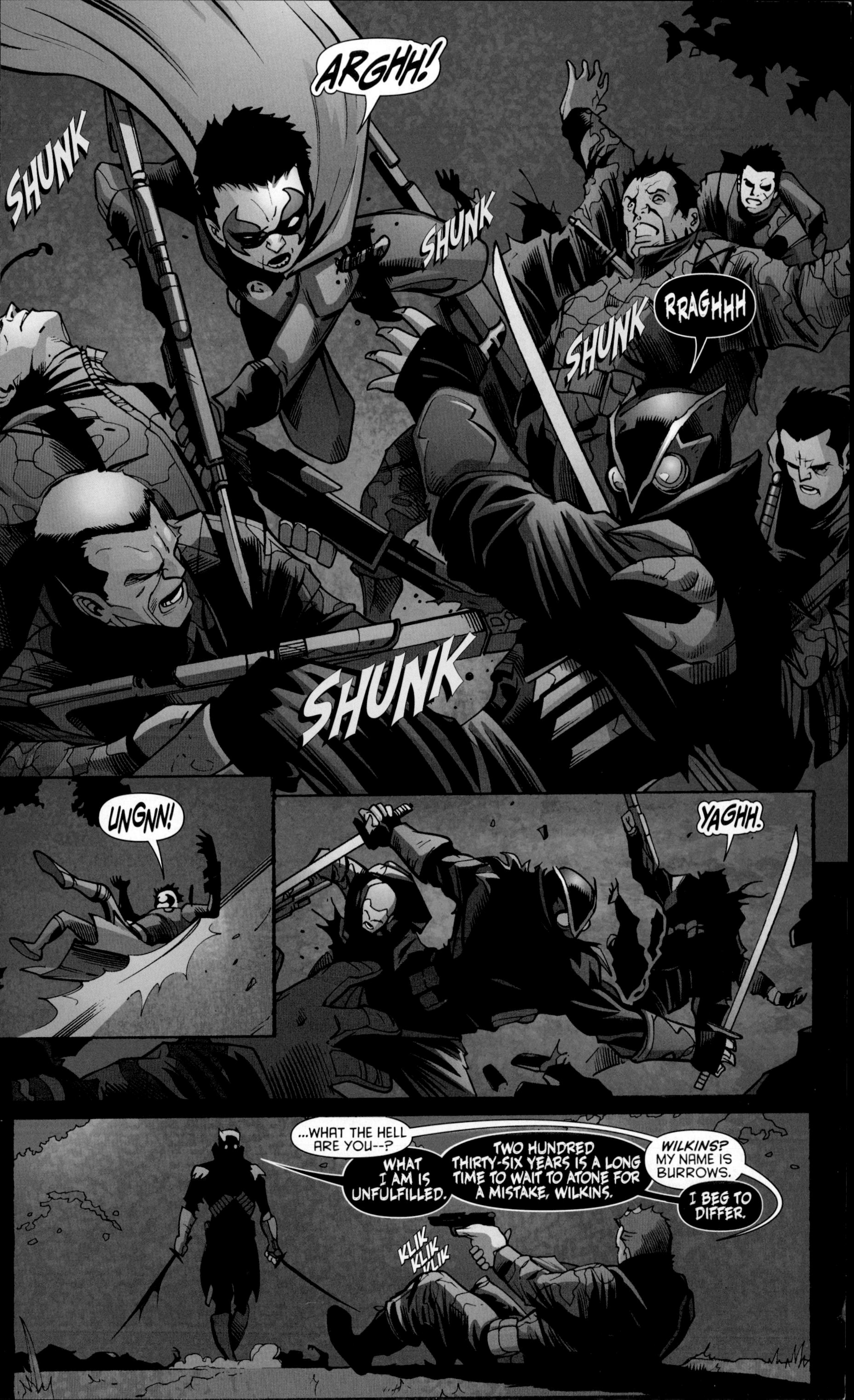

SHUNK
ARGHH!
SHUNK
SHUNK
RRAGHHH
SHUNK
UNGNN!
YAGHH.
...WHAT THE HELL ARE YOU--?
WHAT I AM IS UNFULFILLED.
TWO HUNDRED THIRTY-SIX YEARS IS A LONG TIME TO WAIT TO ATONE FOR A MISTAKE, WILKINS.
WILKINS? MY NAME IS BURROWS.
I BEG TO DIFFER.
KLIK KLIK KLIK

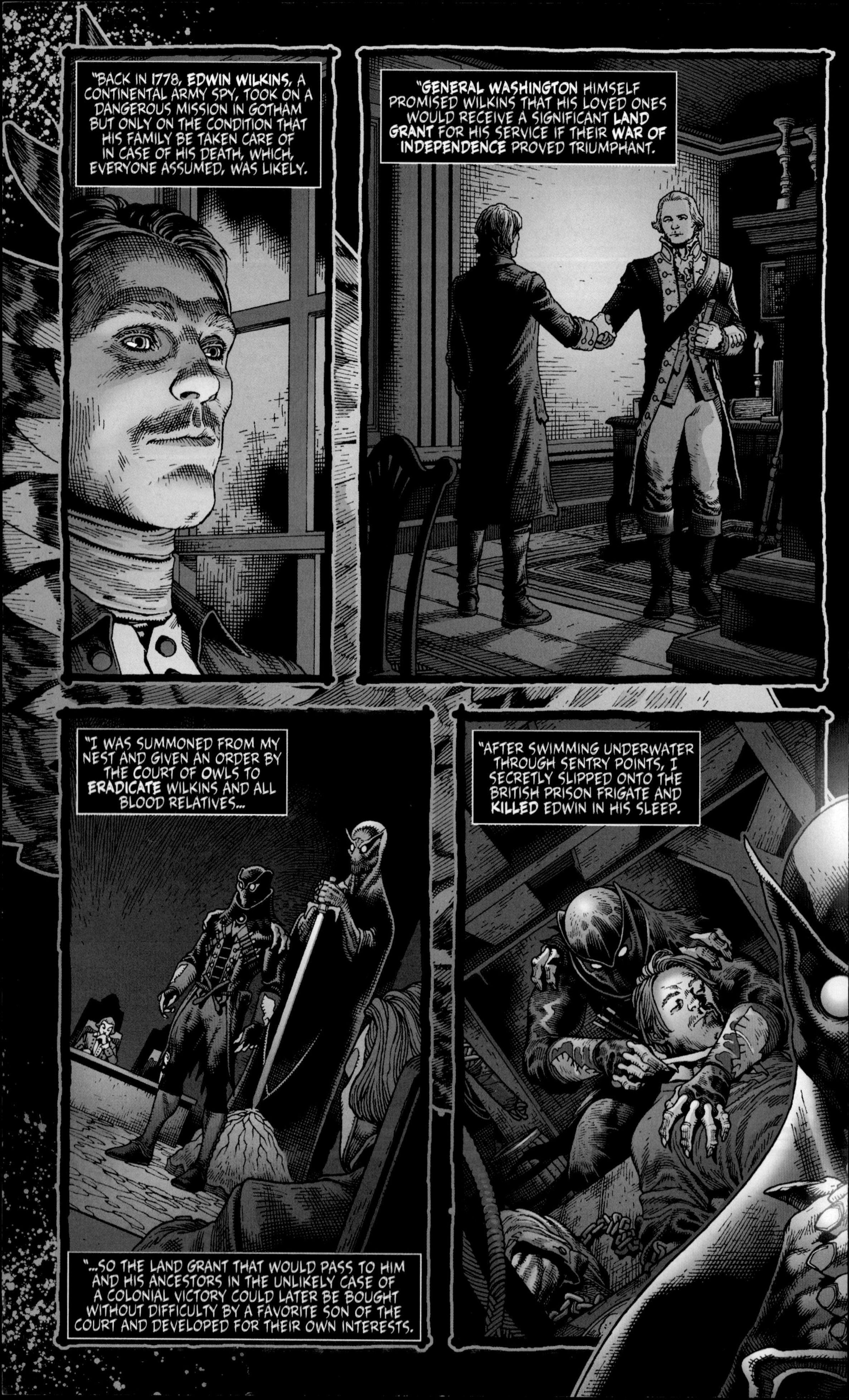
"BACK IN 1778, **EDWIN WILKINS**, A CONTINENTAL ARMY SPY, TOOK ON A DANGEROUS MISSION IN GOTHAM BUT ONLY ON THE CONDITION THAT HIS FAMILY BE TAKEN CARE OF IN CASE OF HIS DEATH, WHICH, EVERYONE ASSUMED, WAS LIKELY.
"**GENERAL WASHINGTON** HIMSELF PROMISED WILKINS THAT HIS LOVED ONES WOULD RECEIVE A SIGNIFICANT **LAND GRANT** FOR HIS SERVICE IF THEIR **WAR OF INDEPENDENCE** PROVED TRIUMPHANT.
"I WAS SUMMONED FROM MY NEST AND GIVEN AN ORDER BY THE **COURT** OF **OWLS** TO **ERADICATE** WILKINS AND ALL BLOOD RELATIVES...
"...SO THE LAND GRANT THAT WOULD PASS TO HIM AND HIS ANCESTORS IN THE UNLIKELY CASE OF A COLONIAL VICTORY COULD LATER BE BOUGHT WITHOUT DIFFICULTY BY A FAVORITE SON OF THE COURT AND DEVELOPED FOR THEIR OWN INTERESTS.
"AFTER SWIMMING UNDERWATER THROUGH SENTRY POINTS, I SECRETLY SLIPPED ONTO THE BRITISH PRISON FRIGATE AND **KILLED** EDWIN IN HIS SLEEP.

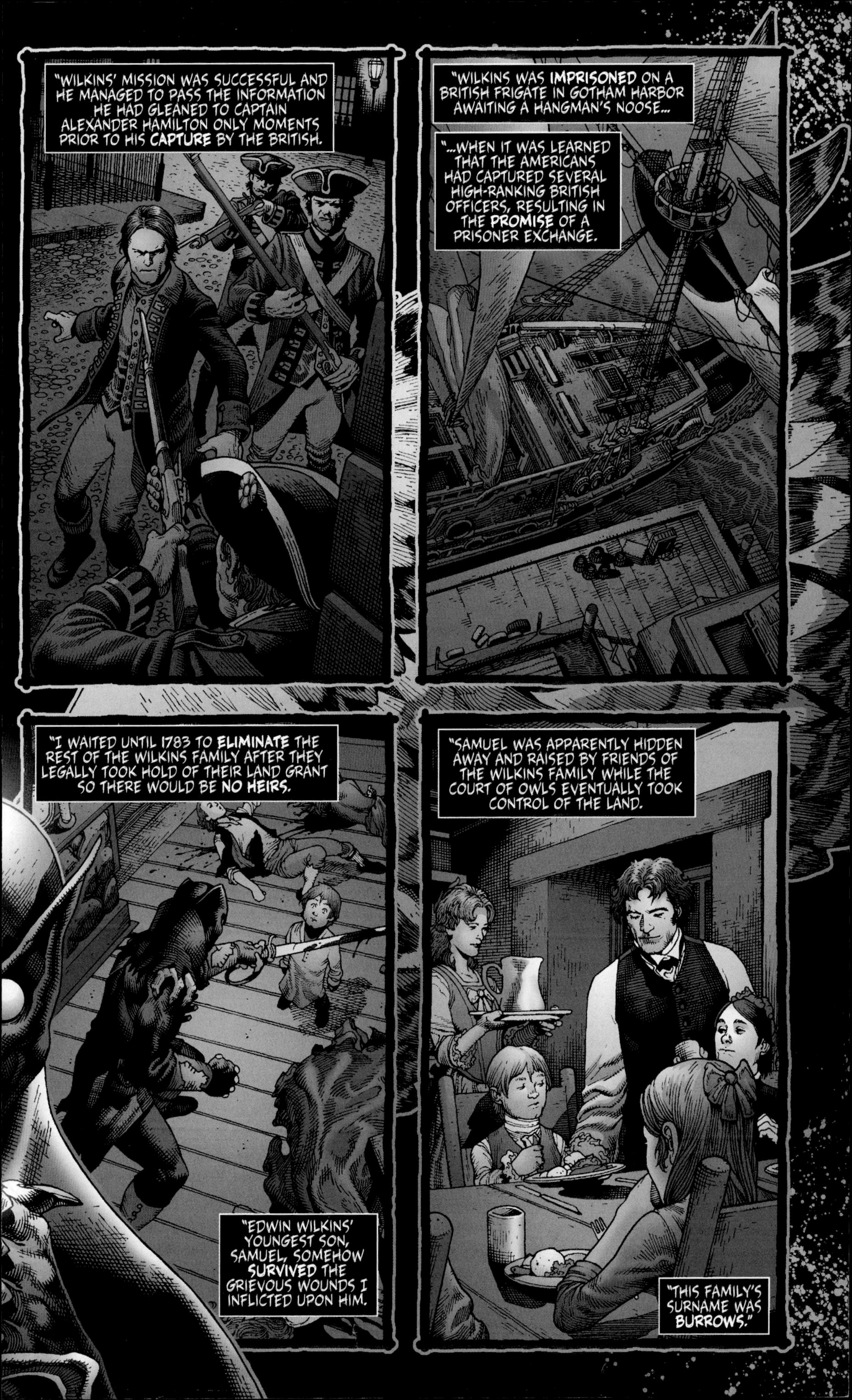
"WILKINS' MISSION WAS SUCCESSFUL AND HE MANAGED TO PASS THE INFORMATION HE HAD GLEANED TO CAPTAIN ALEXANDER HAMILTON ONLY MOMENTS PRIOR TO HIS CAPTURE BY THE BRITISH.
"WILKINS WAS IMPRISONED ON A BRITISH FRIGATE IN GOTHAM HARBOR AWAITING A HANGMAN'S NOOSE...
"...WHEN IT WAS LEARNED THAT THE AMERICANS HAD CAPTURED SEVERAL HIGH-RANKING BRITISH OFFICERS, RESULTING IN THE PROMISE OF A PRISONER EXCHANGE.
"I WAITED UNTIL 1783 TO ELIMINATE THE REST OF THE WILKINS FAMILY AFTER THEY LEGALLY TOOK HOLD OF THEIR LAND GRANT SO THERE WOULD BE NO HEIRS.
"EDWIN WILKINS' YOUNGEST SON, SAMUEL, SOMEHOW SURVIVED THE GRIEVOUS WOUNDS I INFLICTED UPON HIM.
"SAMUEL WAS APPARENTLY HIDDEN AWAY AND RAISED BY FRIENDS OF THE WILKINS FAMILY WHILE THE COURT OF OWLS EVENTUALLY TOOK CONTROL OF THE LAND.
"THIS FAMILY'S SURNAME WAS BURROWS."

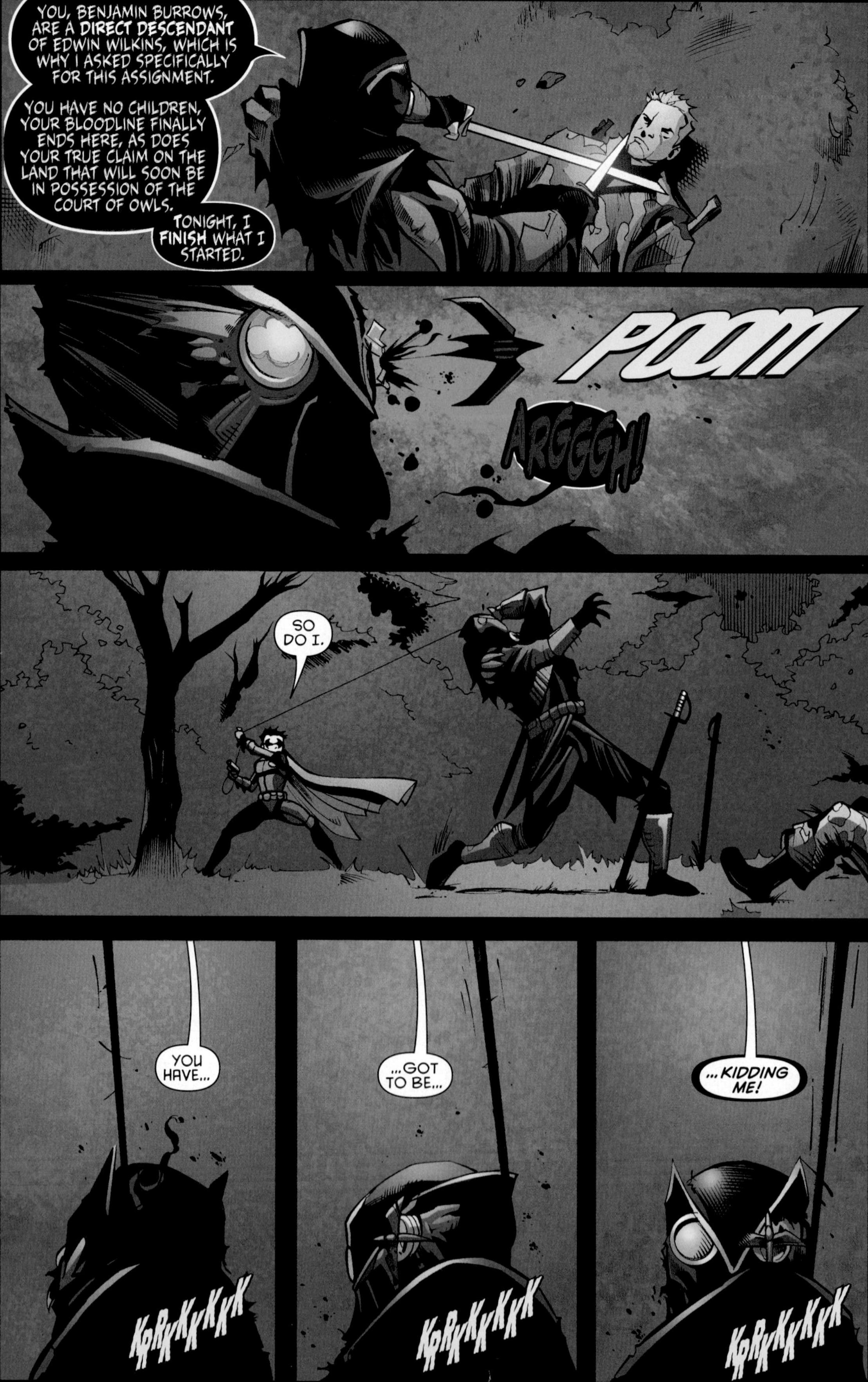
YOU, BENJAMIN BURROWS, ARE A DIRECT DESCENDANT OF EDWIN WILKINS, WHICH IS WHY I ASKED SPECIFICALLY FOR THIS ASSIGNMENT.
YOU HAVE NO CHILDREN, YOUR BLOODLINE FINALLY ENDS HERE, AS DOES YOUR TRUE CLAIM ON THE LAND THAT WILL SOON BE IN POSSESSION OF THE COURT OF OWLS.
TONIGHT, I FINISH WHAT I STARTED.
POOM
ARGGGH!
SO DO I.
YOU HAVE...
KRRKKKKK
...GOT TO BE...
KRRKKKKK
...KIDDING ME!
KRRKKKKK

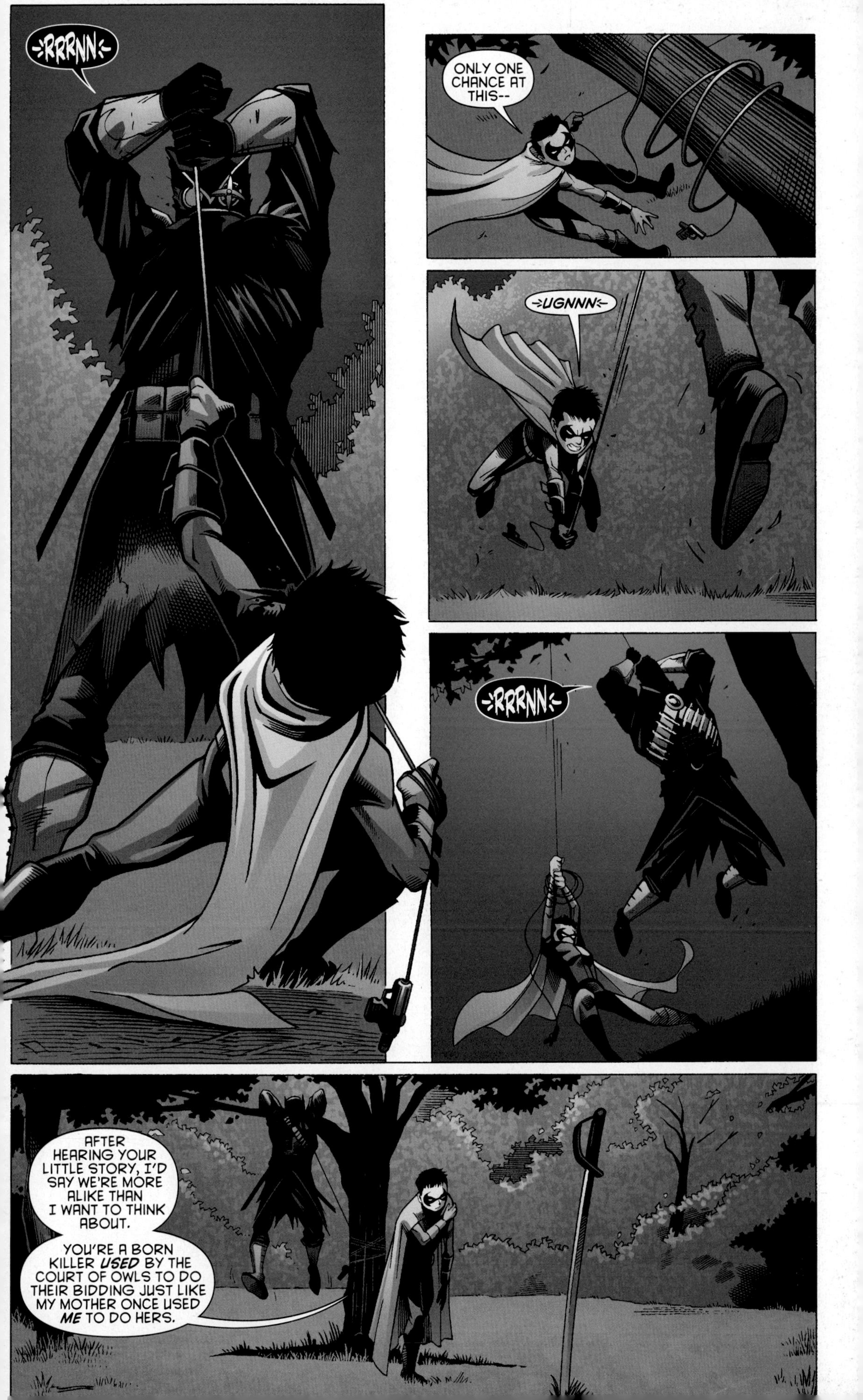
-RRRNN-
ONLY ONE CHANCE AT THIS--
-UGNNN-
-RRRNN-
AFTER HEARING YOUR LITTLE STORY, I'D SAY WE'RE MORE ALIKE THAN I WANT TO THINK ABOUT.
YOU'RE A BORN KILLER *USED* BY THE COURT OF OWLS TO DO THEIR BIDDING JUST LIKE MY MOTHER ONCE USED *ME* TO DO HERS.

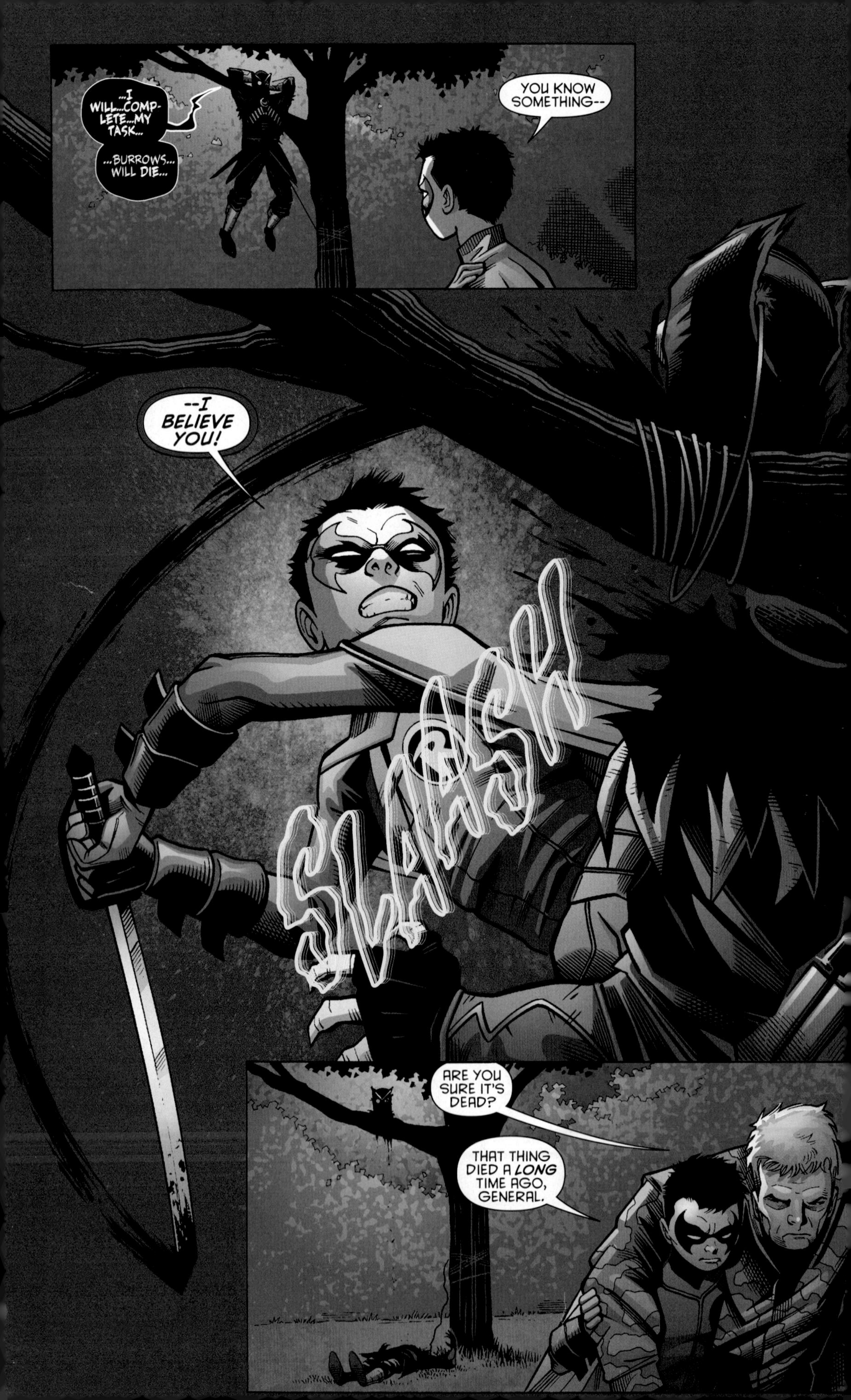

...I WILL...COMP-LETE...MY TASK...
...BURROWS... WILL DIE...
YOU KNOW SOMETHING--
--I BELIEVE YOU!
SLASH
ARE YOU SURE IT'S DEAD?
THAT THING DIED A *LONG* TIME AGO, GENERAL.

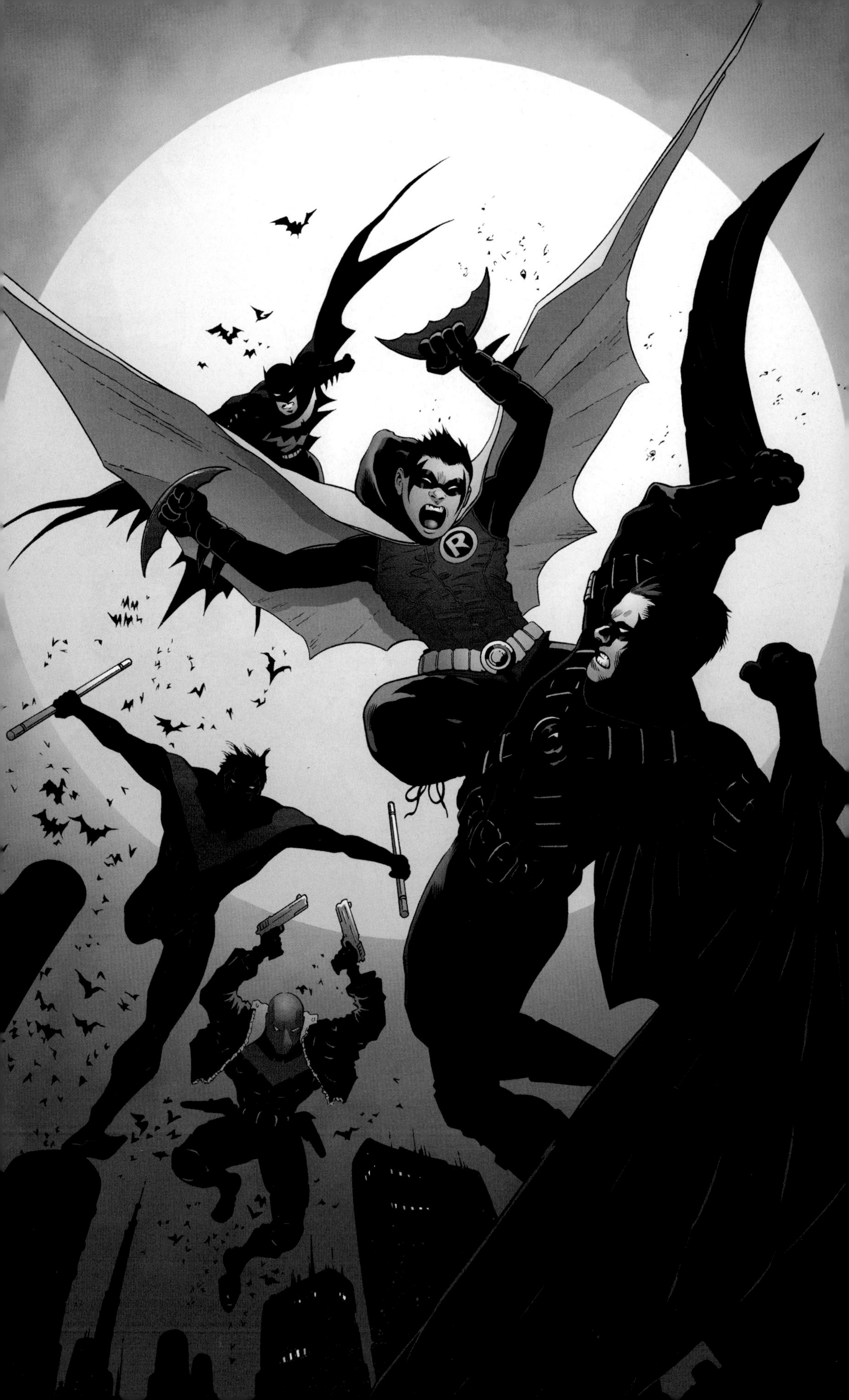

TERMINUS: SCAR OF THE BAT

PETER J. TOMASI writer PATRICK GLEASON penciller MICK GRAY inker

cover by GLEASON, GRAY & KALISZ

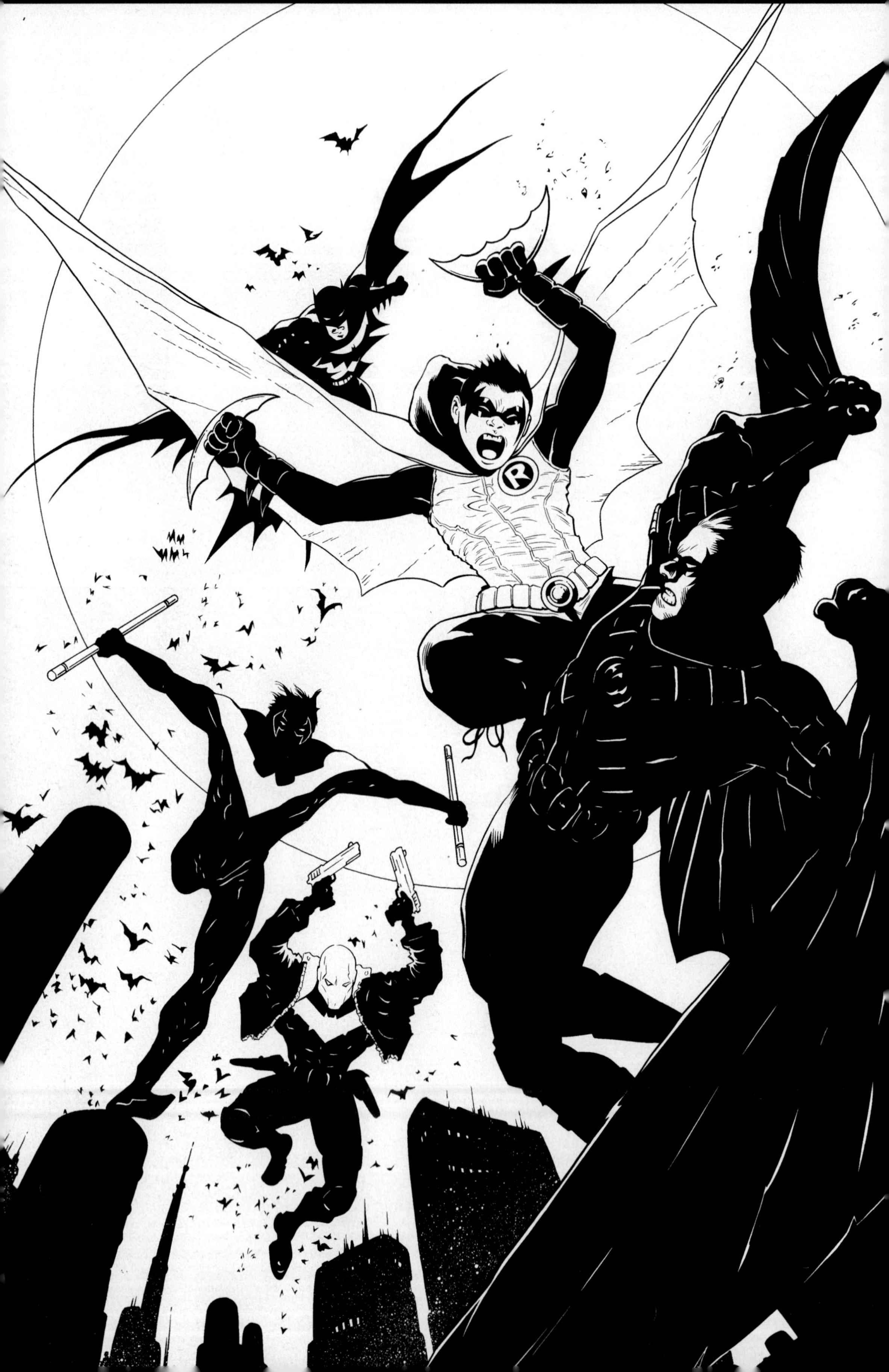

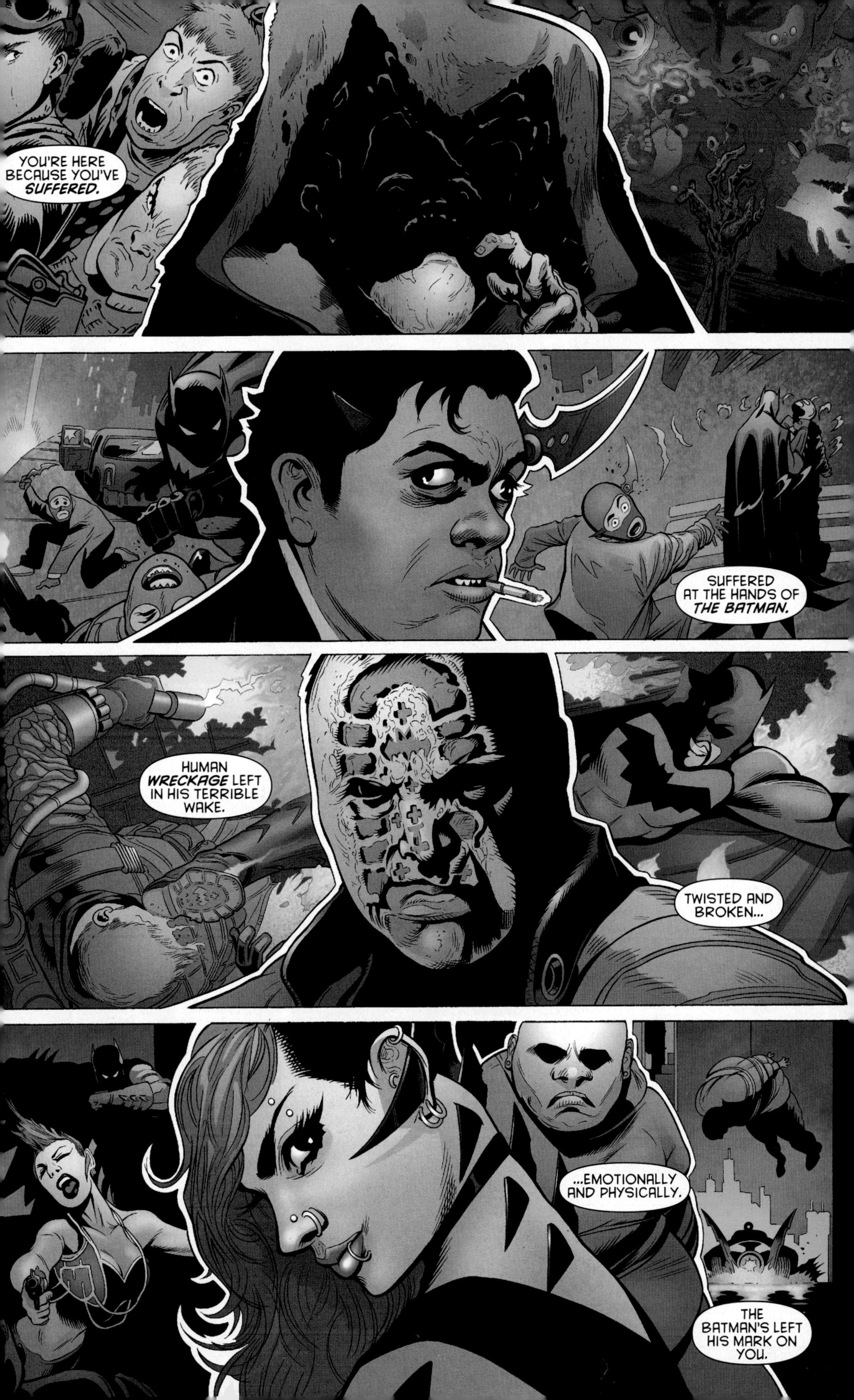

YOU'RE HERE BECAUSE YOU'VE SUFFERED.
SUFFERED AT THE HANDS OF THE BATMAN.
HUMAN WRECKAGE LEFT IN HIS TERRIBLE WAKE.
TWISTED AND BROKEN...
...EMOTIONALLY AND PHYSICALLY.
THE BATMAN'S LEFT HIS MARK ON YOU.

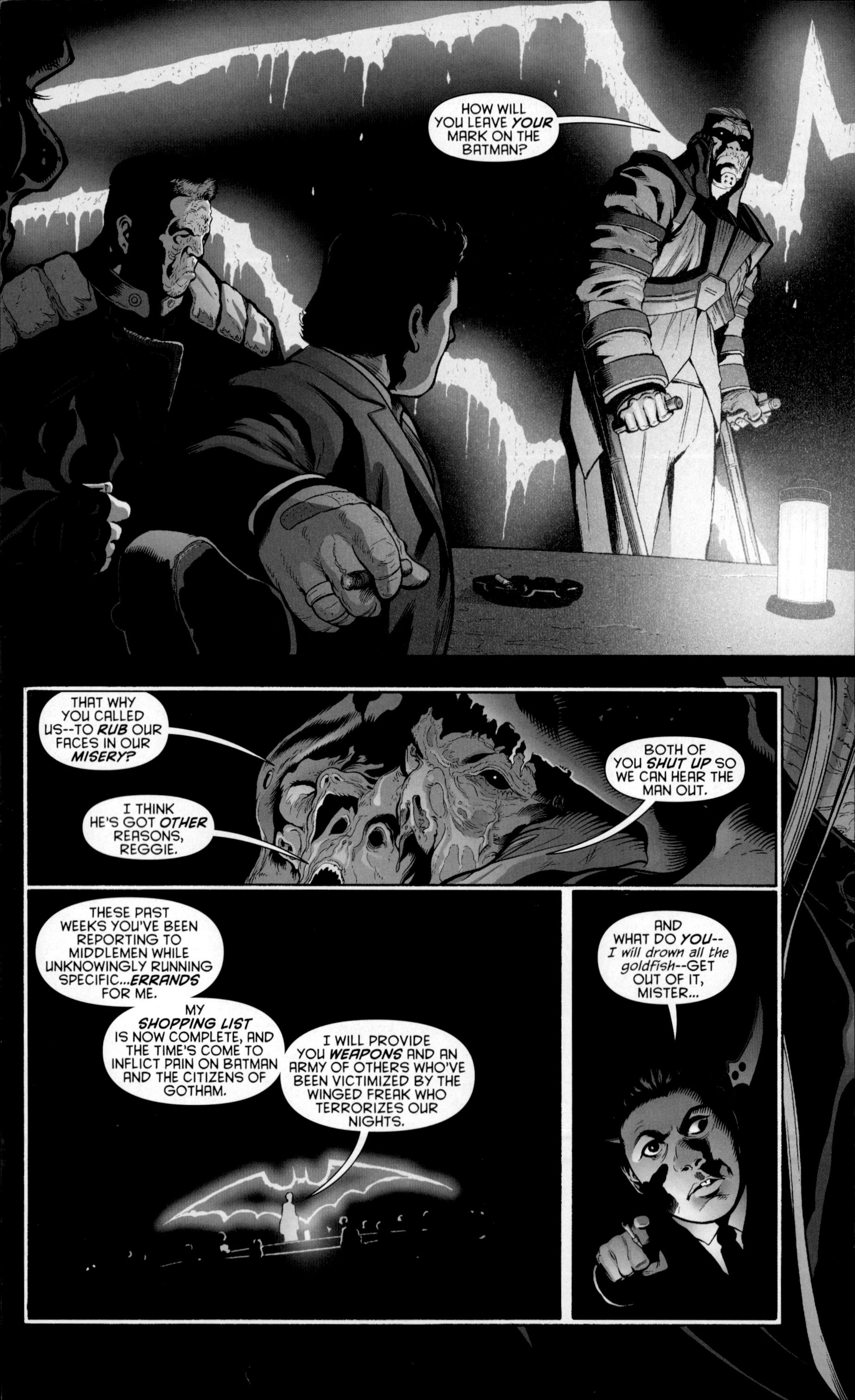
HOW WILL YOU LEAVE YOUR MARK ON THE BATMAN?
THAT WHY YOU CALLED US--TO RUB OUR FACES IN OUR MISERY?
I THINK HE'S GOT OTHER REASONS, REGGIE.
BOTH OF YOU SHUT UP SO WE CAN HEAR THE MAN OUT.
THESE PAST WEEKS YOU'VE BEEN REPORTING TO MIDDLEMEN WHILE UNKNOWINGLY RUNNING SPECIFIC...ERRANDS FOR ME.
MY SHOPPING LIST IS NOW COMPLETE, AND THE TIME'S COME TO INFLICT PAIN ON BATMAN AND THE CITIZENS OF GOTHAM.
I WILL PROVIDE YOU WEAPONS AND AN ARMY OF OTHERS WHO'VE BEEN VICTIMIZED BY THE WINGED FREAK WHO TERRORIZES OUR NIGHTS.
AND WHAT DO YOU-- I will drown all the goldfish--GET OUT OF IT, MISTER...

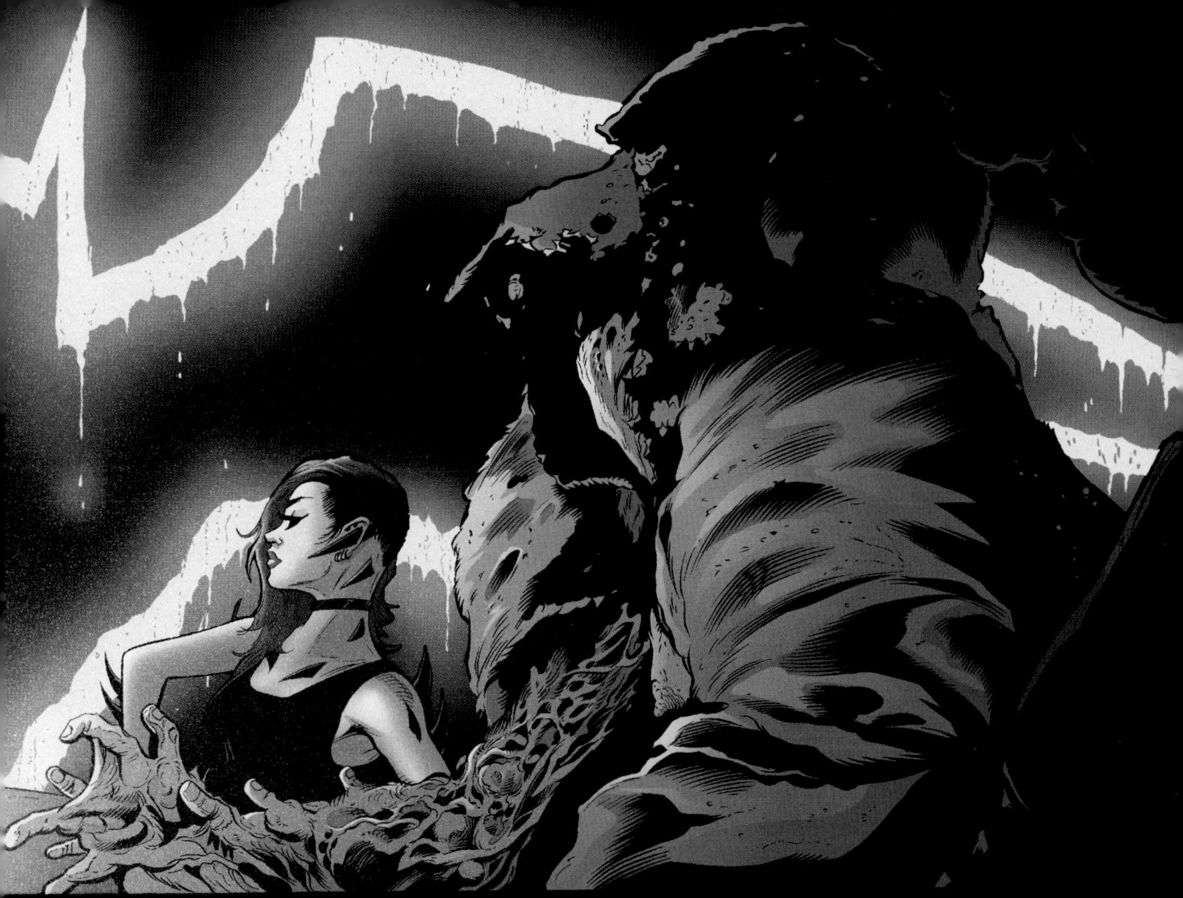

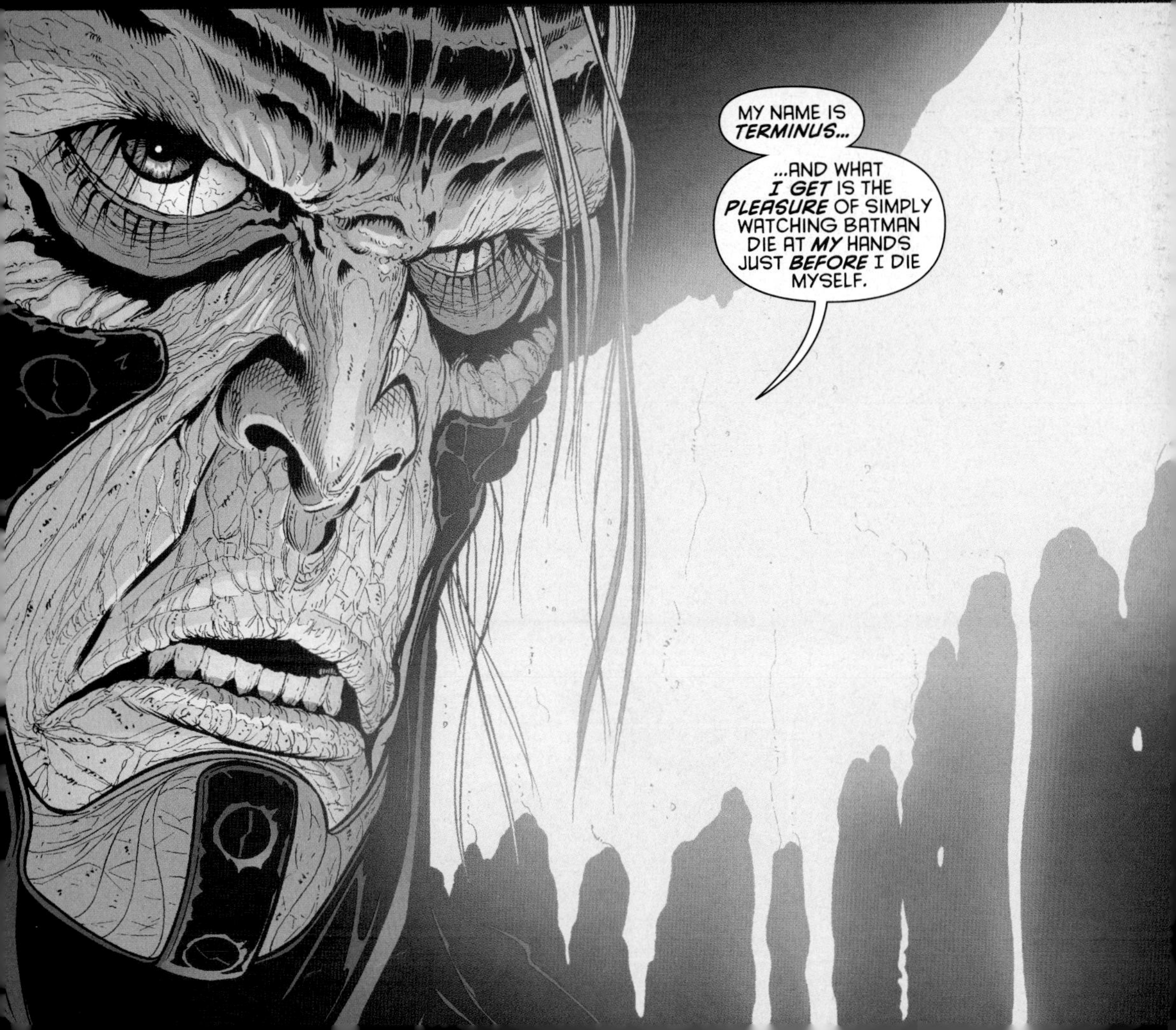
MY NAME IS TERMINUS...
...AND WHAT I GET IS THE PLEASURE OF SIMPLY WATCHING BATMAN DIE AT MY HANDS JUST BEFORE I DIE MYSELF.

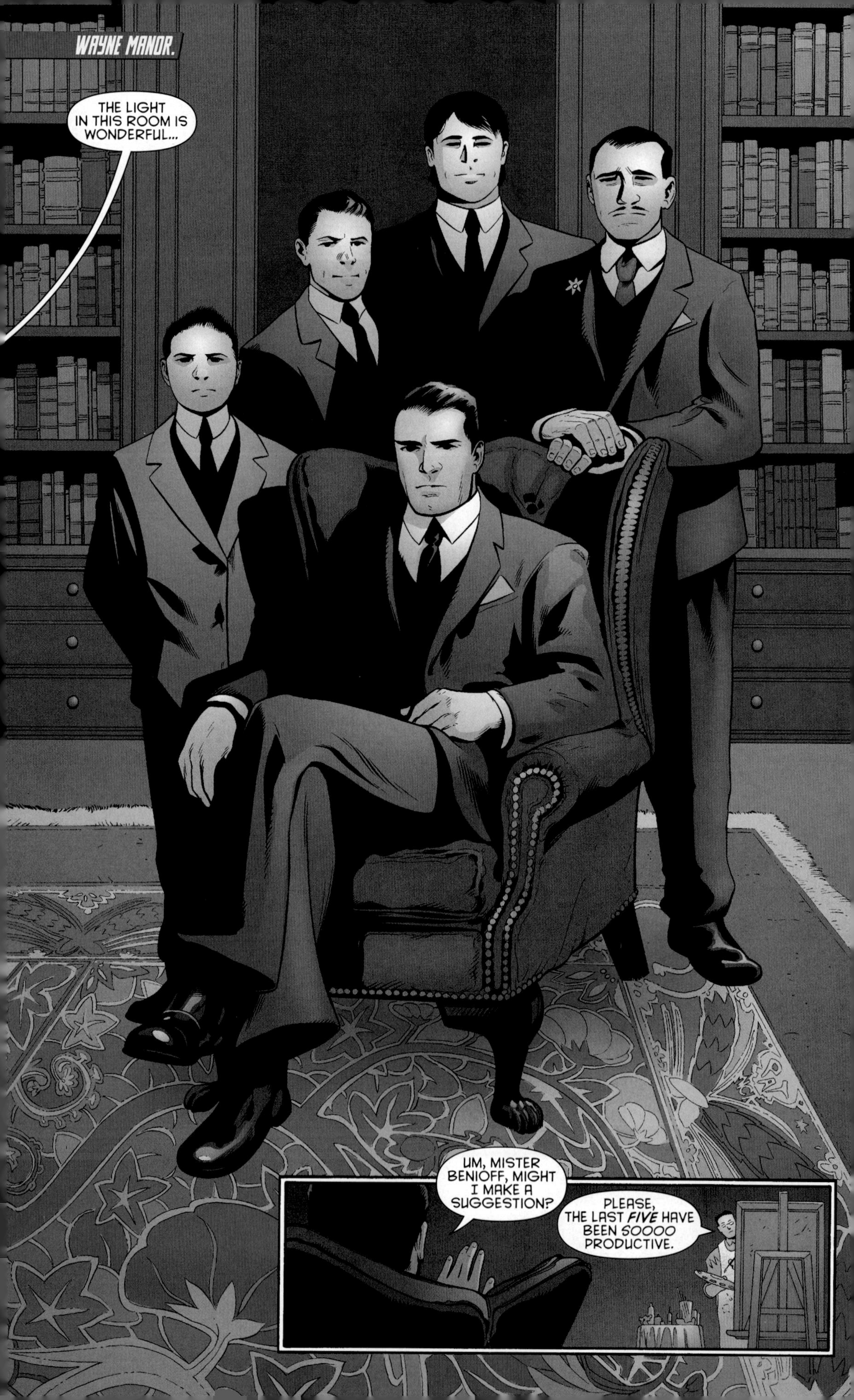
WAYNE MANOR.
THE LIGHT IN THIS ROOM IS WONDERFUL...
UM, MISTER BENIOFF, MIGHT I MAKE A SUGGESTION?
PLEASE, THE LAST FIVE HAVE BEEN SOOOO PRODUCTIVE.

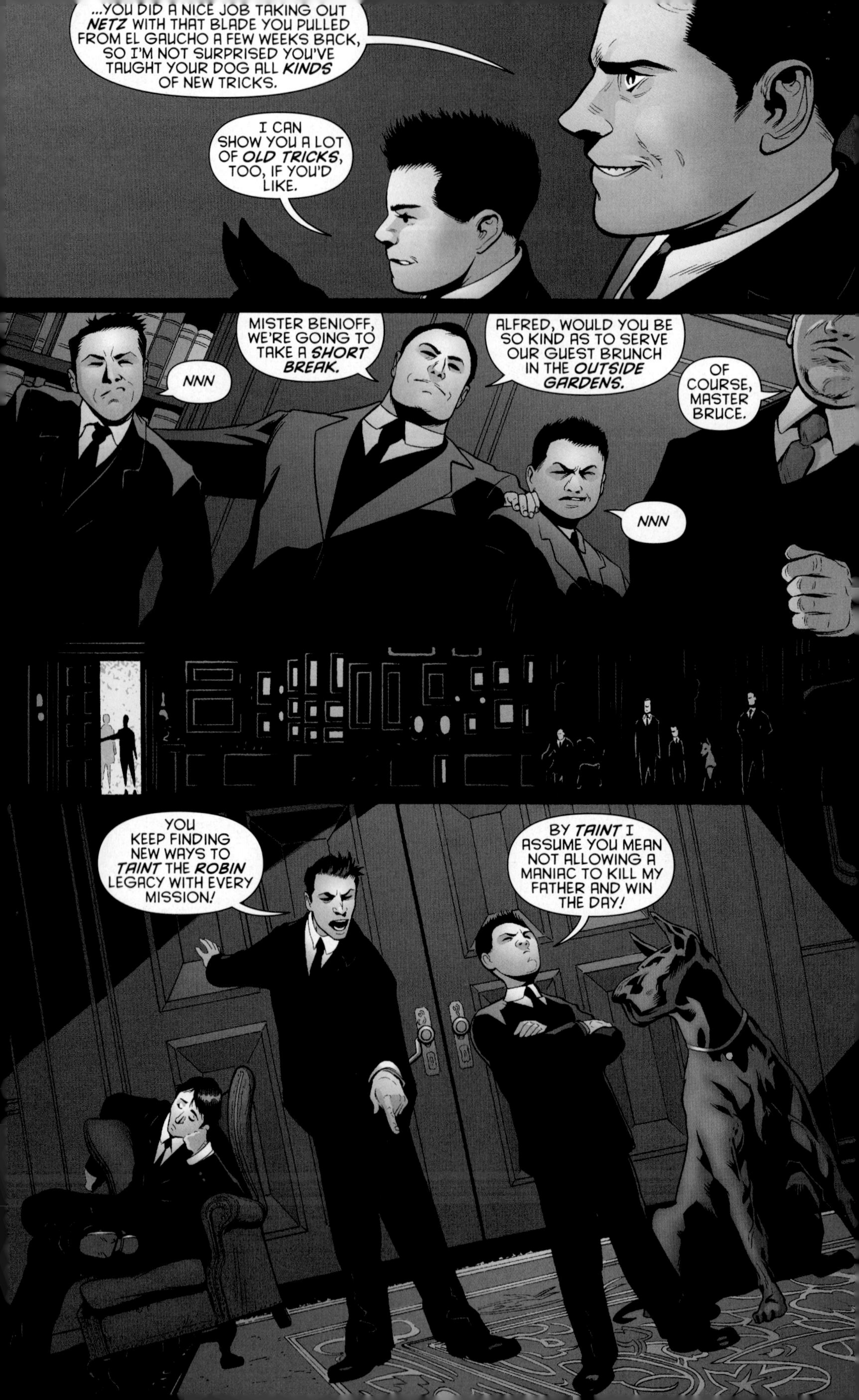
...YOU DID A NICE JOB TAKING OUT NETZ WITH THAT BLADE YOU PULLED FROM EL GAUCHO A FEW WEEKS BACK, SO I'M NOT SURPRISED YOU'VE TAUGHT YOUR DOG ALL KINDS OF NEW TRICKS.
I CAN SHOW YOU A LOT OF OLD TRICKS, TOO, IF YOU'D LIKE.
NNN
MISTER BENIOFF, WE'RE GOING TO TAKE A SHORT BREAK.
ALFRED, WOULD YOU BE SO KIND AS TO SERVE OUR GUEST BRUNCH IN THE OUTSIDE GARDENS.
OF COURSE, MASTER BRUCE.
NNN
YOU KEEP FINDING NEW WAYS TO TAINT THE ROBIN LEGACY WITH EVERY MISSION!
BY TAINT I ASSUME YOU MEAN NOT ALLOWING A MANIAC TO KILL MY FATHER AND WIN THE DAY!

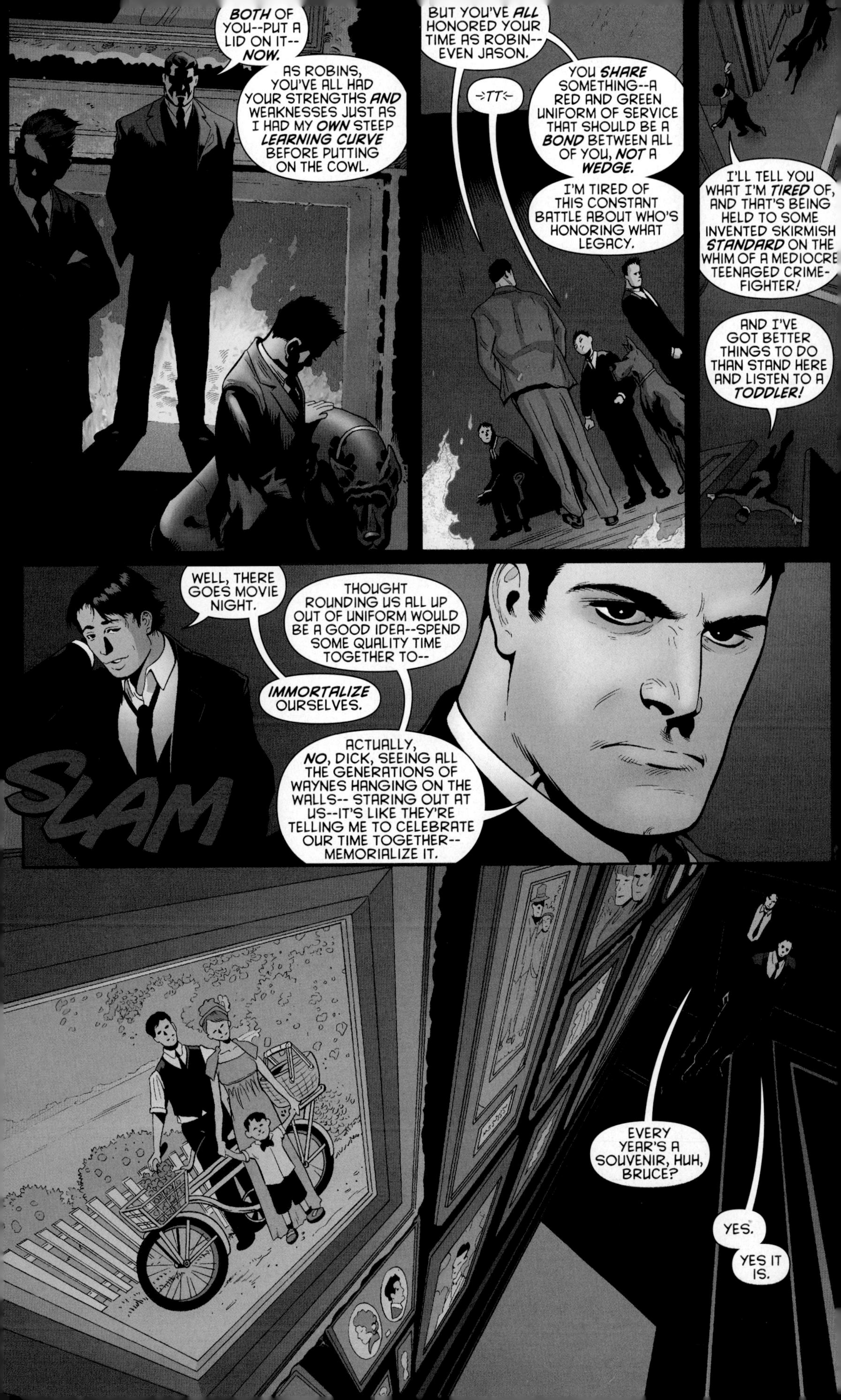
BOTH OF YOU--PUT A LID ON IT--NOW.
AS ROBINS, YOU'VE ALL HAD YOUR STRENGTHS AND WEAKNESSES JUST AS I HAD MY OWN STEEP LEARNING CURVE BEFORE PUTTING ON THE COWL.
BUT YOU'VE ALL HONORED YOUR TIME AS ROBIN--EVEN JASON.
-TT-
YOU SHARE SOMETHING--A RED AND GREEN UNIFORM OF SERVICE THAT SHOULD BE A BOND BETWEEN ALL OF YOU, NOT A WEDGE.
I'M TIRED OF THIS CONSTANT BATTLE ABOUT WHO'S HONORING WHAT LEGACY.
I'LL TELL YOU WHAT I'M TIRED OF, AND THAT'S BEING HELD TO SOME INVENTED SKIRMISH STANDARD ON THE WHIM OF A MEDIOCRE TEENAGED CRIME-FIGHTER!
AND I'VE GOT BETTER THINGS TO DO THAN STAND HERE AND LISTEN TO A TODDLER!
SLAM
WELL, THERE GOES MOVIE NIGHT.
THOUGHT ROUNDING US ALL UP OUT OF UNIFORM WOULD BE A GOOD IDEA--SPEND SOME QUALITY TIME TOGETHER TO--
IMMORTALIZE OURSELVES.
ACTUALLY, NO, DICK, SEEING ALL THE GENERATIONS OF WAYNES HANGING ON THE WALLS-- STARING OUT AT US--IT'S LIKE THEY'RE TELLING ME TO CELEBRATE OUR TIME TOGETHER--MEMORIALIZE IT.
EVERY YEAR'S A SOUVENIR, HUH, BRUCE?
YES.
YES IT IS.

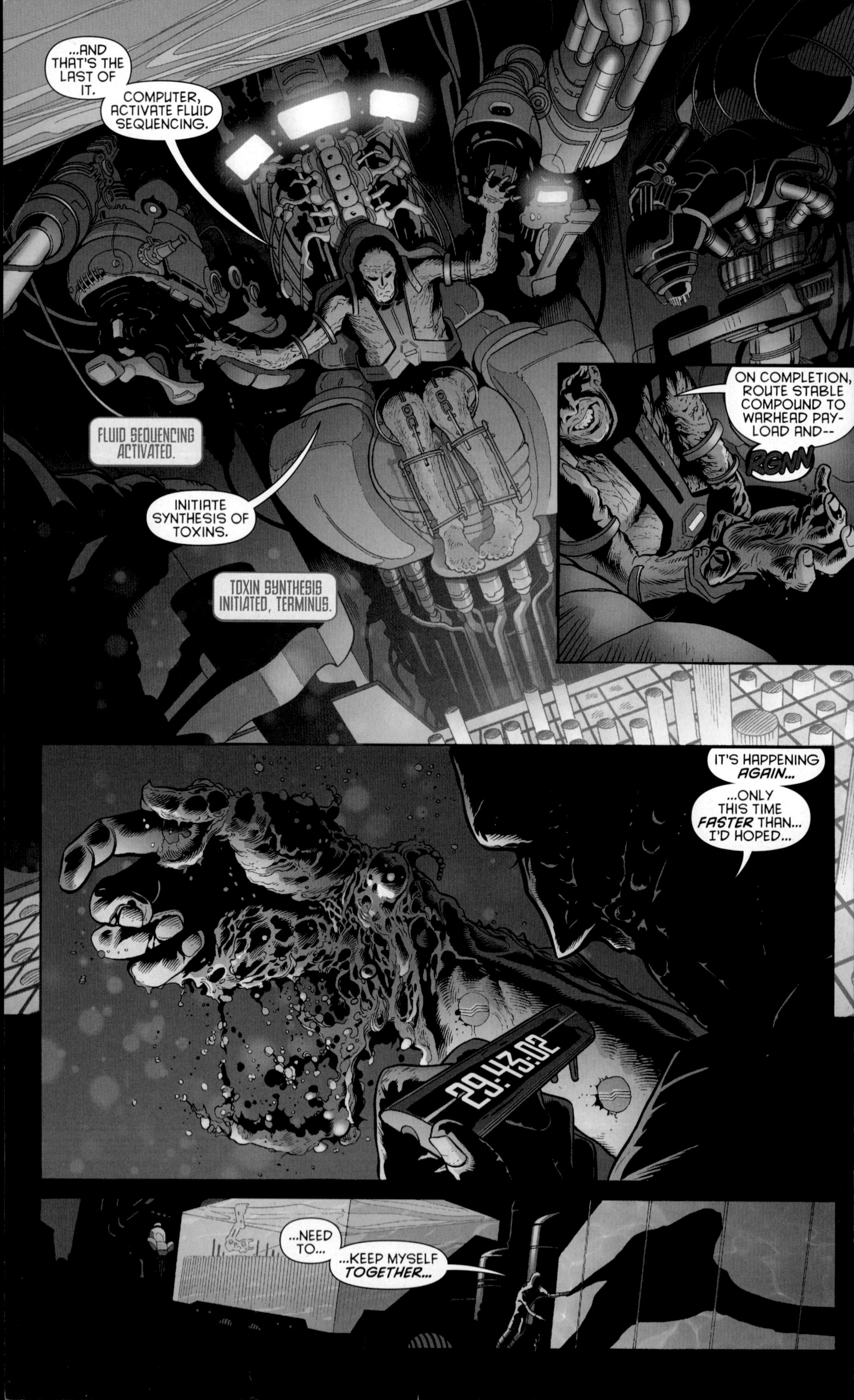
...AND THAT'S THE LAST OF IT.
COMPUTER, ACTIVATE FLUID SEQUENCING.
FLUID SEQUENCING ACTIVATED.
INITIATE SYNTHESIS OF TOXINS.
TOXIN SYNTHESIS INITIATED, TERMINUS.
ON COMPLETION, ROUTE STABLE COMPOUND TO WARHEAD PAY-LOAD AND--
RGNN
IT'S HAPPENING AGAIN...
...ONLY THIS TIME FASTER THAN... I'D HOPED...
29:43:02
...NEED TO...
...KEEP MYSELF TOGETHER...

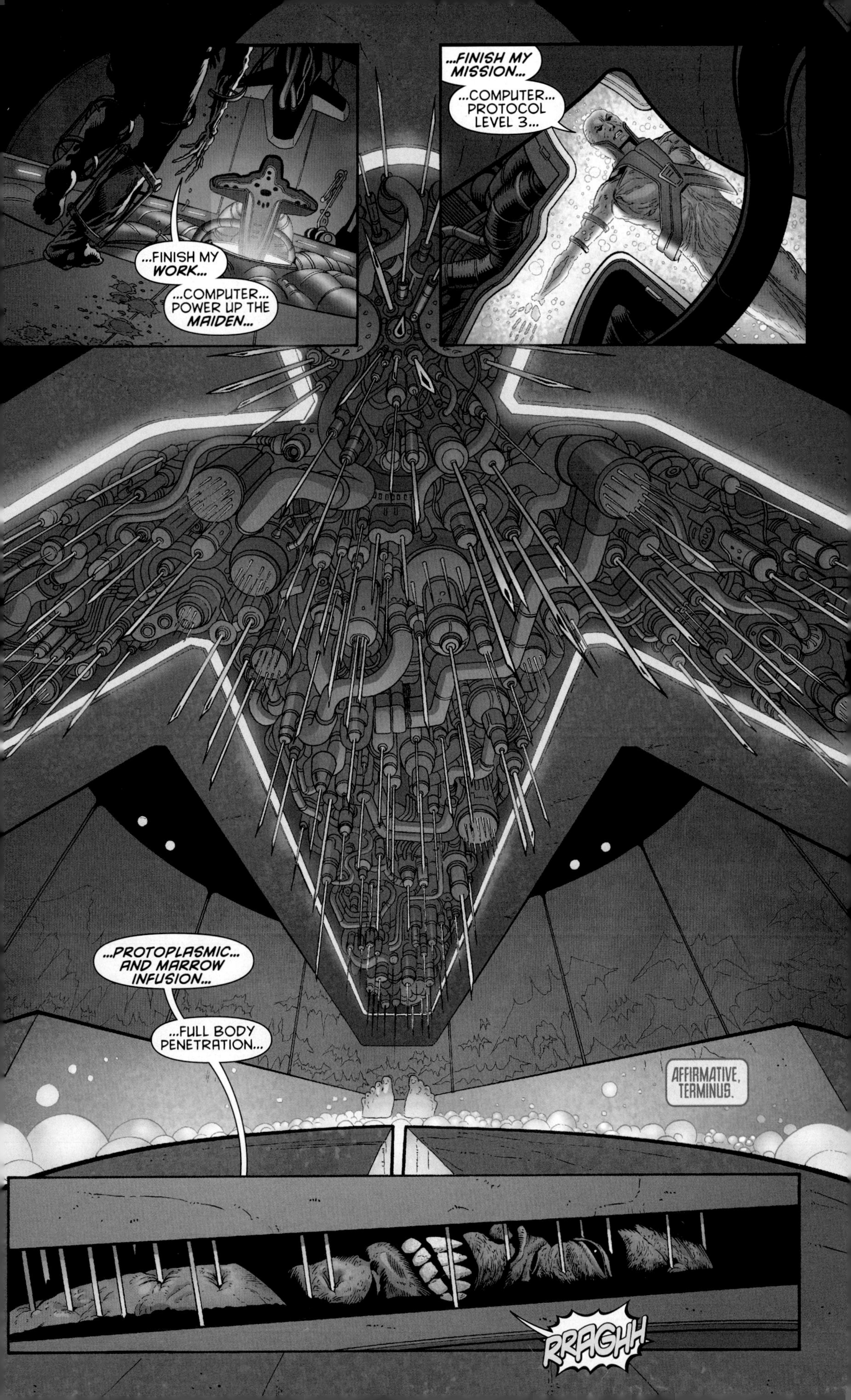
...FINISH MY WORK...
...COMPUTER... POWER UP THE MAIDEN...
...FINISH MY MISSION...
...COMPUTER... PROTOCOL LEVEL 3...
...PROTOPLASMIC... AND MARROW INFUSION...
...FULL BODY PENETRATION...
AFFIRMATIVE, TERMINUS.
RRAGHH

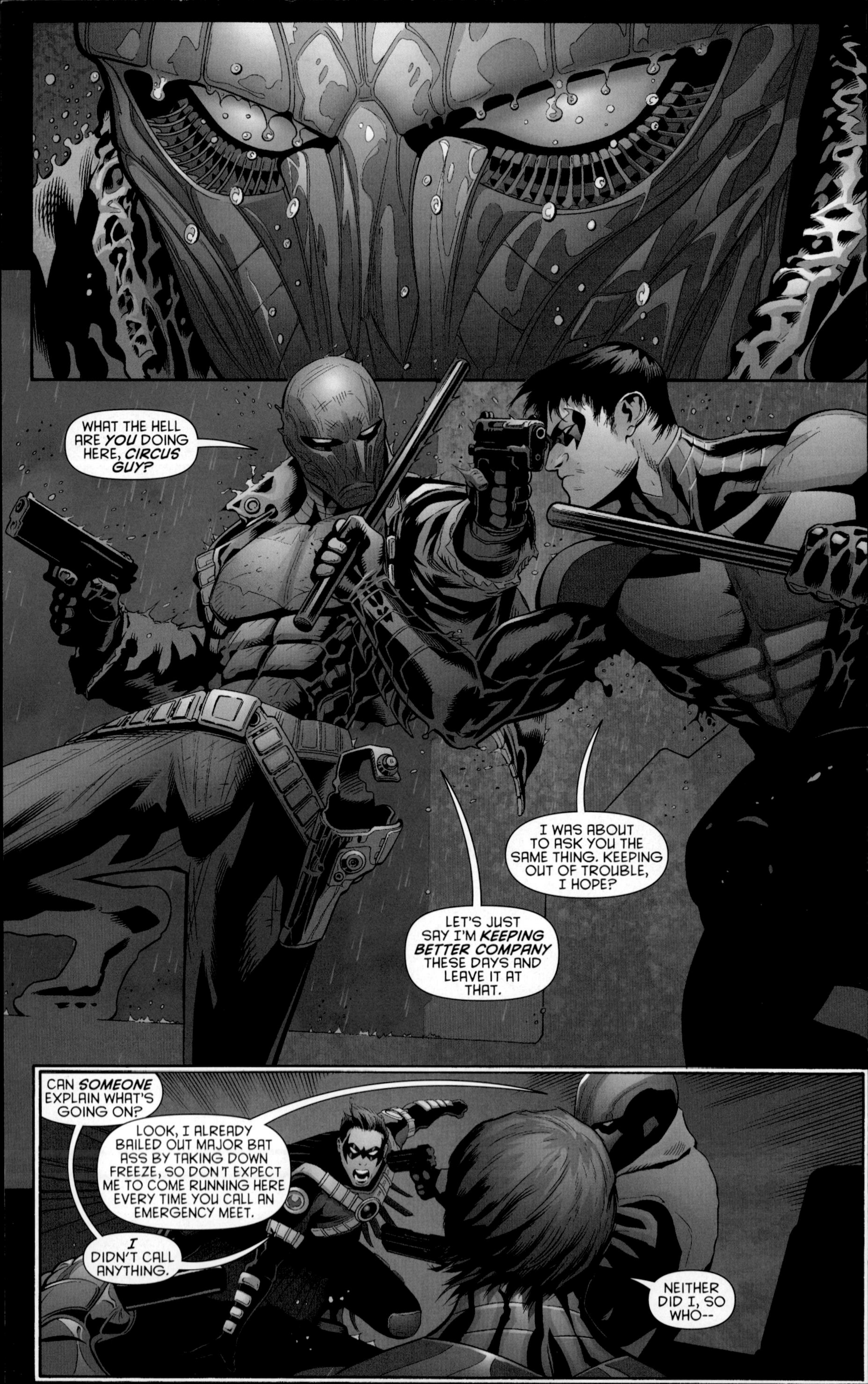
WHAT THE HELL ARE YOU DOING HERE, CIRCUS GUY?
I WAS ABOUT TO ASK YOU THE SAME THING. KEEPING OUT OF TROUBLE, I HOPE?
LET'S JUST SAY I'M KEEPING BETTER COMPANY THESE DAYS AND LEAVE IT AT THAT.
CAN SOMEONE EXPLAIN WHAT'S GOING ON?
LOOK, I ALREADY BAILED OUT MAJOR BAT ASS BY TAKING DOWN FREEZE, SO DON'T EXPECT ME TO COME RUNNING HERE EVERY TIME YOU CALL AN EMERGENCY MEET.
I DIDN'T CALL ANYTHING.
NEITHER DID I, SO WHO--

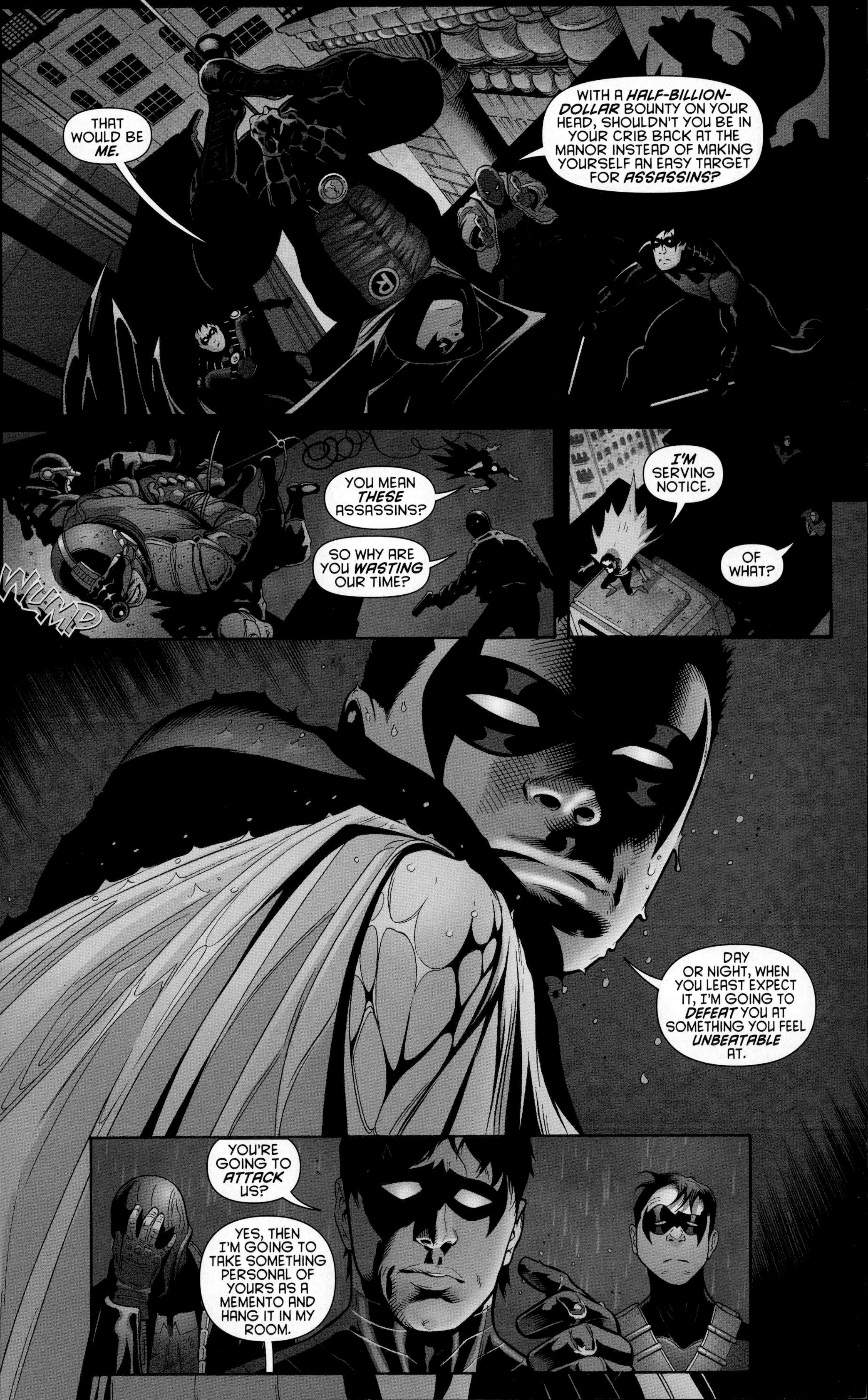

THAT WOULD BE *ME.*
WITH A *HALF-BILLION-DOLLAR* BOUNTY ON YOUR HEAD, SHOULDN'T YOU BE IN YOUR CRIB BACK AT THE MANOR INSTEAD OF MAKING YOURSELF AN EASY TARGET FOR *ASSASSINS?*
WUMP
YOU MEAN *THESE* ASSASSINS?
SO WHY ARE YOU *WASTING* OUR TIME?
*I'M* SERVING NOTICE.
OF WHAT?
DAY OR NIGHT, WHEN YOU LEAST EXPECT IT, I'M GOING TO *DEFEAT* YOU AT SOMETHING YOU FEEL *UNBEATABLE* AT.
YOU'RE GOING TO *ATTACK* US?
YES, THEN I'M GOING TO TAKE SOMETHING PERSONAL OF YOURS AS A MEMENTO AND HANG IT IN MY ROOM.

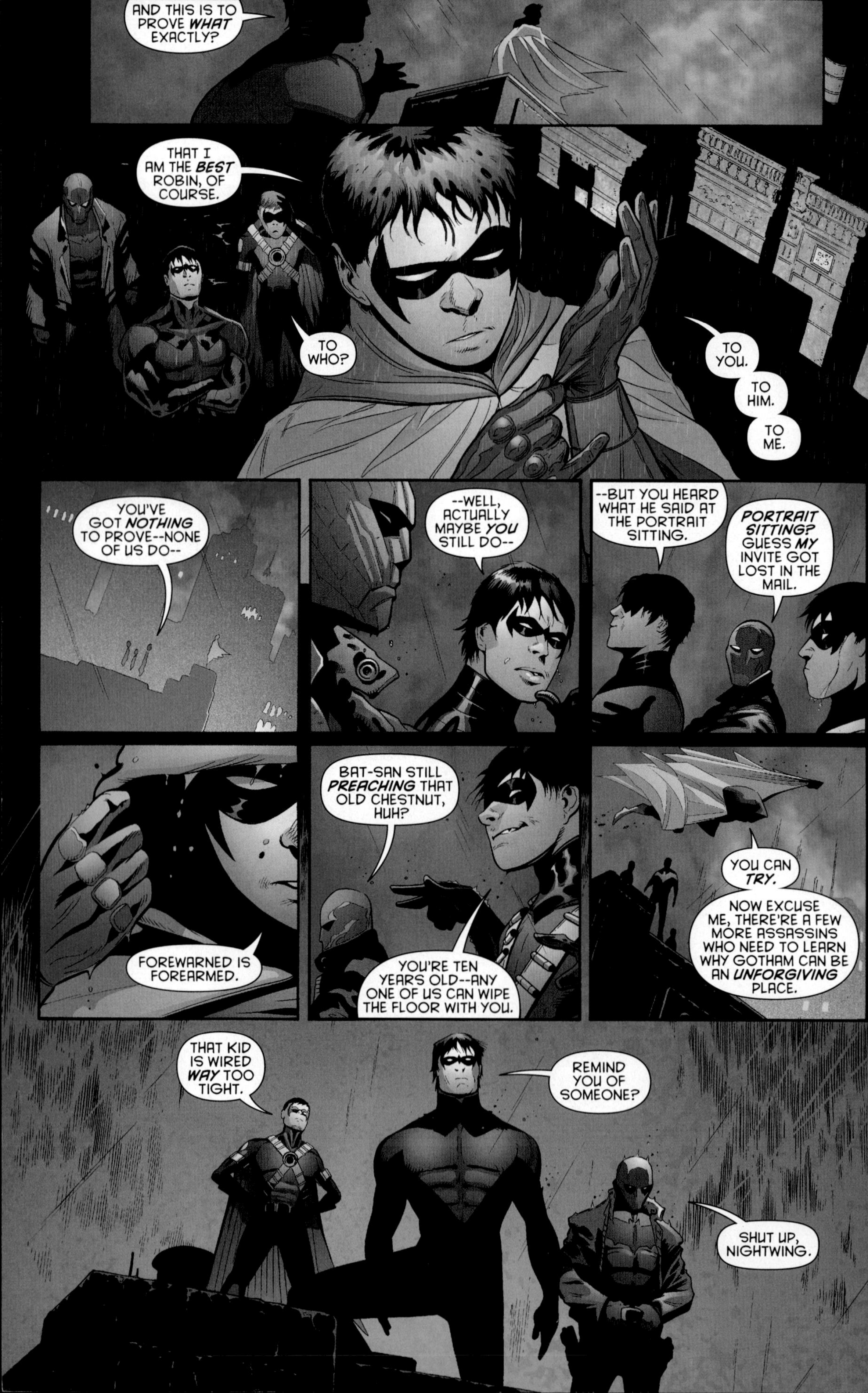
AND THIS IS TO PROVE *WHAT* EXACTLY?
THAT I AM THE *BEST* ROBIN, OF COURSE.
TO WHO?
TO YOU.
TO HIM.
TO ME.
YOU'VE GOT *NOTHING* TO PROVE--NONE OF US DO--
--WELL, ACTUALLY MAYBE *YOU* STILL DO--
--BUT YOU HEARD WHAT HE SAID AT THE PORTRAIT SITTING.
*PORTRAIT SITTING?* GUESS *MY* INVITE GOT LOST IN THE MAIL.
FOREWARNED IS FOREARMED.
BAT-SAN STILL *PREACHING* THAT OLD CHESTNUT, HUH?
YOU'RE TEN YEARS OLD--ANY ONE OF US CAN WIPE THE FLOOR WITH YOU.
YOU CAN *TRY.*
NOW EXCUSE ME, THERE'RE A FEW MORE ASSASSINS WHO NEED TO LEARN WHY GOTHAM CAN BE AN *UNFORGIVING* PLACE.
THAT KID IS WIRED *WAY* TOO TIGHT.
REMIND YOU OF SOMEONE?
SHUT UP, NIGHTWING.

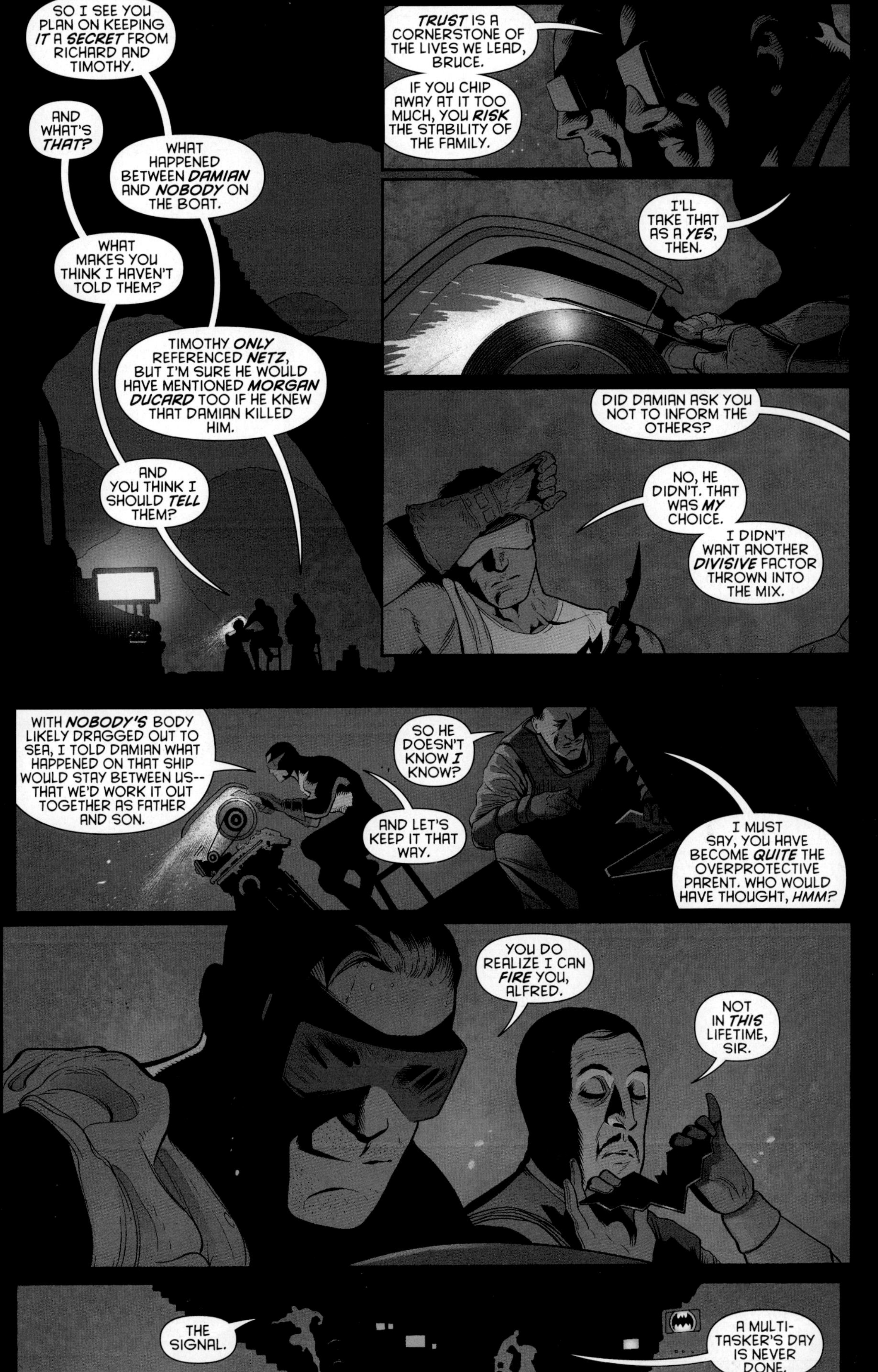

SO I SEE YOU PLAN ON KEEPING IT A SECRET FROM RICHARD AND TIMOTHY.
AND WHAT'S THAT?
WHAT HAPPENED BETWEEN DAMIAN AND NOBODY ON THE BOAT.
WHAT MAKES YOU THINK I HAVEN'T TOLD THEM?
TIMOTHY ONLY REFERENCED NETZ, BUT I'M SURE HE WOULD HAVE MENTIONED MORGAN DUCARD TOO IF HE KNEW THAT DAMIAN KILLED HIM.
AND YOU THINK I SHOULD TELL THEM?
TRUST IS A CORNERSTONE OF THE LIVES WE LEAD, BRUCE.
IF YOU CHIP AWAY AT IT TOO MUCH, YOU RISK THE STABILITY OF THE FAMILY.
I'LL TAKE THAT AS A YES, THEN.
DID DAMIAN ASK YOU NOT TO INFORM THE OTHERS?
NO, HE DIDN'T. THAT WAS MY CHOICE.
I DIDN'T WANT ANOTHER DIVISIVE FACTOR THROWN INTO THE MIX.
WITH NOBODY'S BODY LIKELY DRAGGED OUT TO SEA, I TOLD DAMIAN WHAT HAPPENED ON THAT SHIP WOULD STAY BETWEEN US--THAT WE'D WORK IT OUT TOGETHER AS FATHER AND SON.
SO HE DOESN'T KNOW I KNOW?
AND LET'S KEEP IT THAT WAY.
I MUST SAY, YOU HAVE BECOME QUITE THE OVERPROTECTIVE PARENT. WHO WOULD HAVE THOUGHT, HMM?
YOU DO REALIZE I CAN FIRE YOU, ALFRED.
NOT IN THIS LIFETIME, SIR.
THE SIGNAL.
A MULTI-TASKER'S DAY IS NEVER DONE.

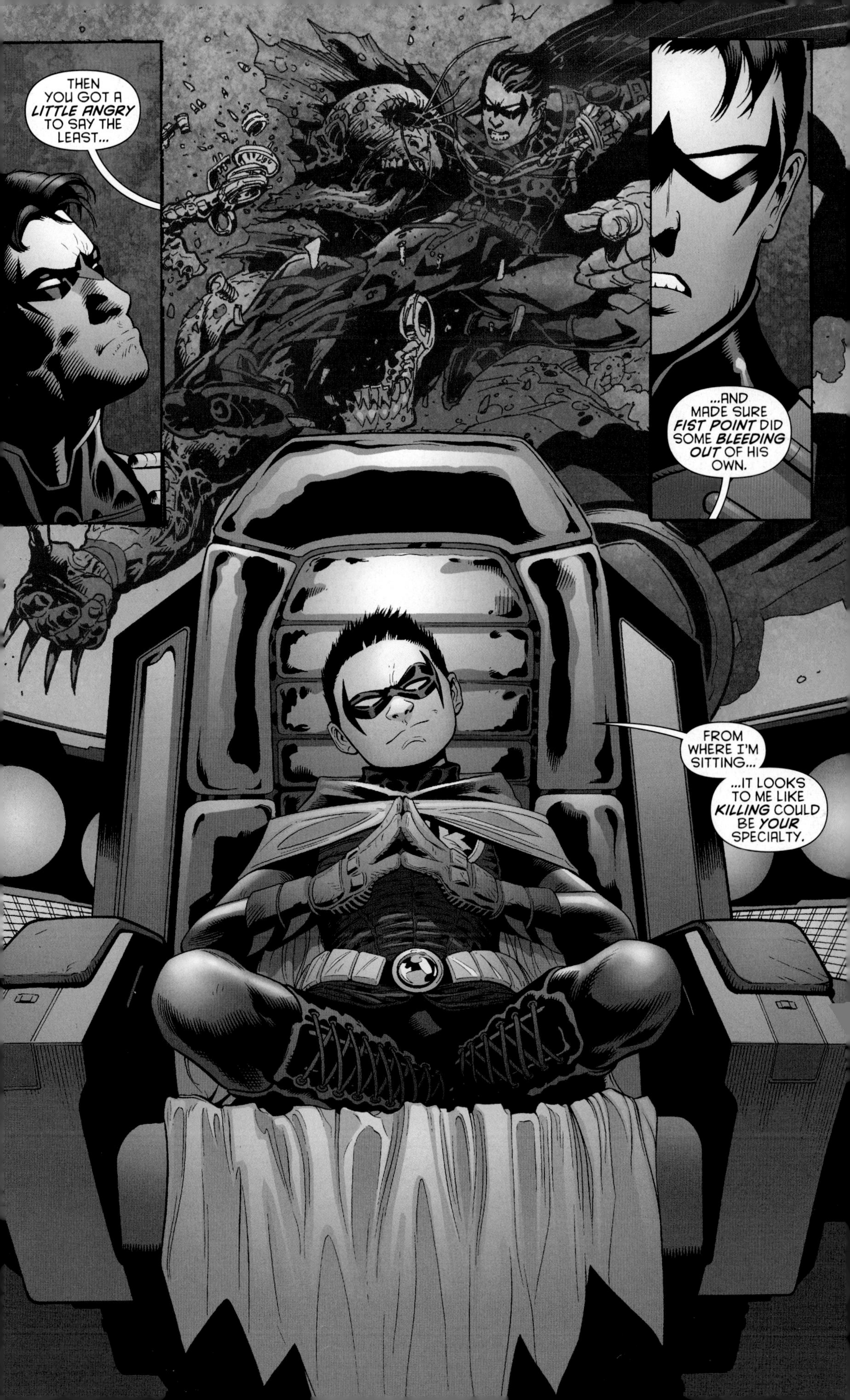
THEN YOU GOT A LITTLE ANGRY TO SAY THE LEAST...
...AND MADE SURE FIST POINT DID SOME BLEEDING OUT OF HIS OWN.
FROM WHERE I'M SITTING...
...IT LOOKS TO ME LIKE KILLING COULD BE YOUR SPECIALTY.

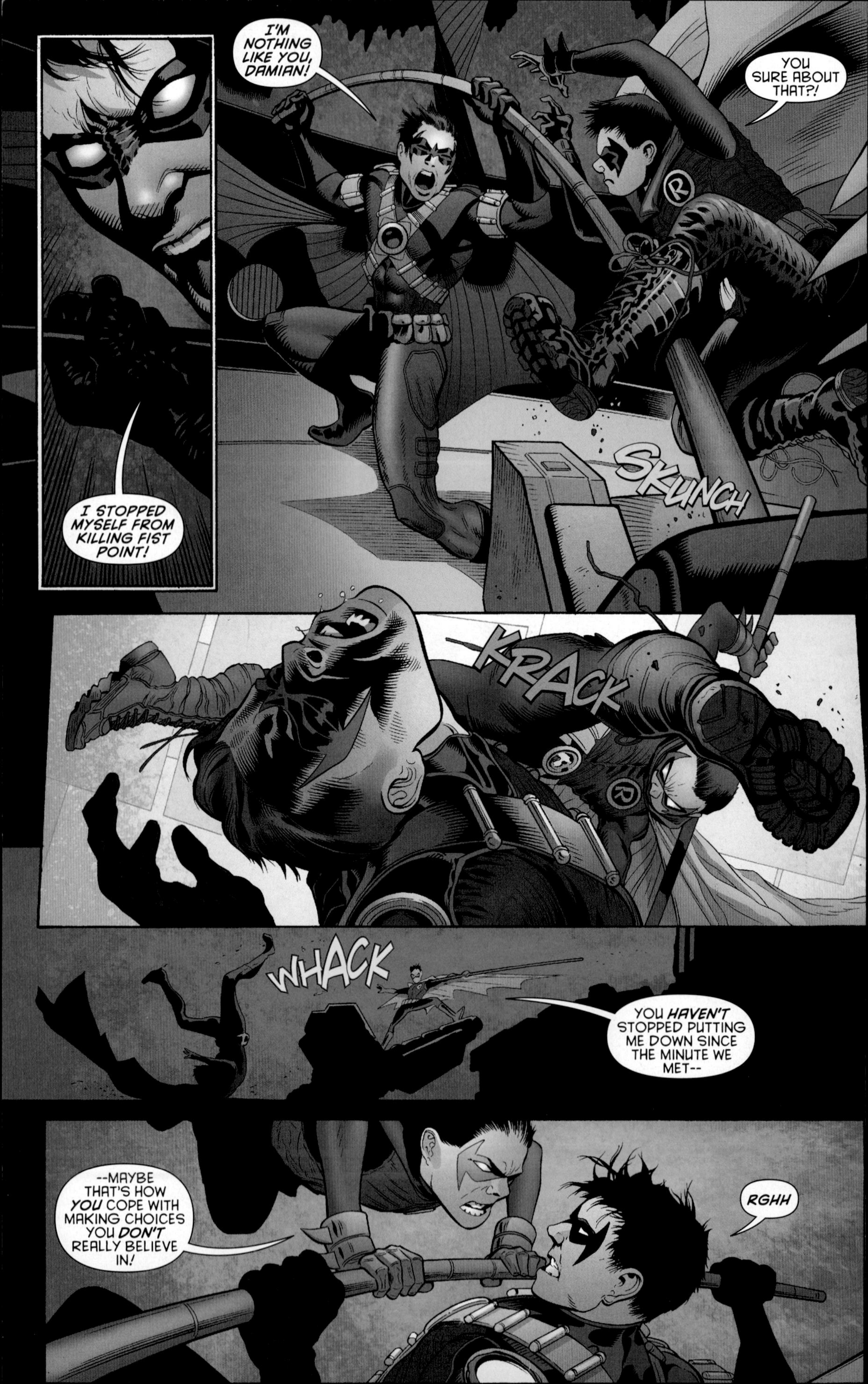
I'M NOTHING LIKE YOU, DAMIAN!
YOU SURE ABOUT THAT?!
I STOPPED MYSELF FROM KILLING FIST POINT!
SKUNCH
KRACK
WHACK
YOU HAVEN'T STOPPED PUTTING ME DOWN SINCE THE MINUTE WE MET--
--MAYBE THAT'S HOW YOU COPE WITH MAKING CHOICES YOU DON'T REALLY BELIEVE IN!
RGHH

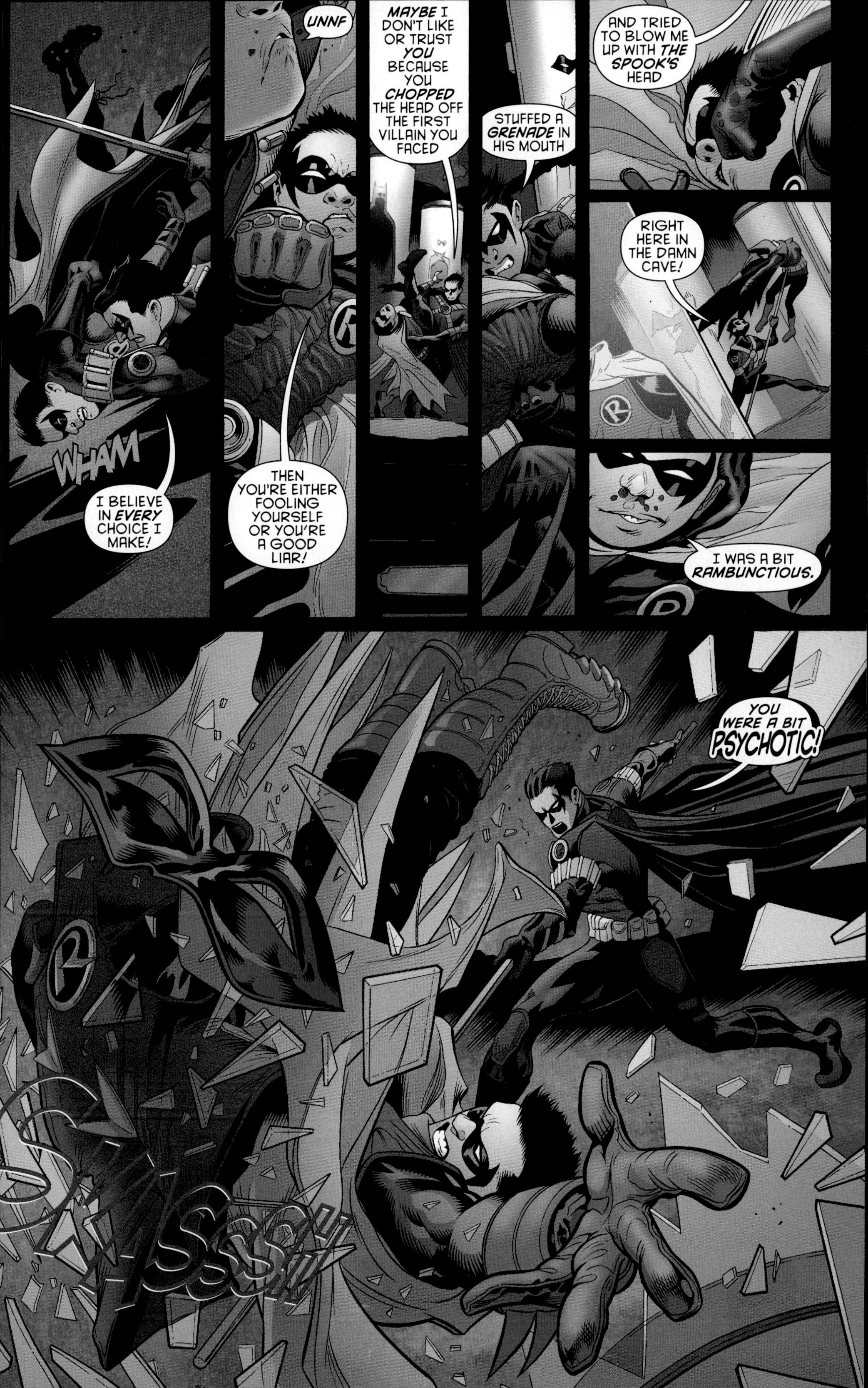

WHAM
I BELIEVE IN *EVERY* CHOICE I MAKE!
UNNF
THEN YOU'RE EITHER FOOLING YOURSELF OR YOU'RE A GOOD LIAR!
*MAYBE* I DON'T LIKE OR TRUST *YOU* BECAUSE YOU *CHOPPED* THE HEAD OFF THE FIRST VILLAIN YOU FACED
STUFFED A *GRENADE* IN HIS MOUTH
AND TRIED TO BLOW ME UP WITH *THE SPOOK'S* HEAD
RIGHT HERE IN THE DAMN CAVE!
I WAS A BIT *RAMBUNCTIOUS.*
*YOU* WERE A BIT PSYCHOTIC!

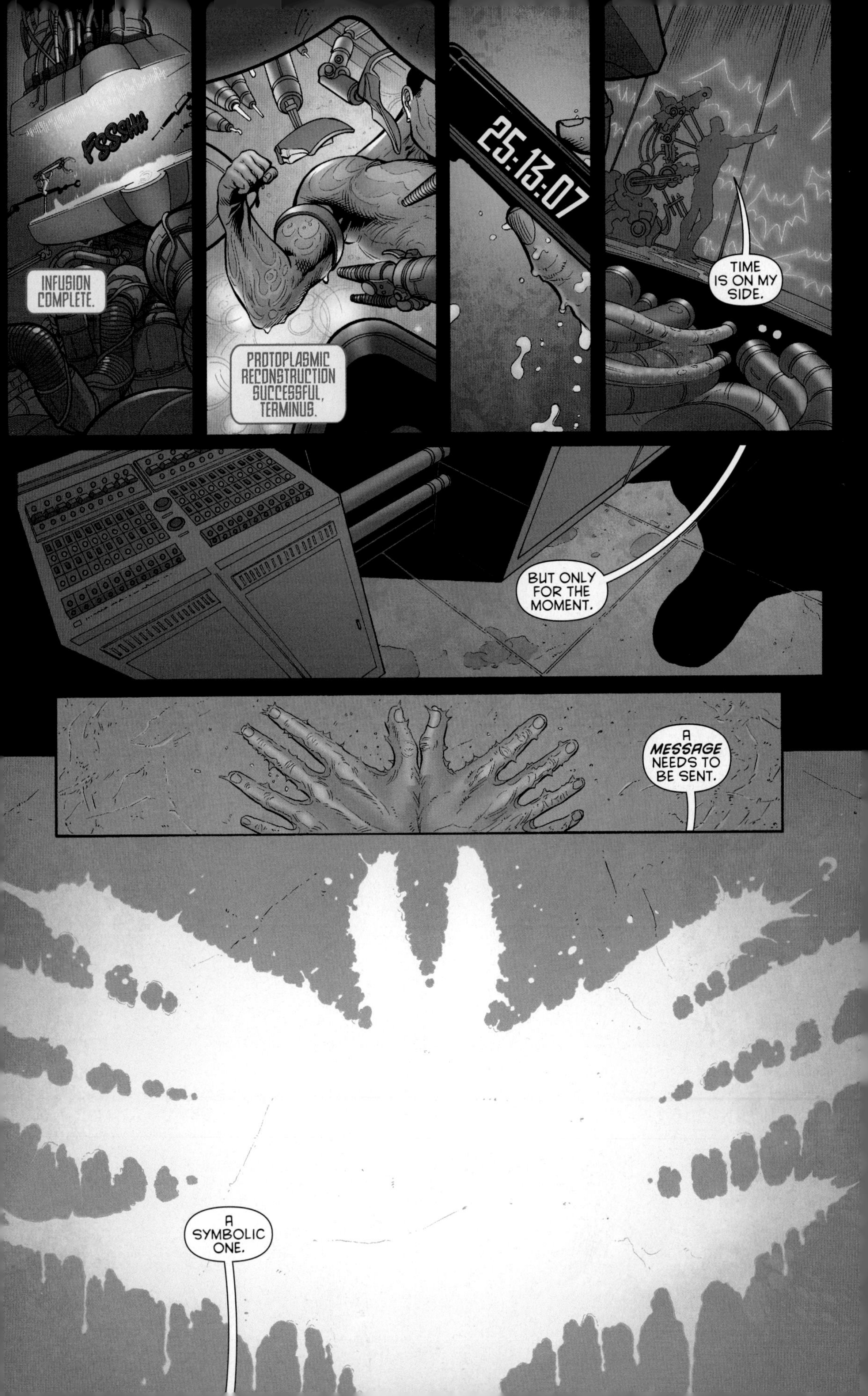
FSSSHH
INFUSION COMPLETE.
PROTOPLASMIC RECONSTRUCTION SUCCESSFUL, TERMINUS.
25:13:07
TIME IS ON MY SIDE.
BUT ONLY FOR THE MOMENT.
A *MESSAGE* NEEDS TO BE SENT.
A SYMBOLIC ONE.

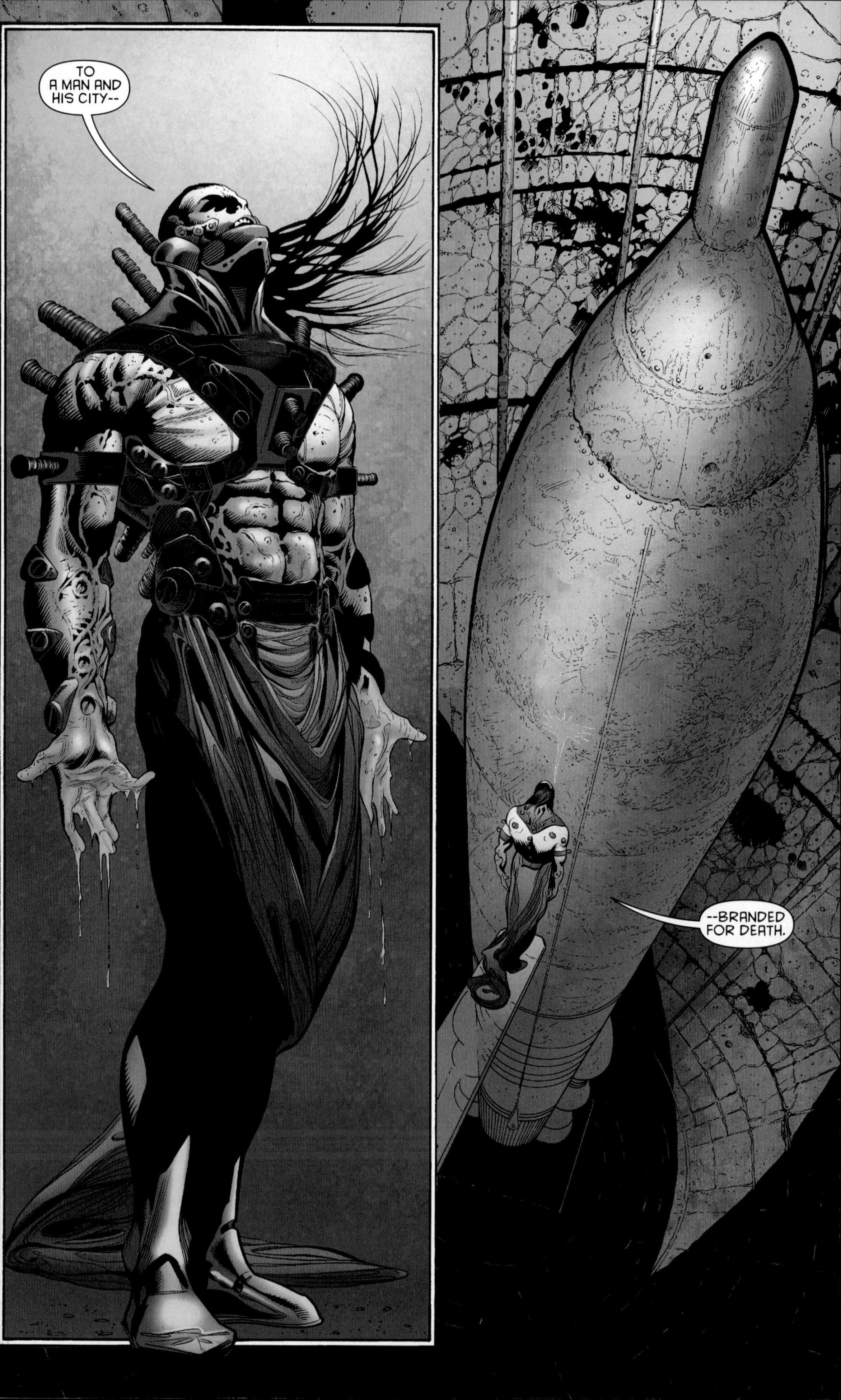
TO A MAN AND HIS CITY--
--BRANDED FOR DEATH.

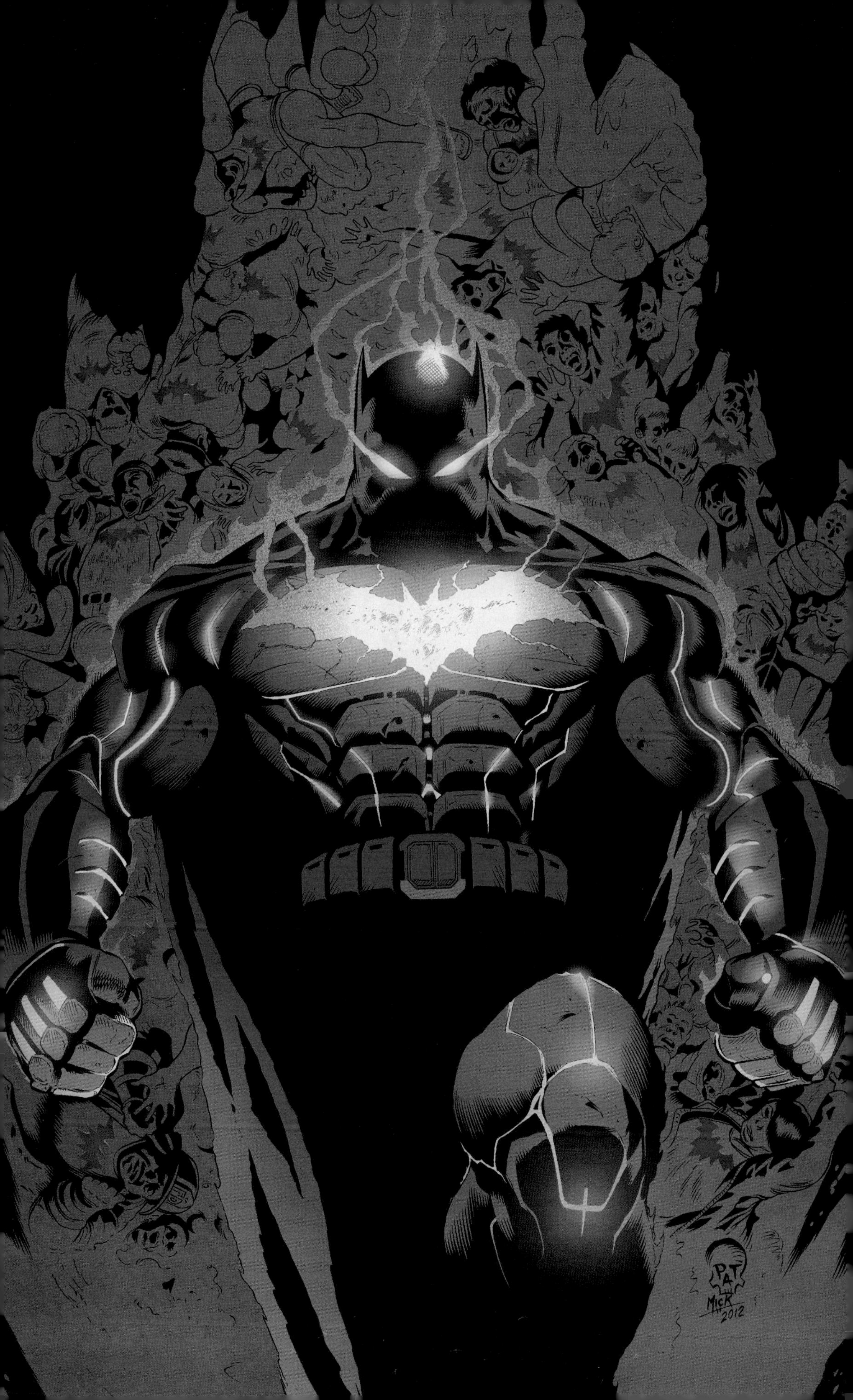
PAT
MICK
2012

# TERMINUS: BRANDED

**PETER J. TOMASI** writer **PATRICK GLEASON** penciller **MICK GRAY, KEITH CHAMPAGNE & TOM NGUYEN** inkers
cover by **GLEASON, GRAY & KALISZ**

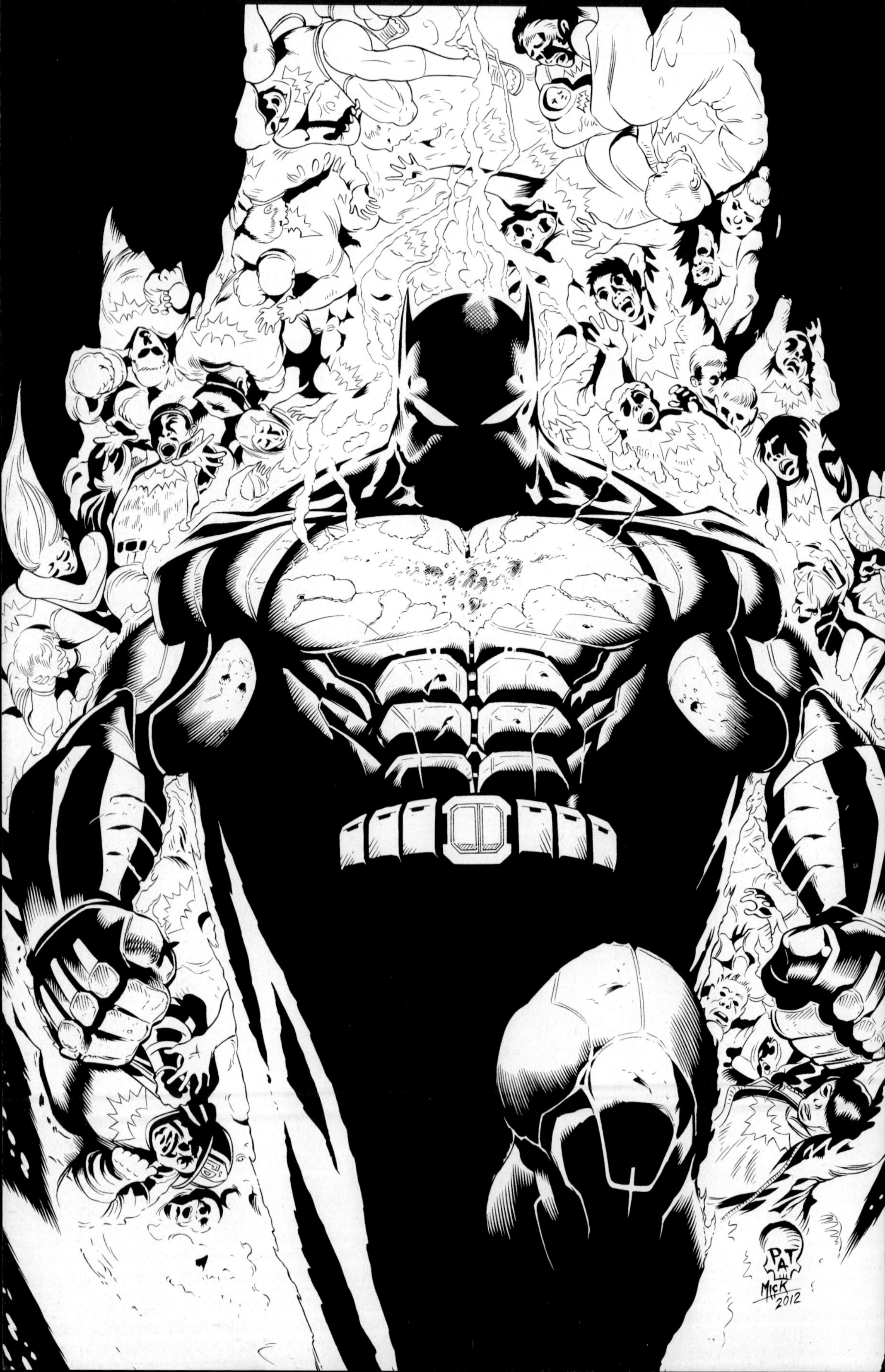
PAT
MICK
2012

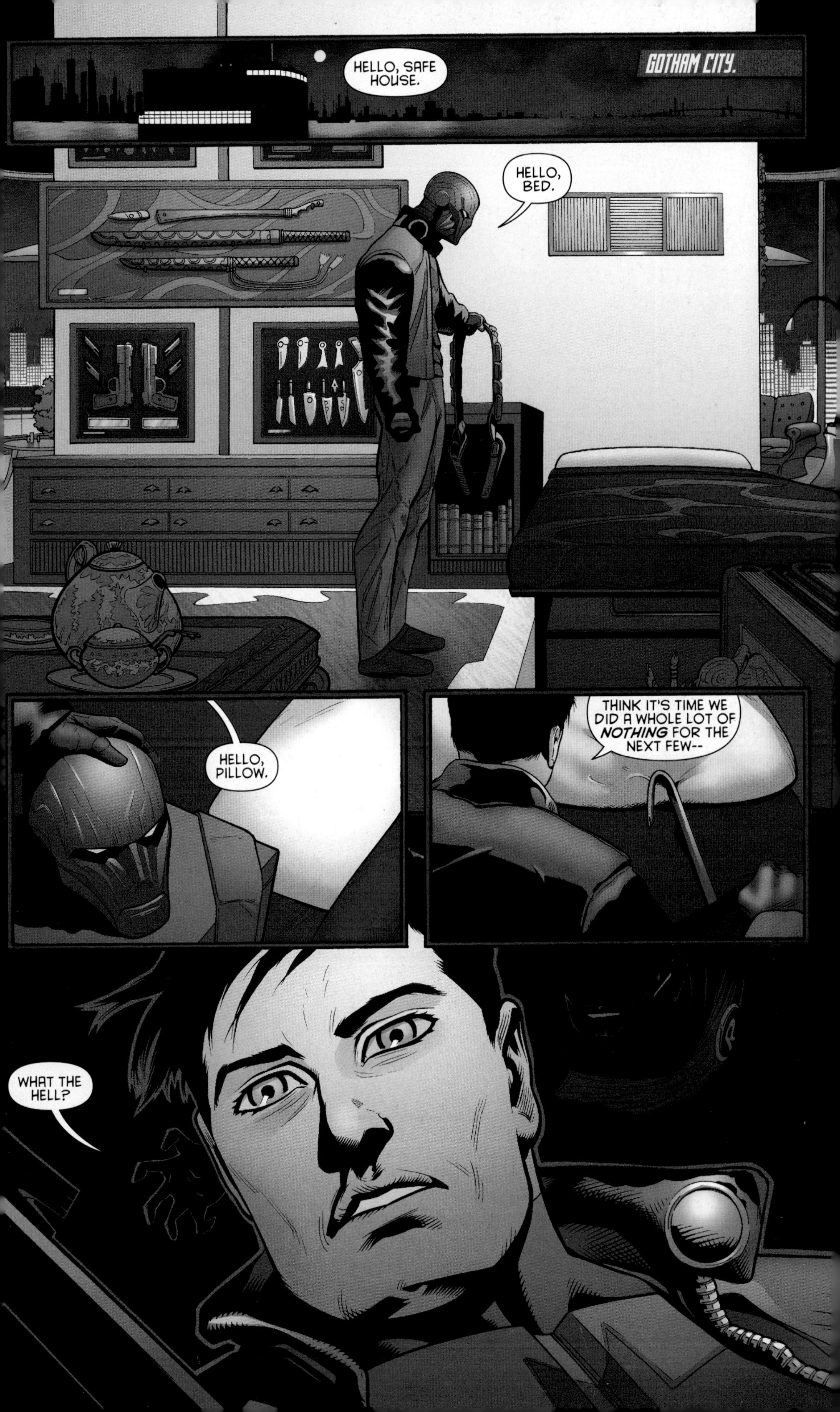
GOTHAM CITY.
HELLO, SAFE HOUSE.
HELLO, BED.
HELLO, PILLOW.
THINK IT'S TIME WE DID A WHOLE LOT OF *NOTHING* FOR THE NEXT FEW--
WHAT THE HELL?

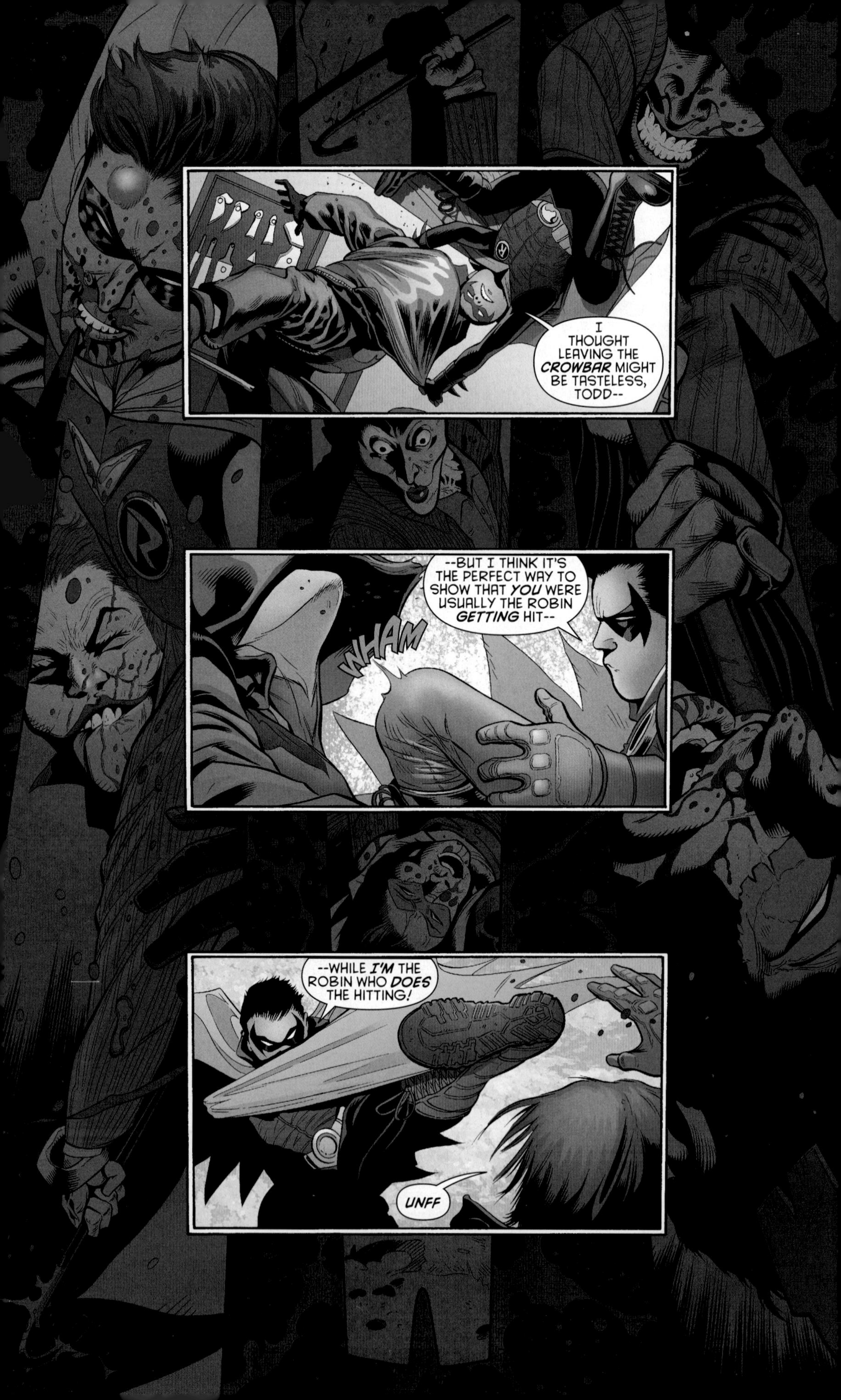

I THOUGHT LEAVING THE CROWBAR MIGHT BE TASTELESS, TODD--
--BUT I THINK IT'S THE PERFECT WAY TO SHOW THAT YOU WERE USUALLY THE ROBIN GETTING HIT--
WHAM
--WHILE I'M THE ROBIN WHO DOES THE HITTING!
UNFF

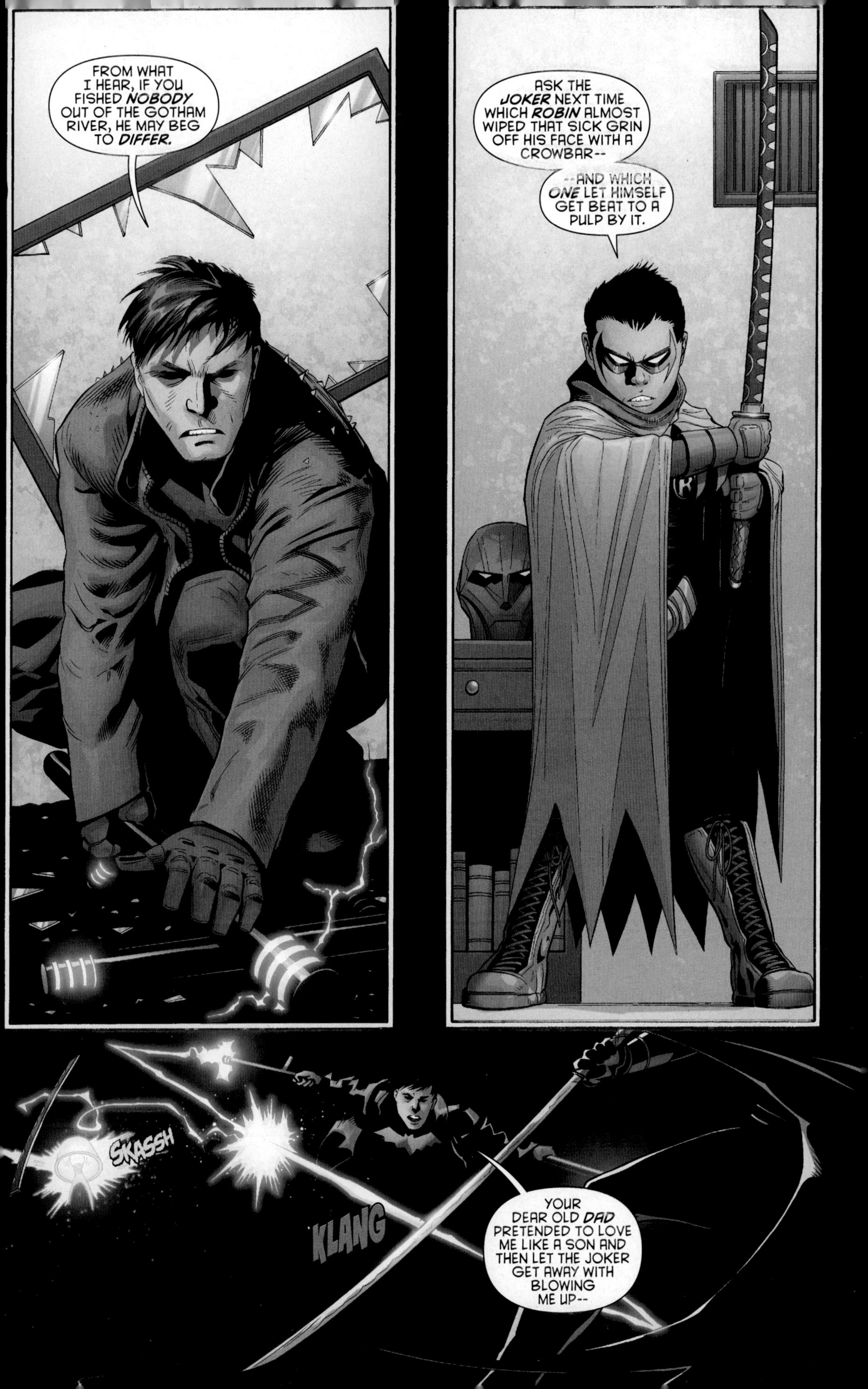
FROM WHAT I HEAR, IF YOU FISHED NOBODY OUT OF THE GOTHAM RIVER, HE MAY BEG TO DIFFER.
ASK THE JOKER NEXT TIME WHICH ROBIN ALMOST WIPED THAT SICK GRIN OFF HIS FACE WITH A CROWBAR--
--AND WHICH ONE LET HIMSELF GET BEAT TO A PULP BY IT.
SKASSH
KLANG
YOUR DEAR OLD DAD PRETENDED TO LOVE ME LIKE A SON AND THEN LET THE JOKER GET AWAY WITH BLOWING ME UP--

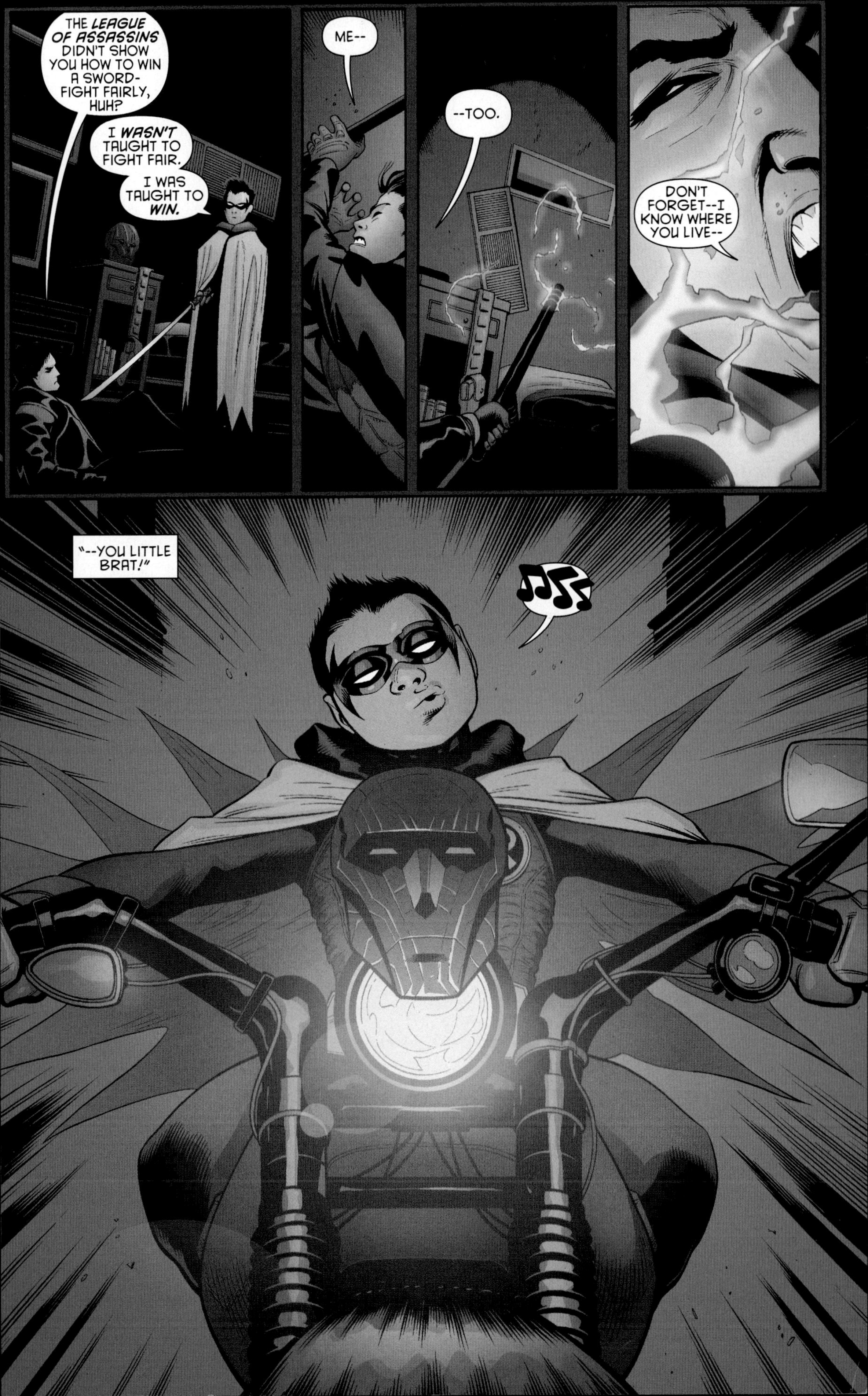
THE LEAGUE OF ASSASSINS DIDN'T SHOW YOU HOW TO WIN A SWORD-FIGHT FAIRLY, HUH?
I WASN'T TAUGHT TO FIGHT FAIR.
I WAS TAUGHT TO WIN.
ME--
--TOO.
DON'T FORGET--I KNOW WHERE YOU LIVE--
"--YOU LITTLE BRAT!"

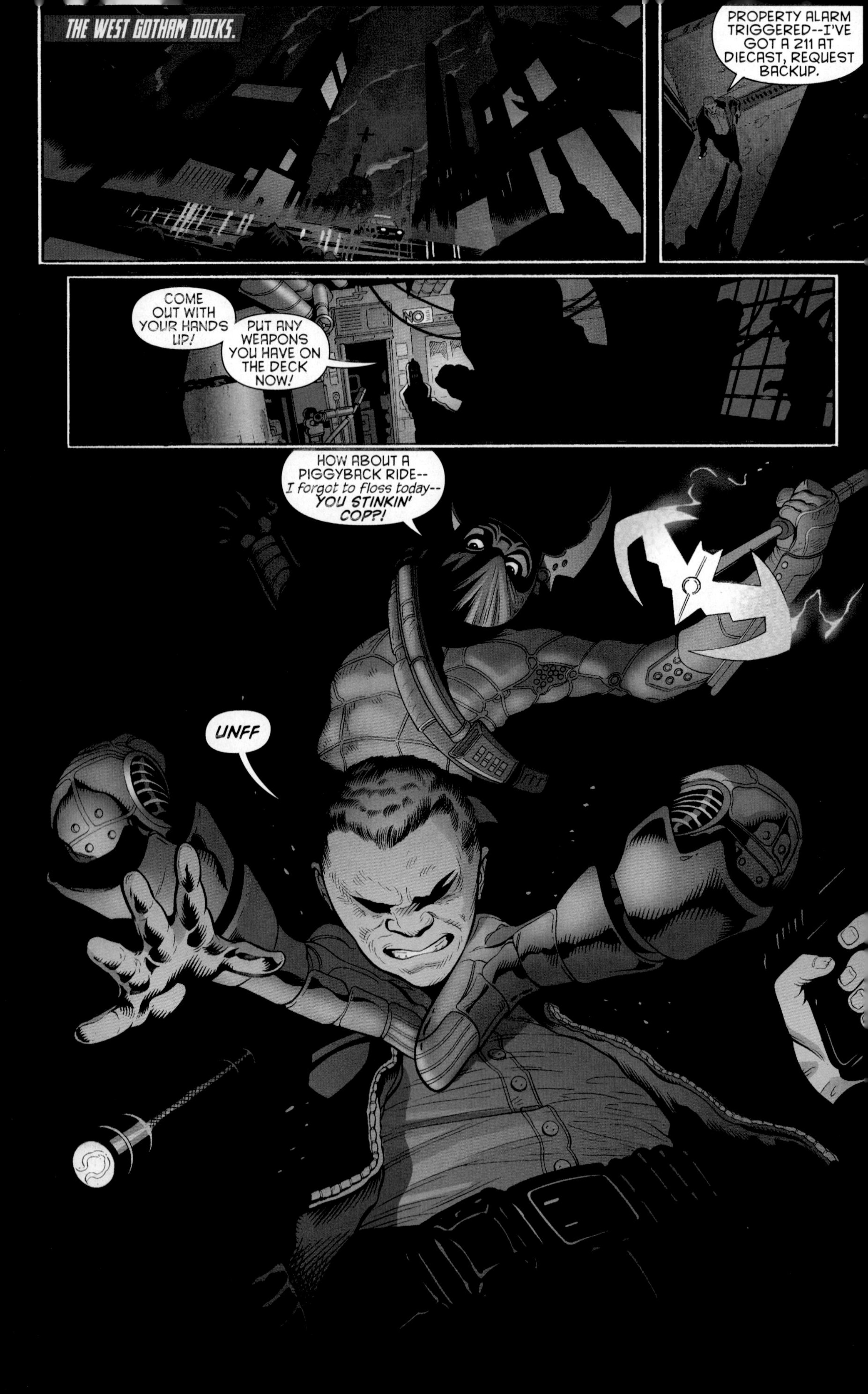
THE WEST GOTHAM DOCKS.
PROPERTY ALARM TRIGGERED--I'VE GOT A 211 AT DIECAST, REQUEST BACKUP.
COME OUT WITH YOUR HANDS UP!
PUT ANY WEAPONS YOU HAVE ON THE DECK NOW!
NO
HOW ABOUT A PIGGYBACK RIDE-- I forgot to floss today-- YOU STINKIN' COPP?!
UNFF

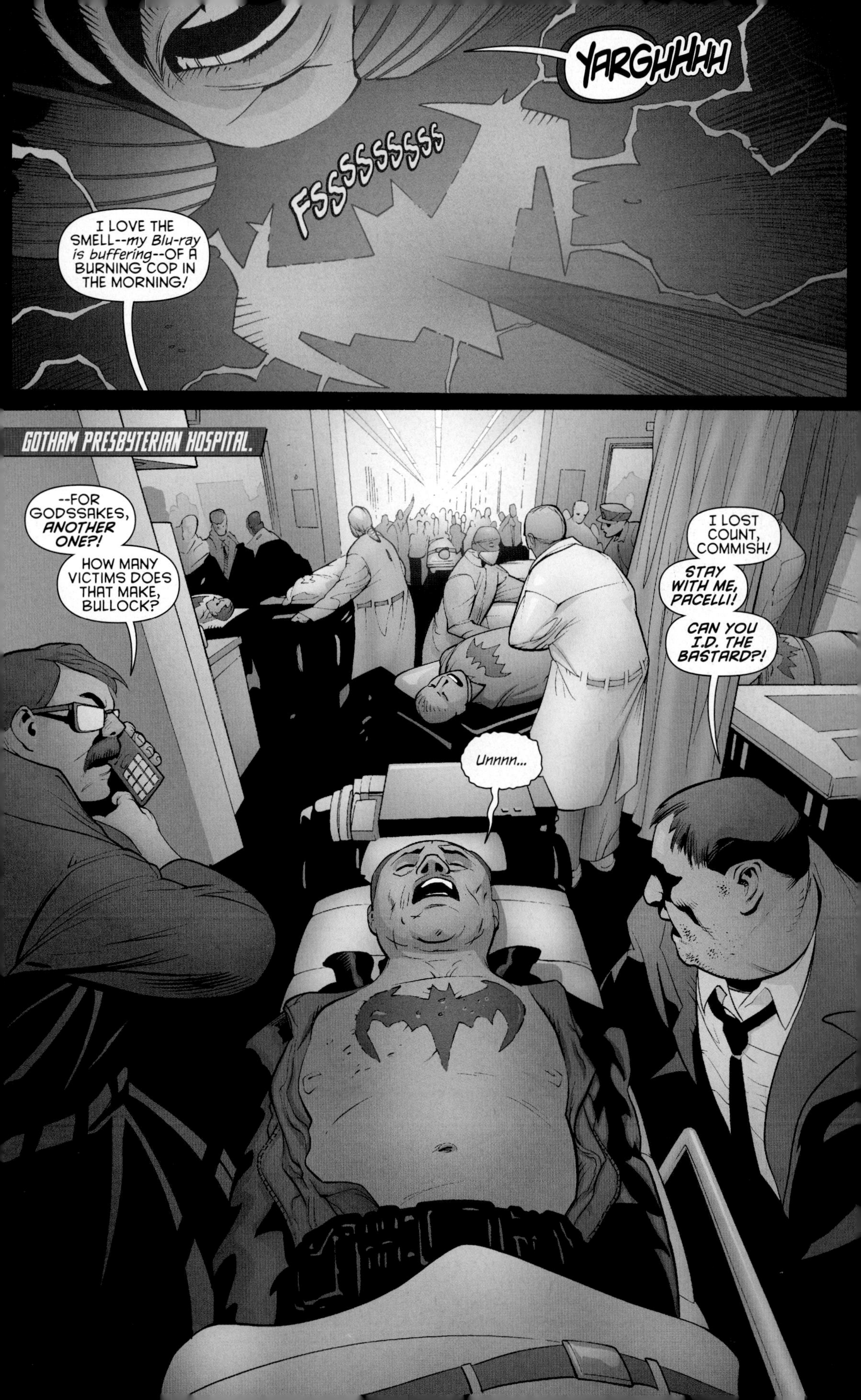
YARGHHHH
FSSSSSSSSS
I LOVE THE SMELL--my Blu-ray is buffering--OF A BURNING COP IN THE MORNING!
GOTHAM PRESBYTERIAN HOSPITAL.
--FOR GODSSAKES, ANOTHER ONE?!
HOW MANY VICTIMS DOES THAT MAKE, BULLOCK?
I LOST COUNT, COMMISH!
STAY WITH ME, PACELLI!
CAN YOU I.D. THE BASTARD?!
Unnnn...

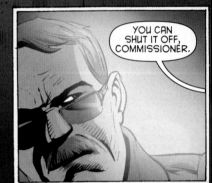

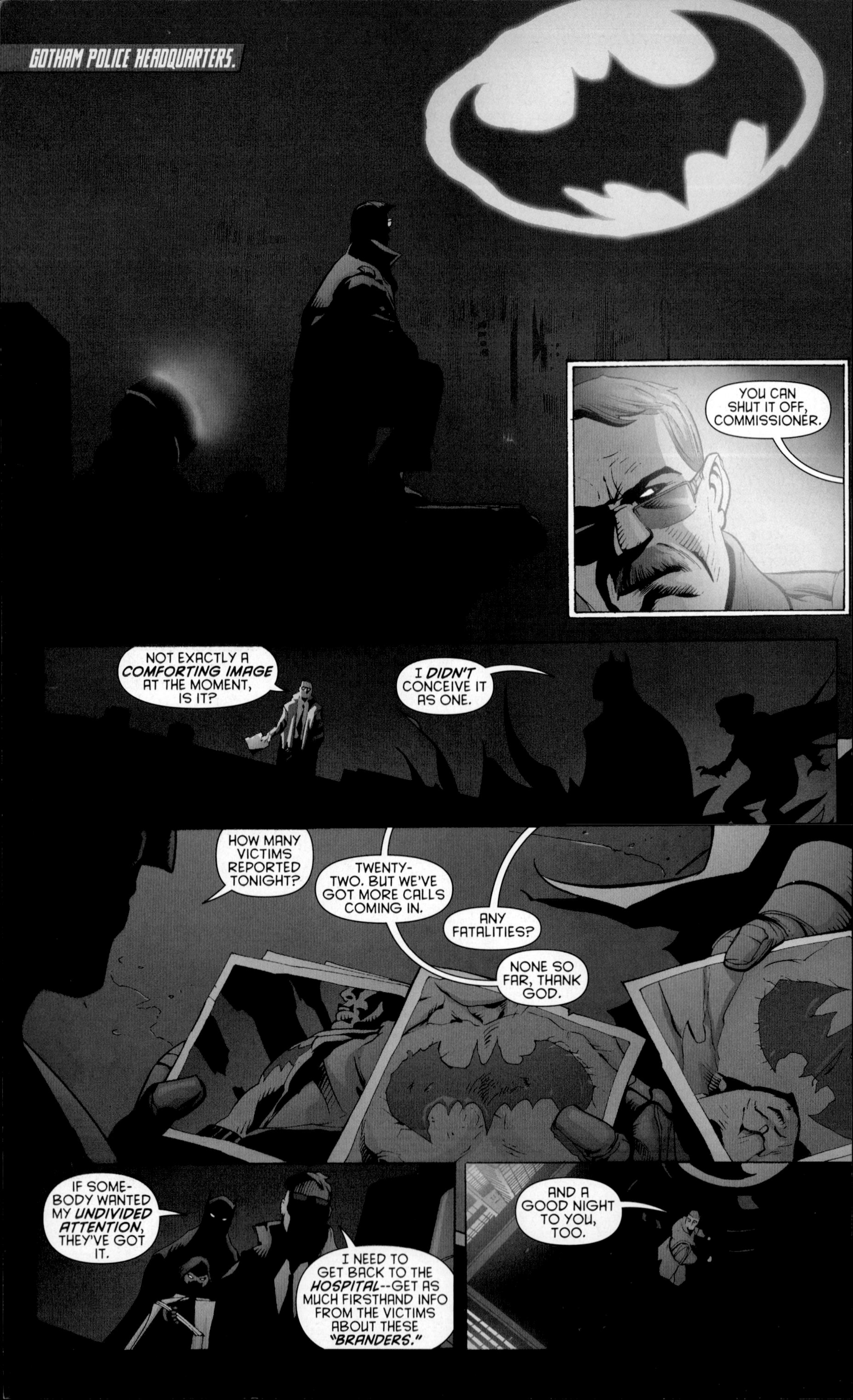
GOTHAM POLICE HEADQUARTERS.
YOU CAN SHUT IT OFF, COMMISSIONER.
NOT EXACTLY A COMFORTING IMAGE AT THE MOMENT, IS IT?
I DIDN'T CONCEIVE IT AS ONE.
HOW MANY VICTIMS REPORTED TONIGHT?
TWENTY-TWO. BUT WE'VE GOT MORE CALLS COMING IN.
ANY FATALITIES?
NONE SO FAR, THANK GOD.
IF SOMEBODY WANTED MY UNDIVIDED ATTENTION, THEY'VE GOT IT.
I NEED TO GET BACK TO THE HOSPITAL--GET AS MUCH FIRSTHAND INFO FROM THE VICTIMS ABOUT THESE "BRANDERS."
AND A GOOD NIGHT TO YOU, TOO.

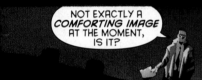

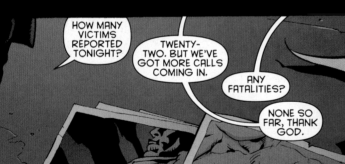

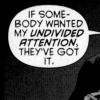

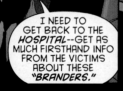

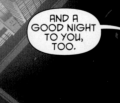

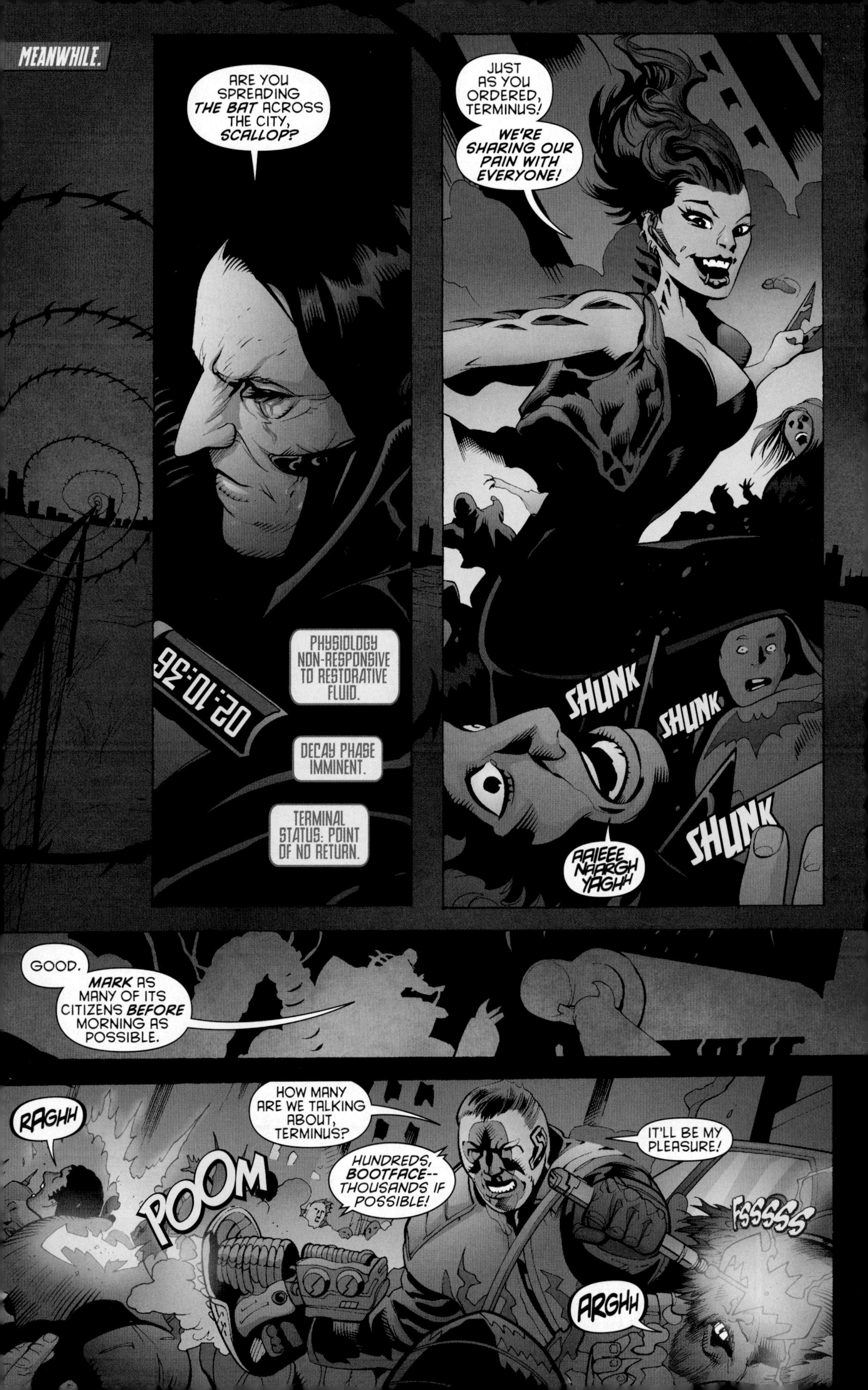
MEANWHILE.
ARE YOU SPREADING *THE BAT* ACROSS THE CITY, *SCALLOP?*
JUST AS YOU ORDERED, TERMINUS!
*WE'RE SHARING OUR PAIN WITH EVERYONE!*
02:10:36
PHYSIOLOGY NON-RESPONSIVE TO RESTORATIVE FLUID.
DECAY PHASE IMMINENT.
TERMINAL STATUS: POINT OF NO RETURN.
SHUNK
SHUNK
SHUNK
AAIEEE NAARGH YAGHH
GOOD. *MARK* AS MANY OF ITS CITIZENS *BEFORE* MORNING AS POSSIBLE.
RAGHH
POOM
HOW MANY ARE WE TALKING ABOUT, TERMINUS?
HUNDREDS, *BOOTFACE*-- THOUSANDS IF POSSIBLE!
IT'LL BE MY PLEASURE!
FSSSSS
ARGHH

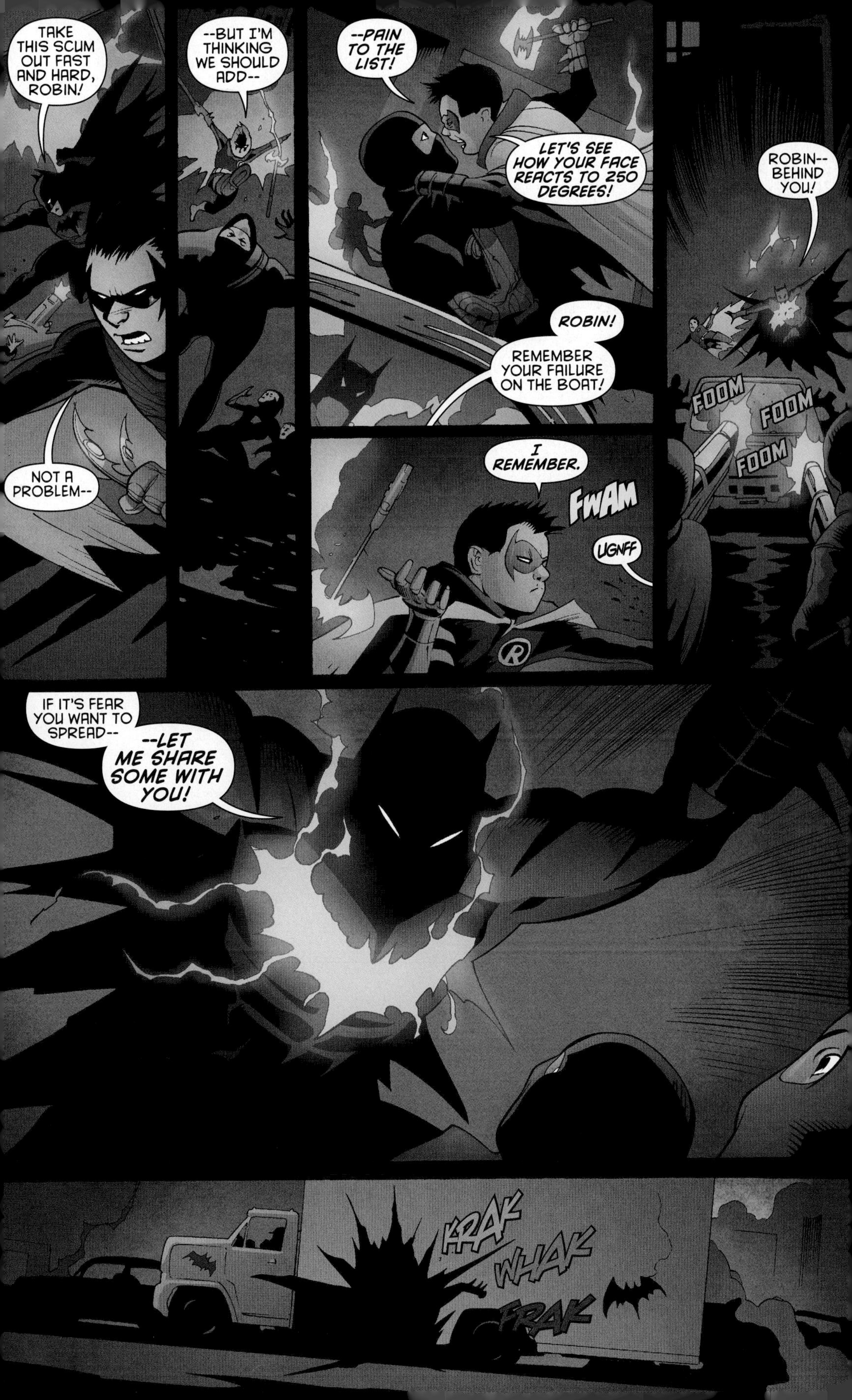
TAKE THIS SCUM OUT FAST AND HARD, ROBIN!
NOT A PROBLEM--
--BUT I'M THINKING WE SHOULD ADD--
--PAIN TO THE LIST!
LET'S SEE HOW YOUR FACE REACTS TO 250 DEGREES!
ROBIN!
REMEMBER YOUR FAILURE ON THE BOAT!
I REMEMBER.
FWAM
UGNFF
ROBIN-- BEHIND YOU!
FOOM
FOOM
FOOM
IF IT'S FEAR YOU WANT TO SPREAD--
--LET ME SHARE SOME WITH YOU!
KRAK
WHAK
FRAK

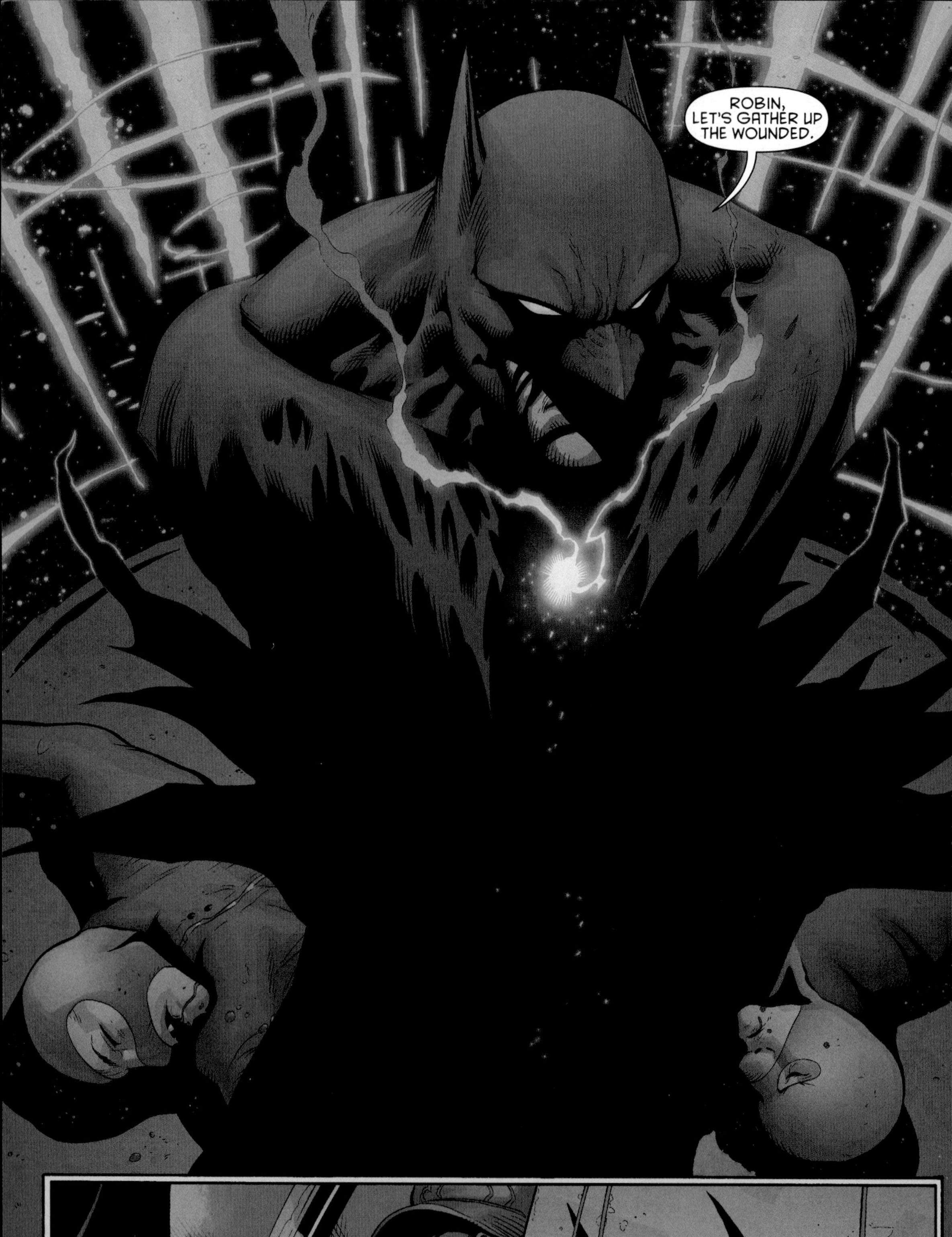
ROBIN, LET'S GATHER UP THE WOUNDED.

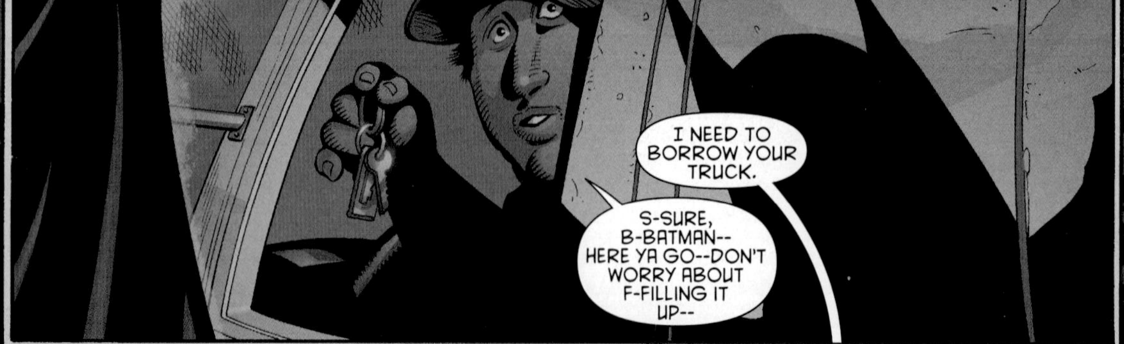
I NEED TO BORROW YOUR TRUCK.
S-SURE, B-BATMAN-- HERE YA GO--DON'T WORRY ABOUT F-FILLING IT UP--

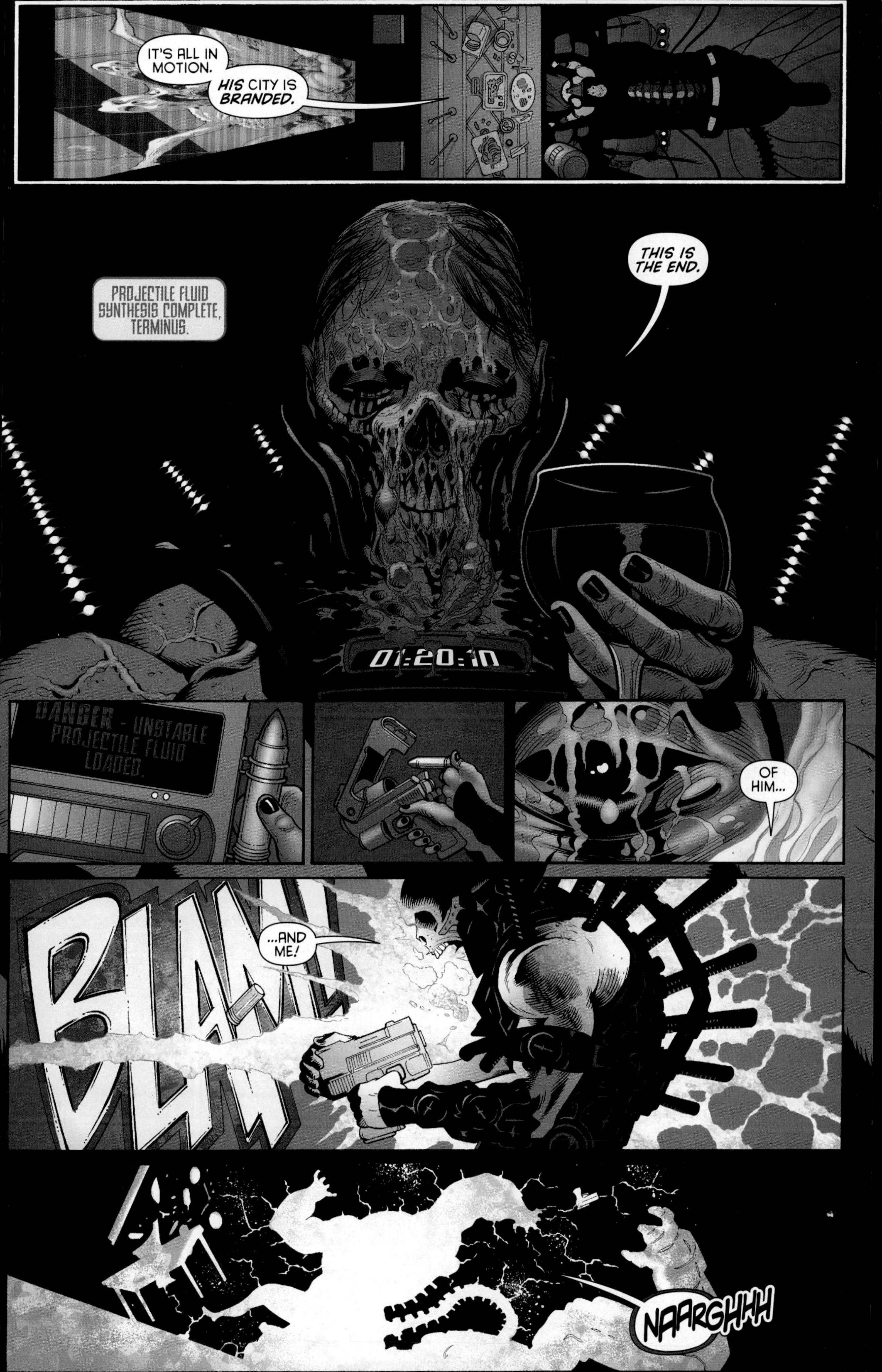
IT'S ALL IN MOTION.
HIS CITY IS BRANDED.
PROJECTILE FLUID SYNTHESIS COMPLETE, TERMINUS.
THIS IS THE END.
01:20:10
DANGER - UNSTABLE PROJECTILE FLUID LOADED.
OF HIM...
...AND ME!
NAARGHHH

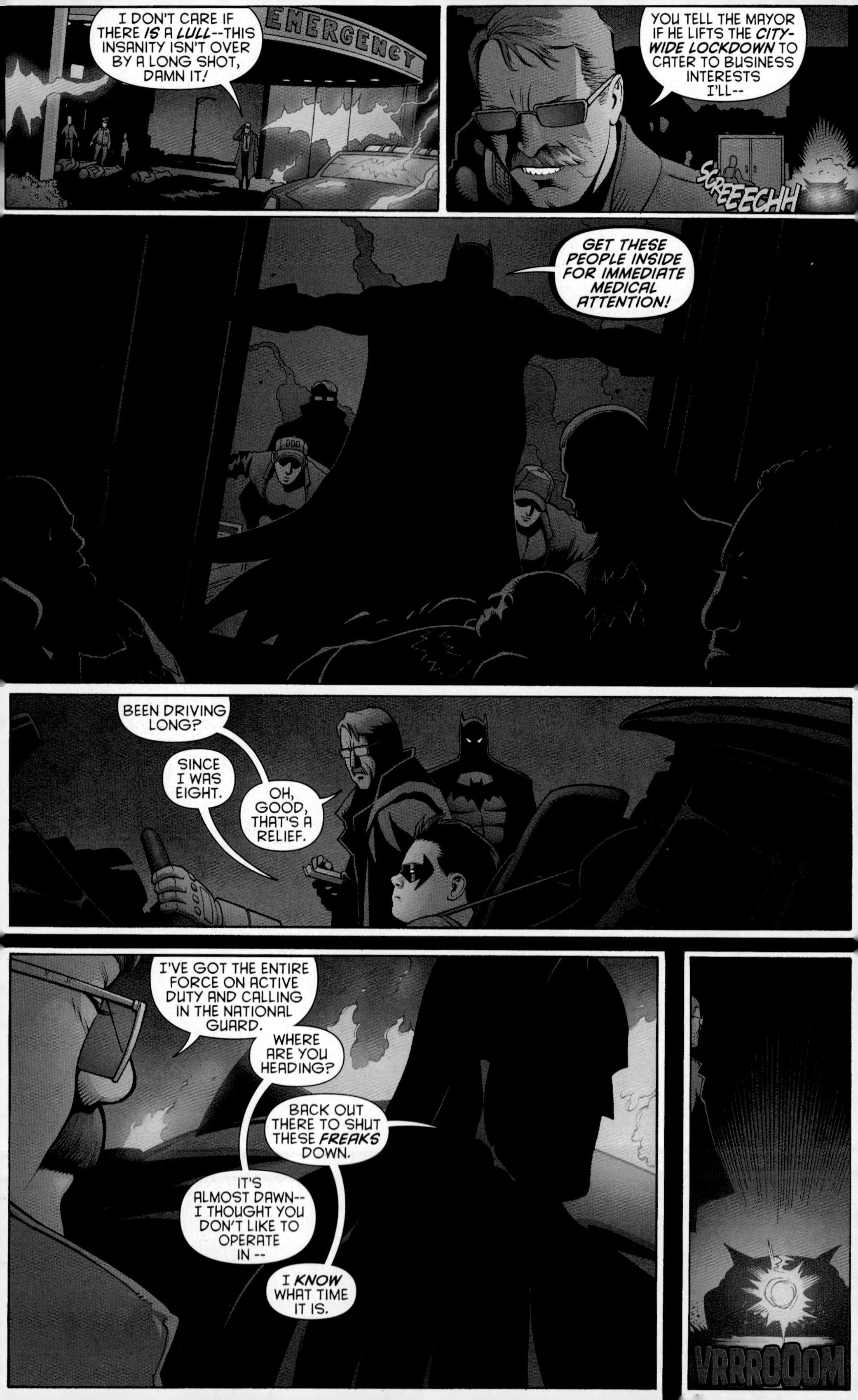
EMERGENCY
I DON'T CARE IF THERE *IS* A *LULL*--THIS INSANITY ISN'T OVER BY A LONG SHOT, DAMN IT!
YOU TELL THE MAYOR IF HE LIFTS THE *CITY-WIDE LOCKDOWN* TO CATER TO BUSINESS INTERESTS I'LL--
SCREEECHH
GET THESE PEOPLE INSIDE FOR IMMEDIATE MEDICAL ATTENTION!
BEEN DRIVING LONG?
SINCE I WAS EIGHT.
OH, GOOD, THAT'S A RELIEF.
I'VE GOT THE ENTIRE FORCE ON ACTIVE DUTY AND CALLING IN THE NATIONAL GUARD.
WHERE ARE YOU HEADING?
BACK OUT THERE TO SHUT THESE *FREAKS* DOWN.
IT'S ALMOST DAWN-- I THOUGHT YOU DON'T LIKE TO OPERATE IN --
I *KNOW* WHAT TIME IT IS.
VRRROOOM

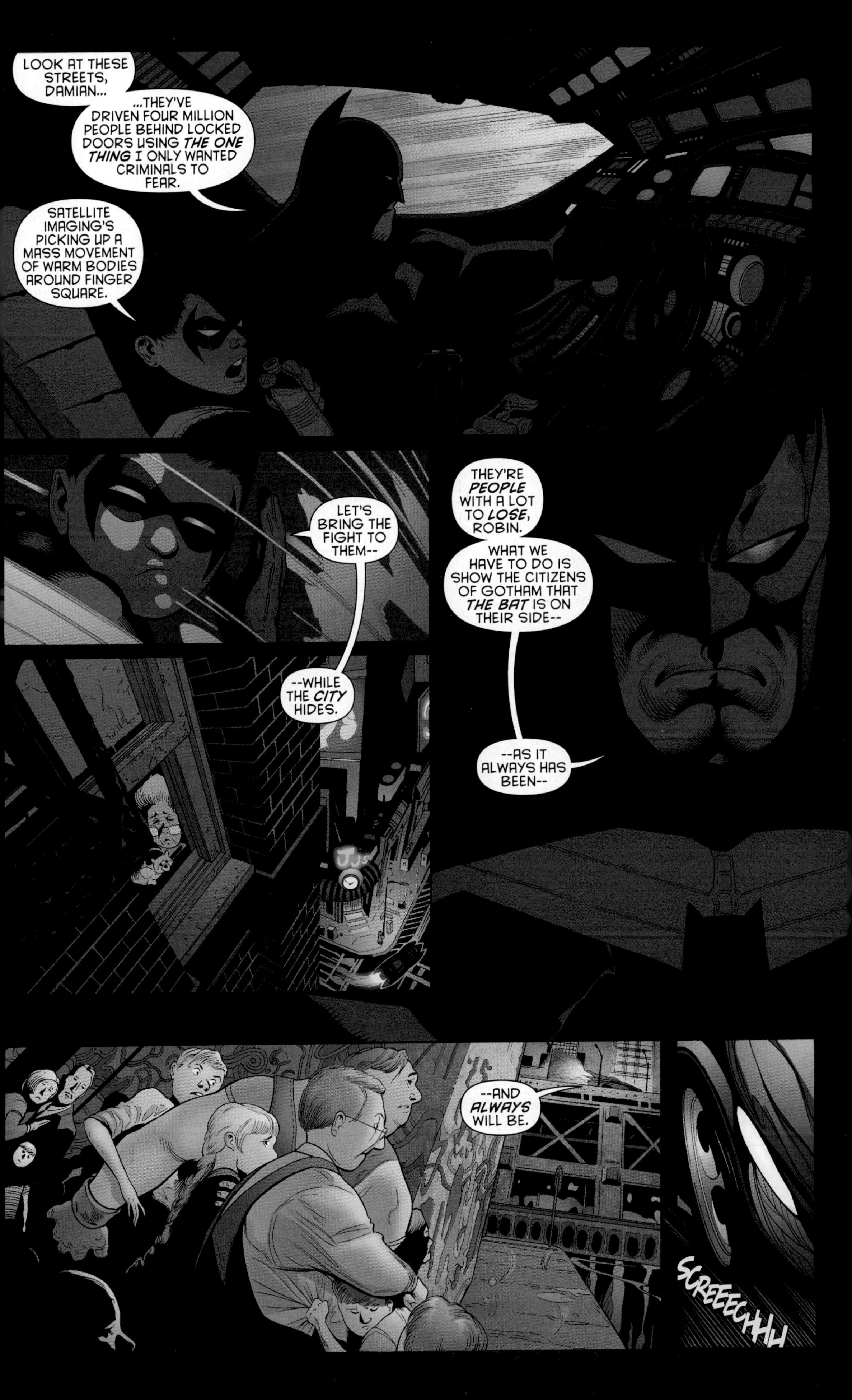
LOOK AT THESE STREETS, DAMIAN...
...THEY'VE DRIVEN FOUR MILLION PEOPLE BEHIND LOCKED DOORS USING *THE ONE THING* I ONLY WANTED CRIMINALS TO FEAR.
SATELLITE IMAGING'S PICKING UP A MASS MOVEMENT OF WARM BODIES AROUND FINGER SQUARE.
LET'S BRING THE FIGHT TO THEM--
--WHILE THE *CITY* HIDES.
THEY'RE *PEOPLE* WITH A LOT TO *LOSE*, ROBIN.
WHAT WE HAVE TO DO IS SHOW THE CITIZENS OF GOTHAM THAT *THE BAT* IS ON THEIR SIDE--
--AS IT ALWAYS HAS BEEN--
--AND *ALWAYS* WILL BE.
SCREEEGHHH

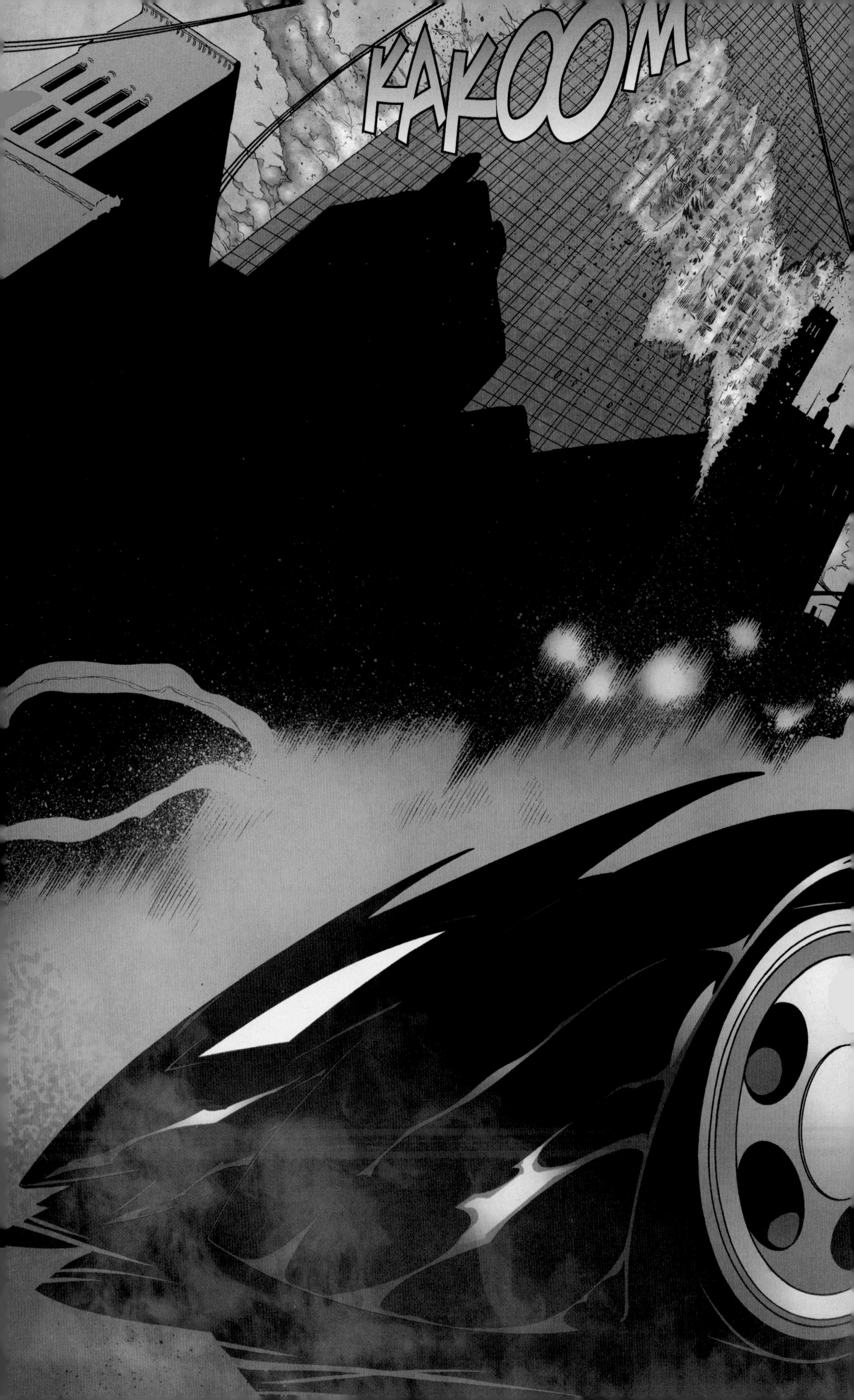
KAKOOM

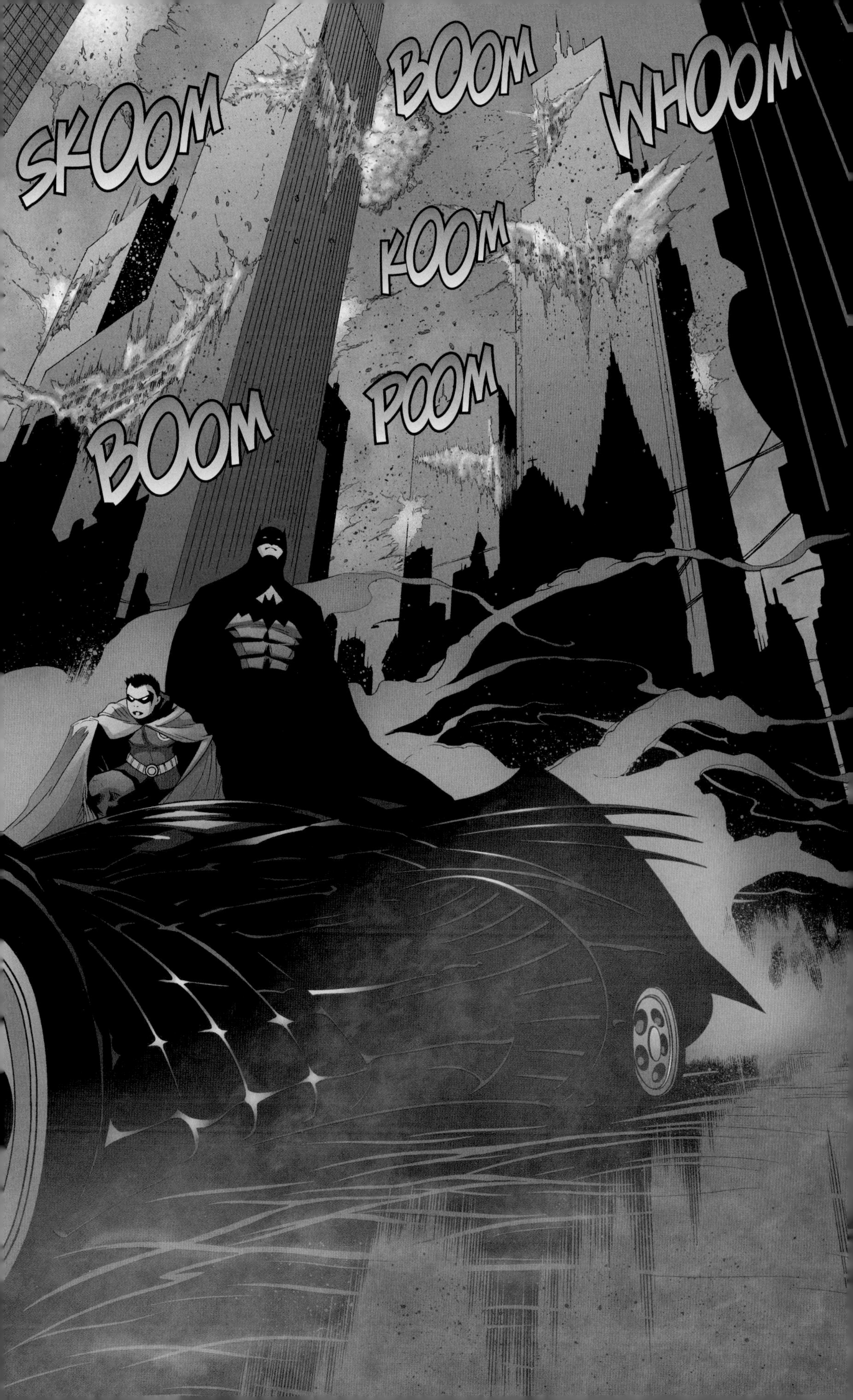
SKOOM
BOOM
WHOOM
KOOM
BOOM
POOM

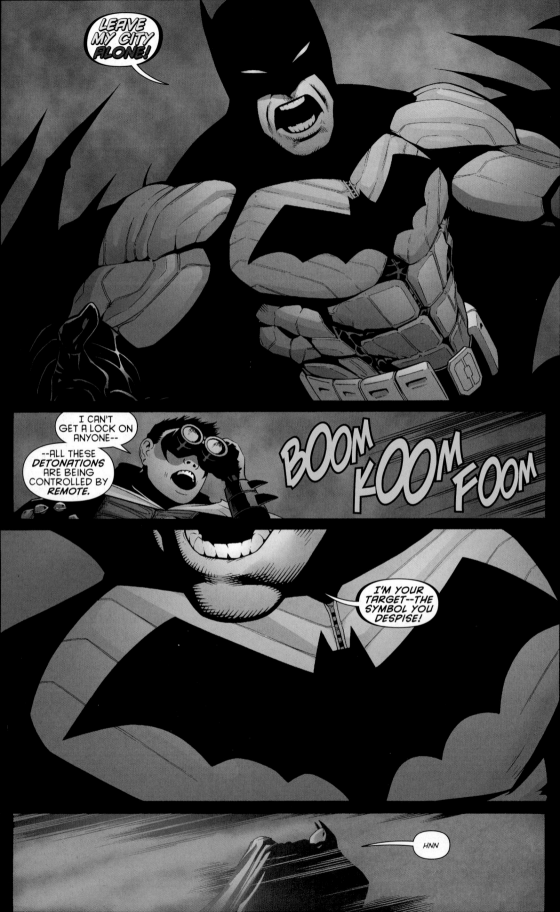

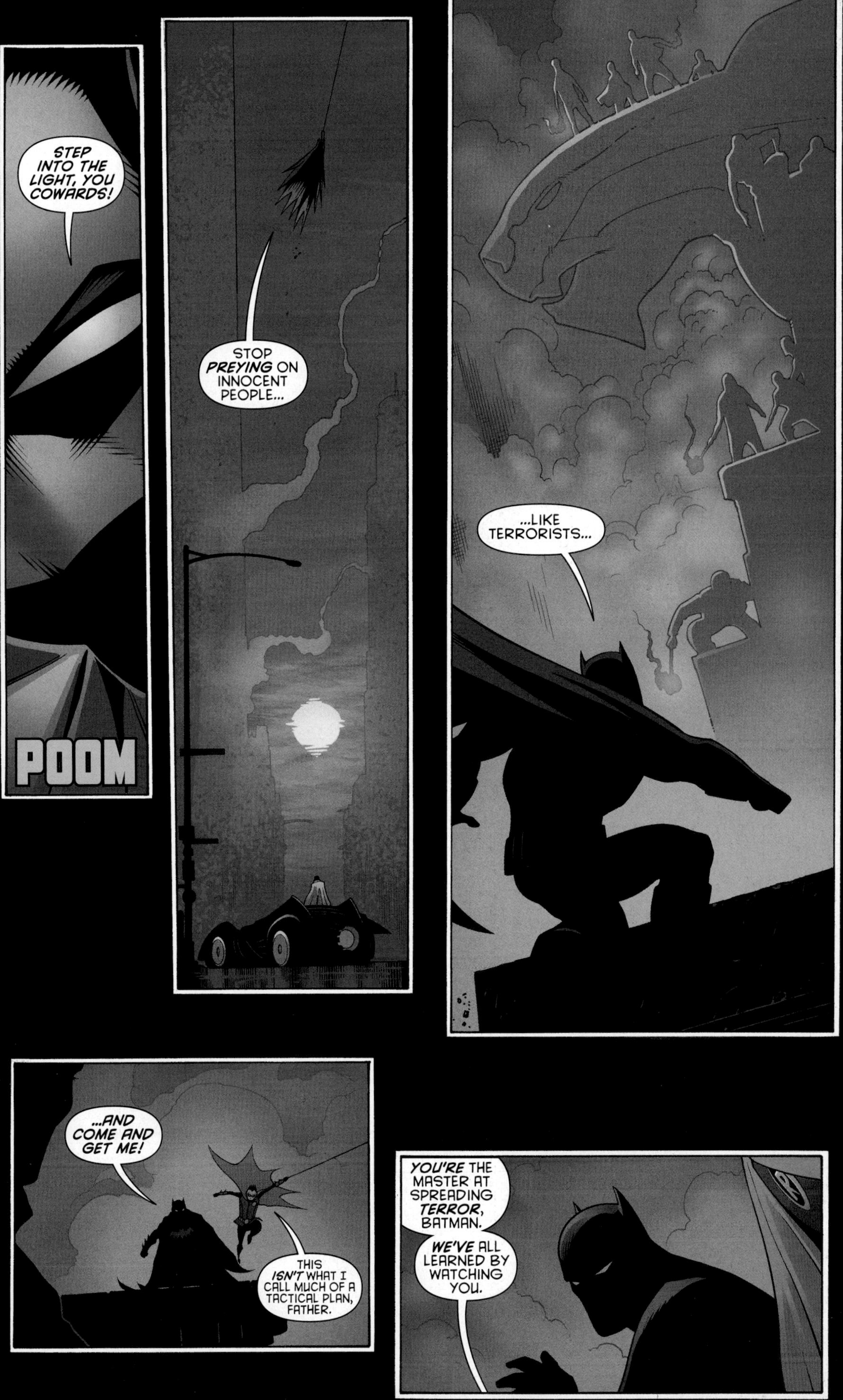

STEP INTO THE LIGHT, YOU COWARDS!
POOM
STOP PREYING ON INNOCENT PEOPLE...
...LIKE TERRORISTS...
...AND COME AND GET ME!
THIS ISN'T WHAT I CALL MUCH OF A TACTICAL PLAN, FATHER.
YOU'RE THE MASTER AT SPREADING TERROR, BATMAN.
WE'VE ALL LEARNED BY WATCHING YOU.

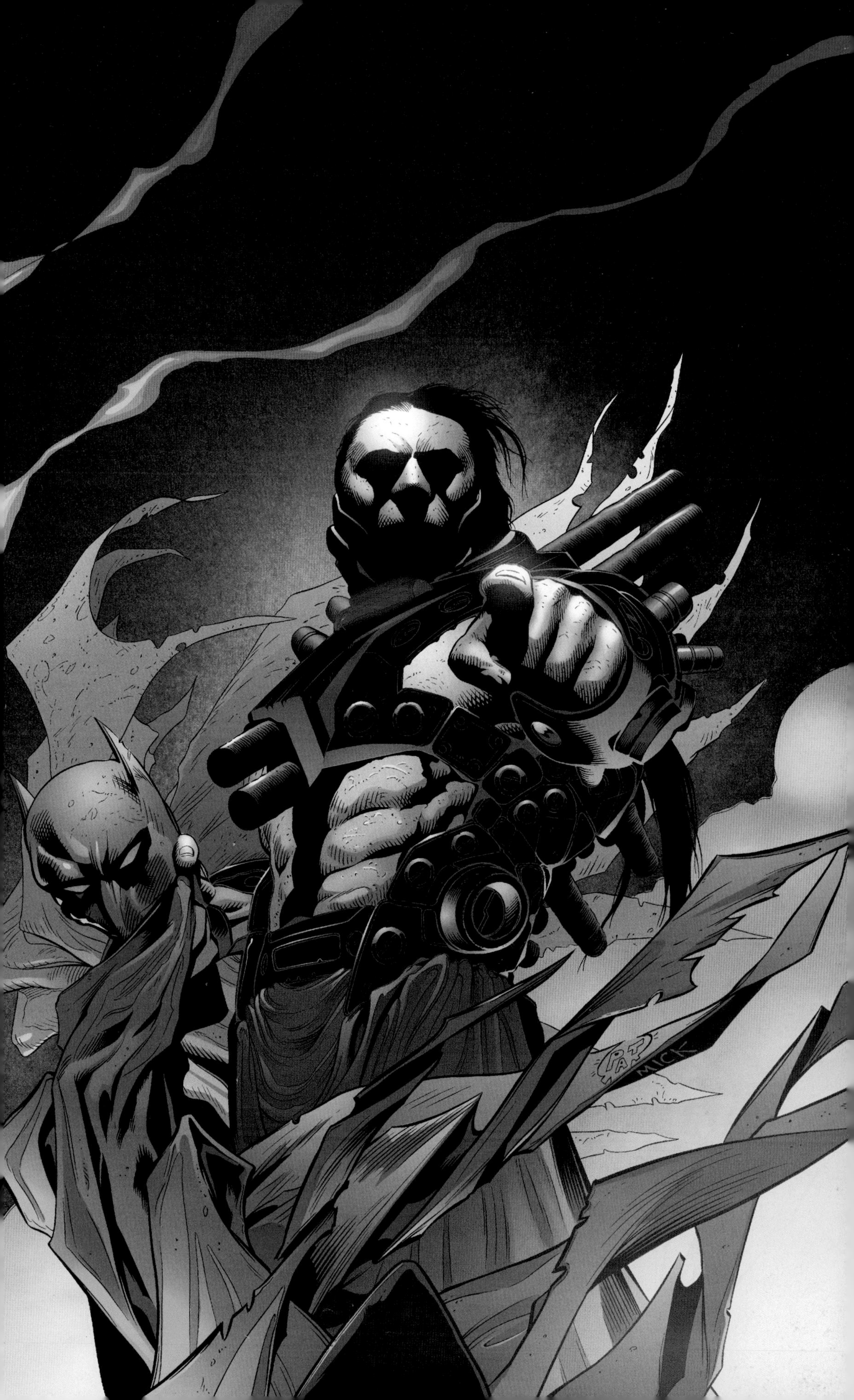

**TERMINUS: LAST GASP**

**PETER J. TOMASI** writer **PATRICK GLEASON** penciller **MICK GRAY** inker

cover by **GLEASON, GRAY & KALISZ**

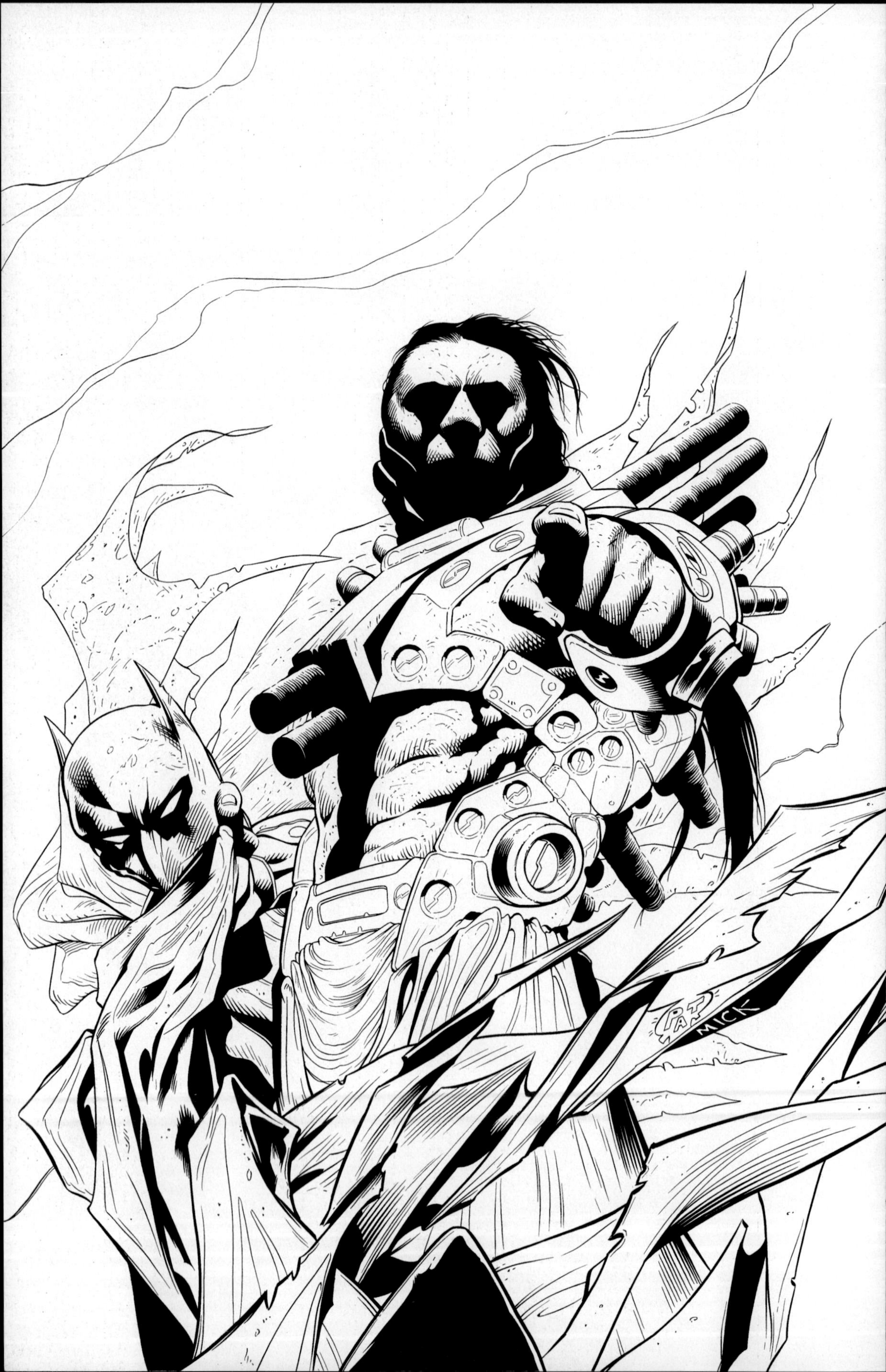
PAT
MICK

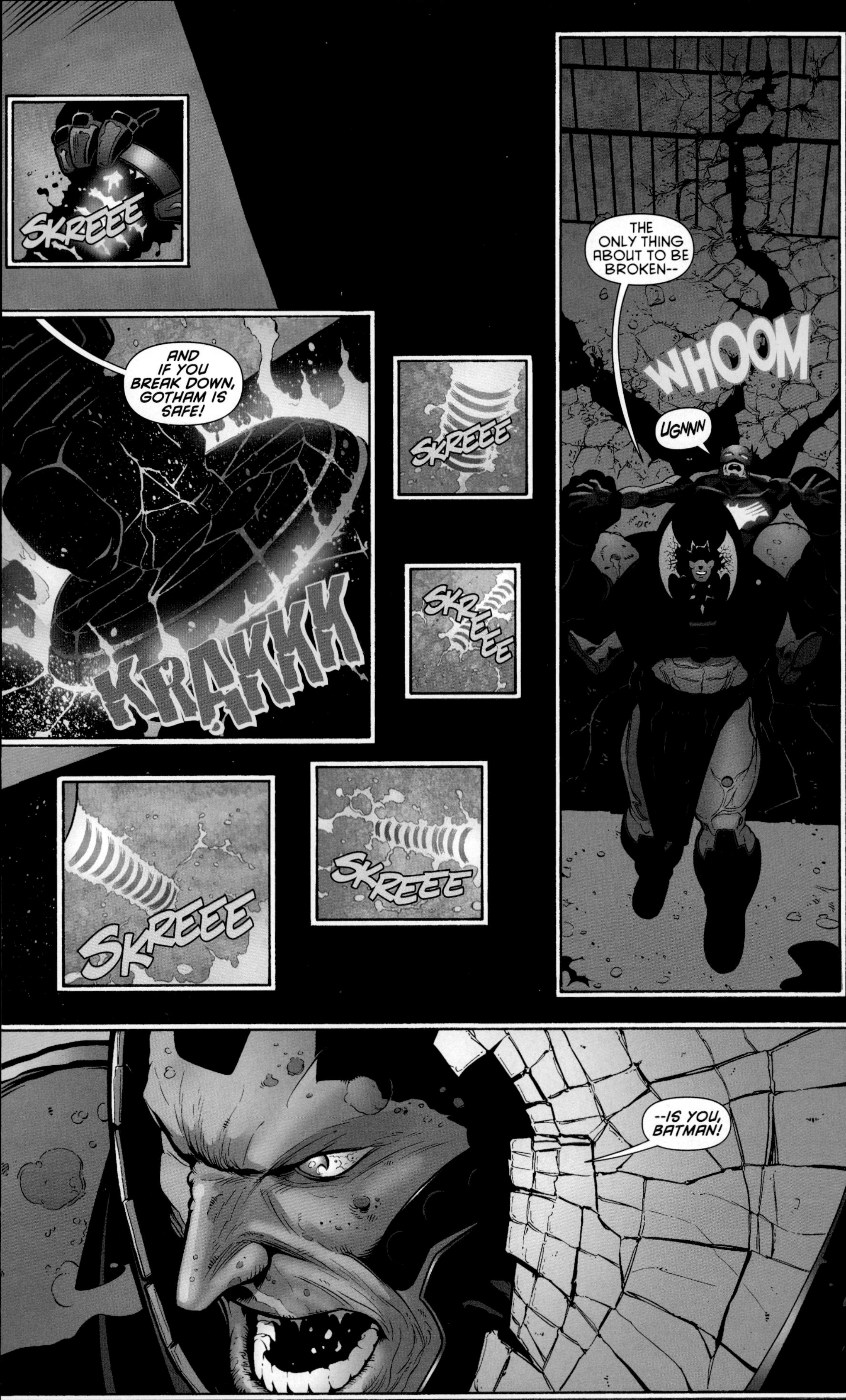
SKREEE
AND IF YOU BREAK DOWN, GOTHAM IS SAFE!
KRAKKK
SKREEE
SKREEEE
SKREEE
SKREEE
THE ONLY THING ABOUT TO BE BROKEN--
WHOOM
UGNNN
--IS YOU, BATMAN!

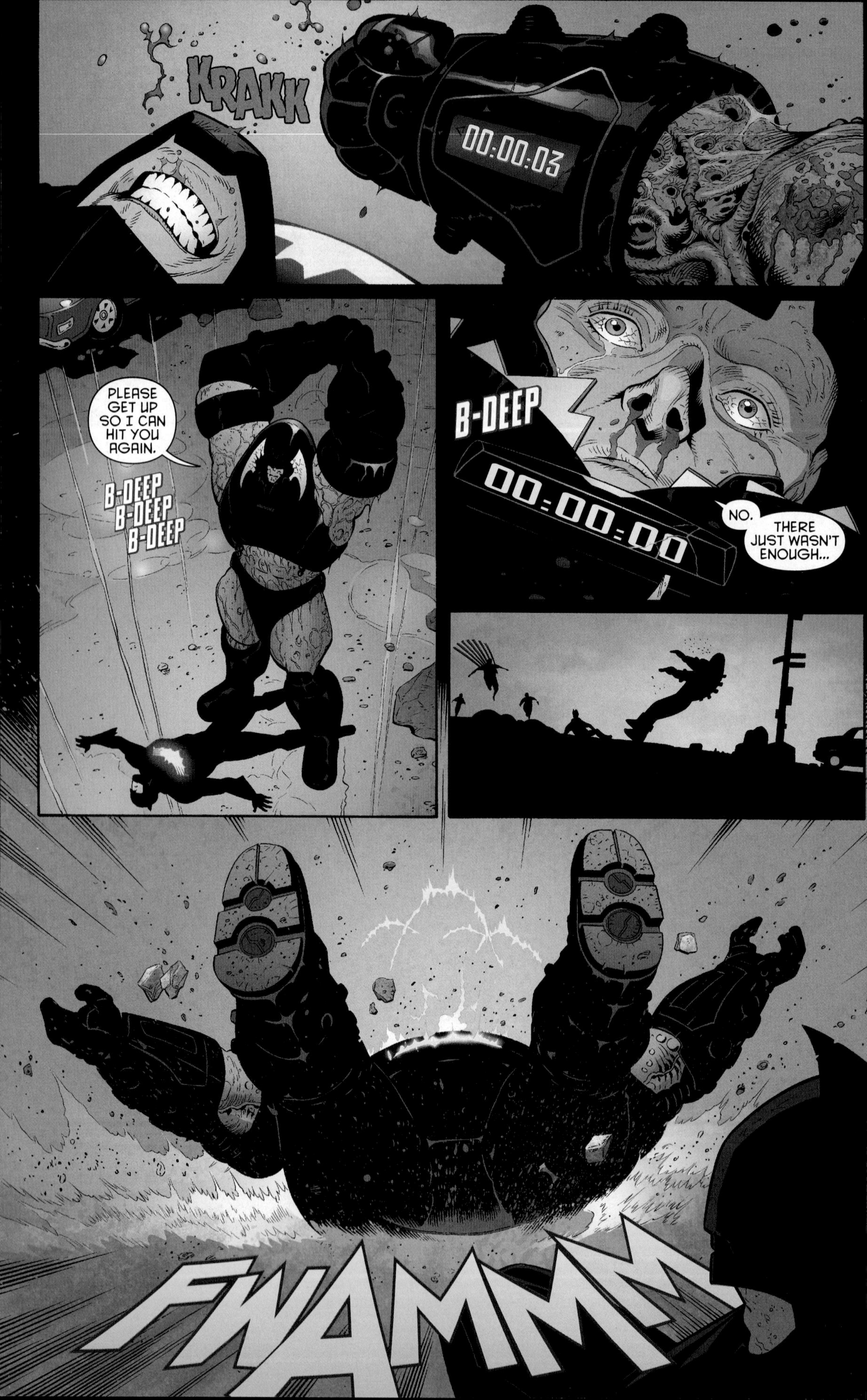
KRAKK
00:00:03
PLEASE GET UP SO I CAN HIT YOU AGAIN.
B-DEEP
B-DEEP
B-DEEP
B-DEEP
00:00:00
NO.
THERE JUST WASN'T ENOUGH...
FWAMMM

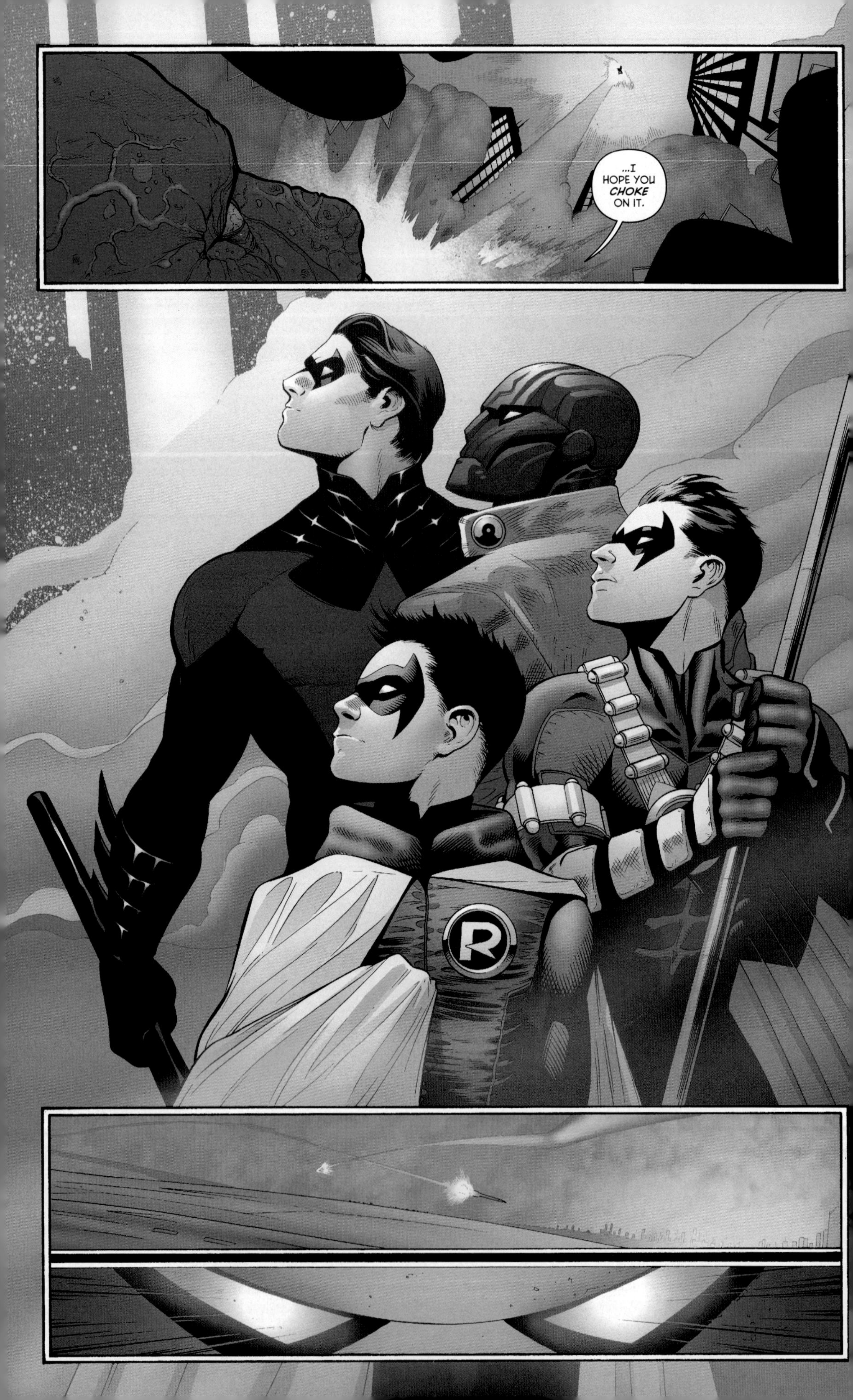
...I HOPE YOU CHOKE ON IT.

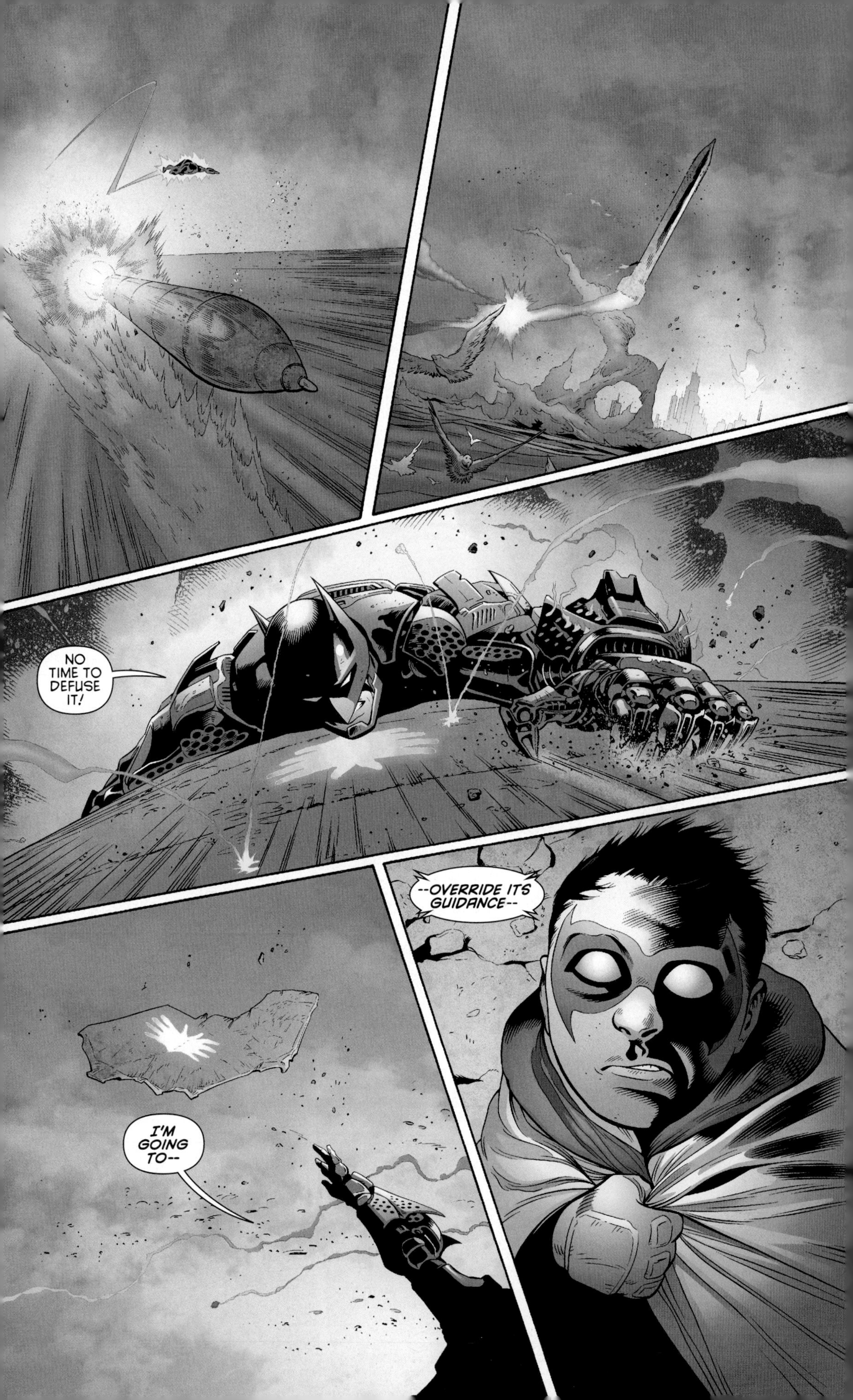
NO TIME TO DEFUSE IT!
--OVERRIDE ITS GUIDANCE--
I'M GOING TO--

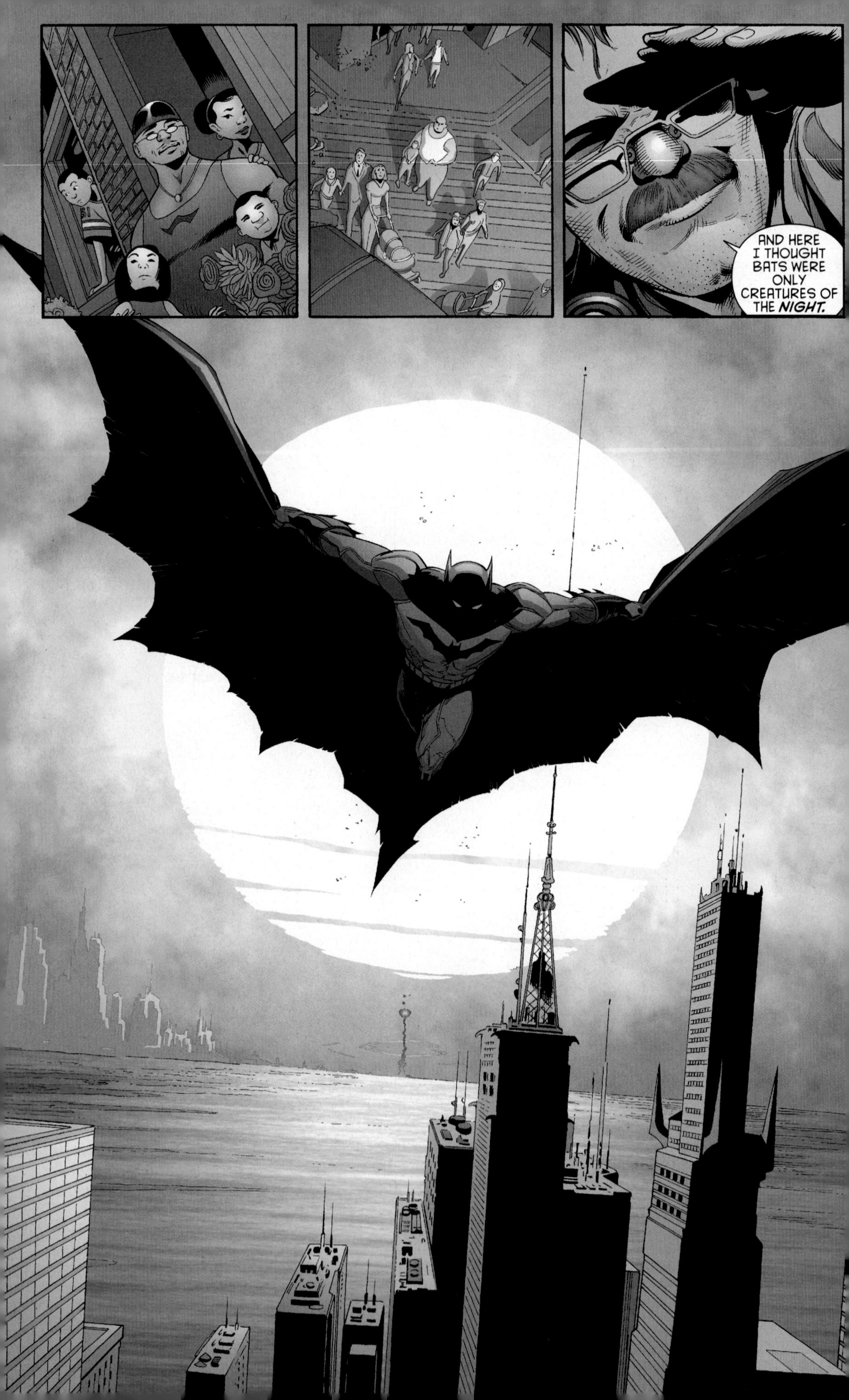
AND HERE I THOUGHT BATS WERE ONLY CREATURES OF THE *NIGHT.*

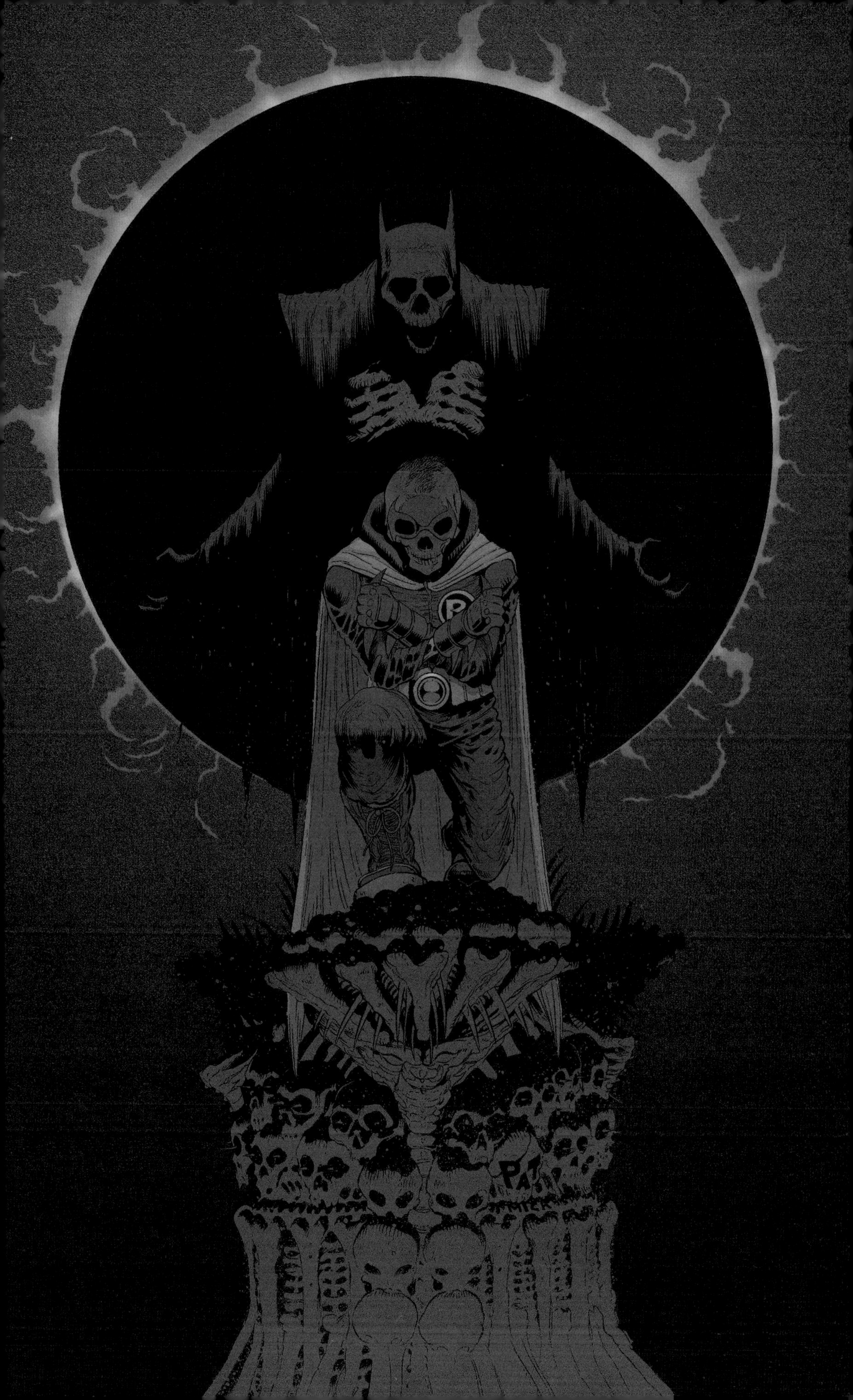

**PETER J. TOMASI** writer **PATRICK GLEASON** penciller, pages 1-15 **TOMAS GIORELLO** artist, pages 16-20 **MICK GRAY** inker, pages 1-15
cover by **GLEASON, GRAY & KALISZ**

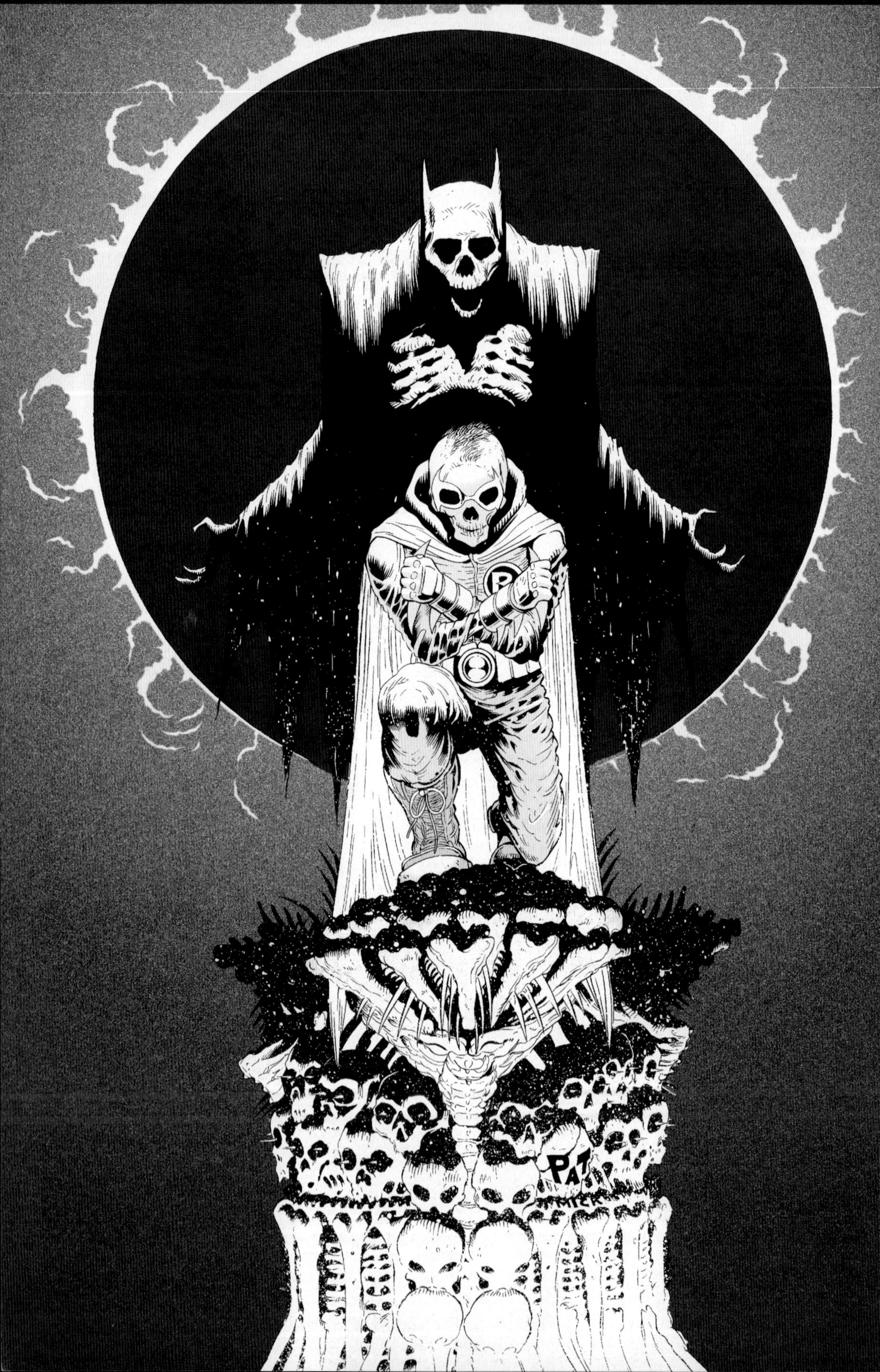
PAT
MICK

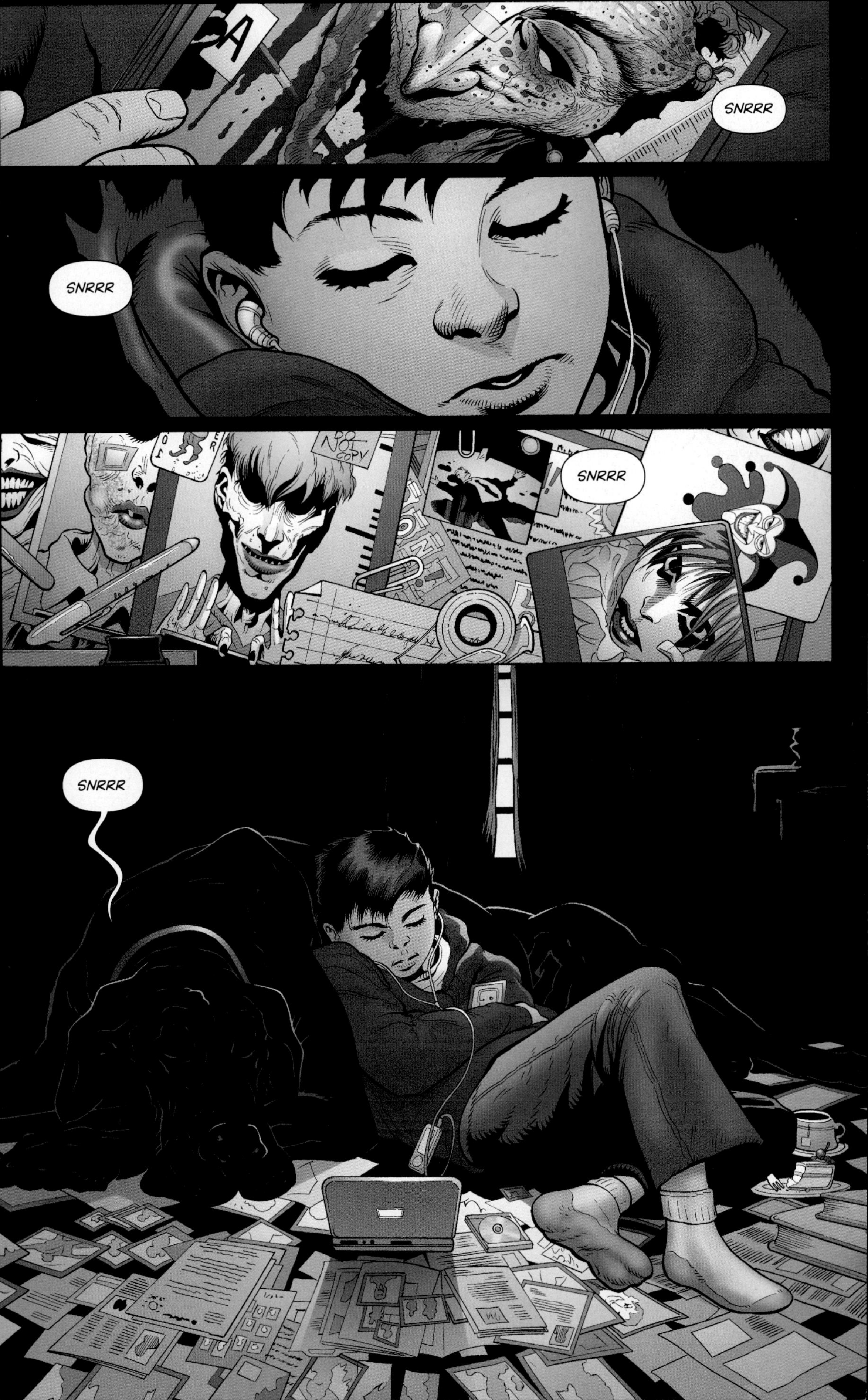
SNRRR
SNRRR
SNRRR
SNRRR

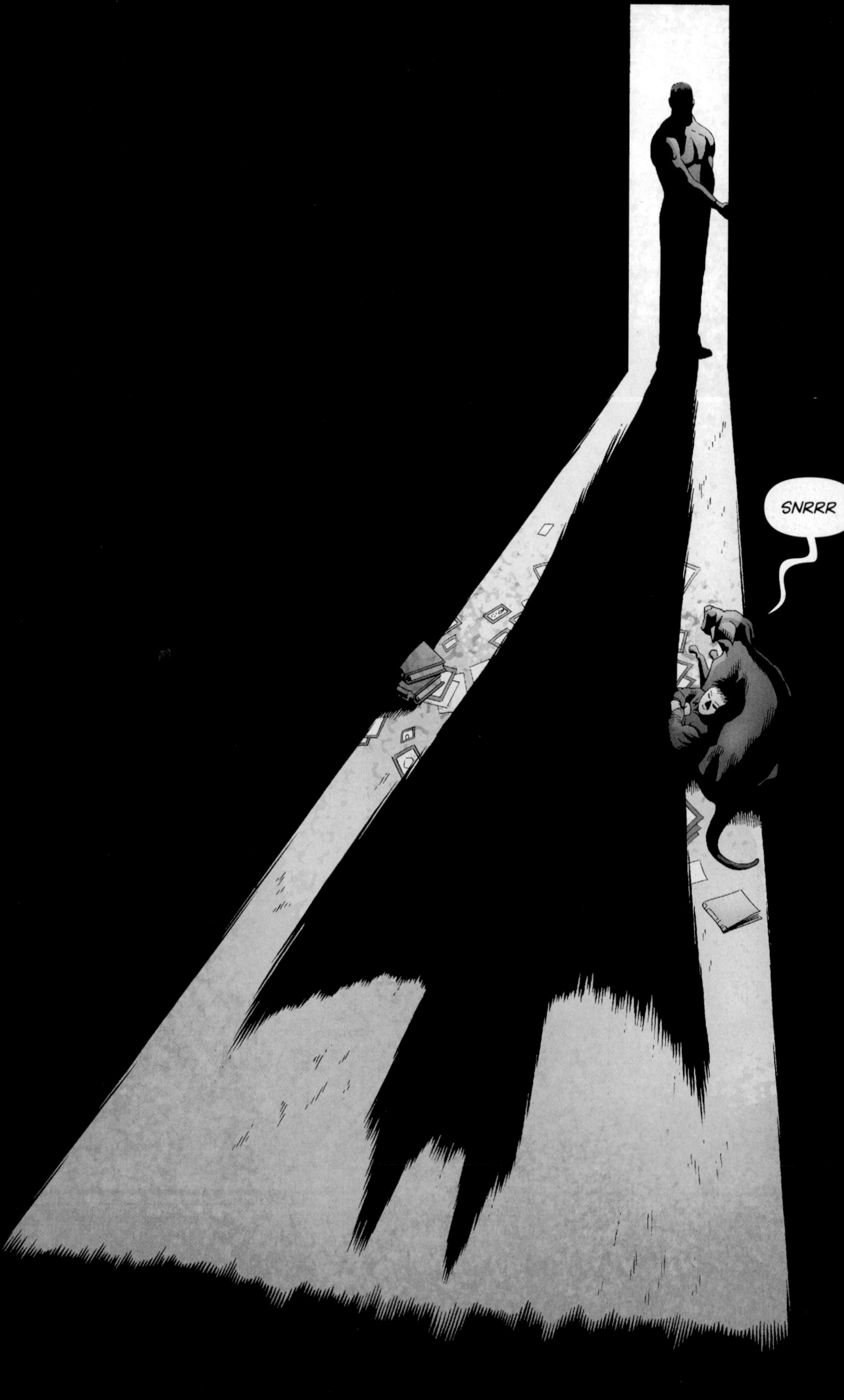
SNRRR

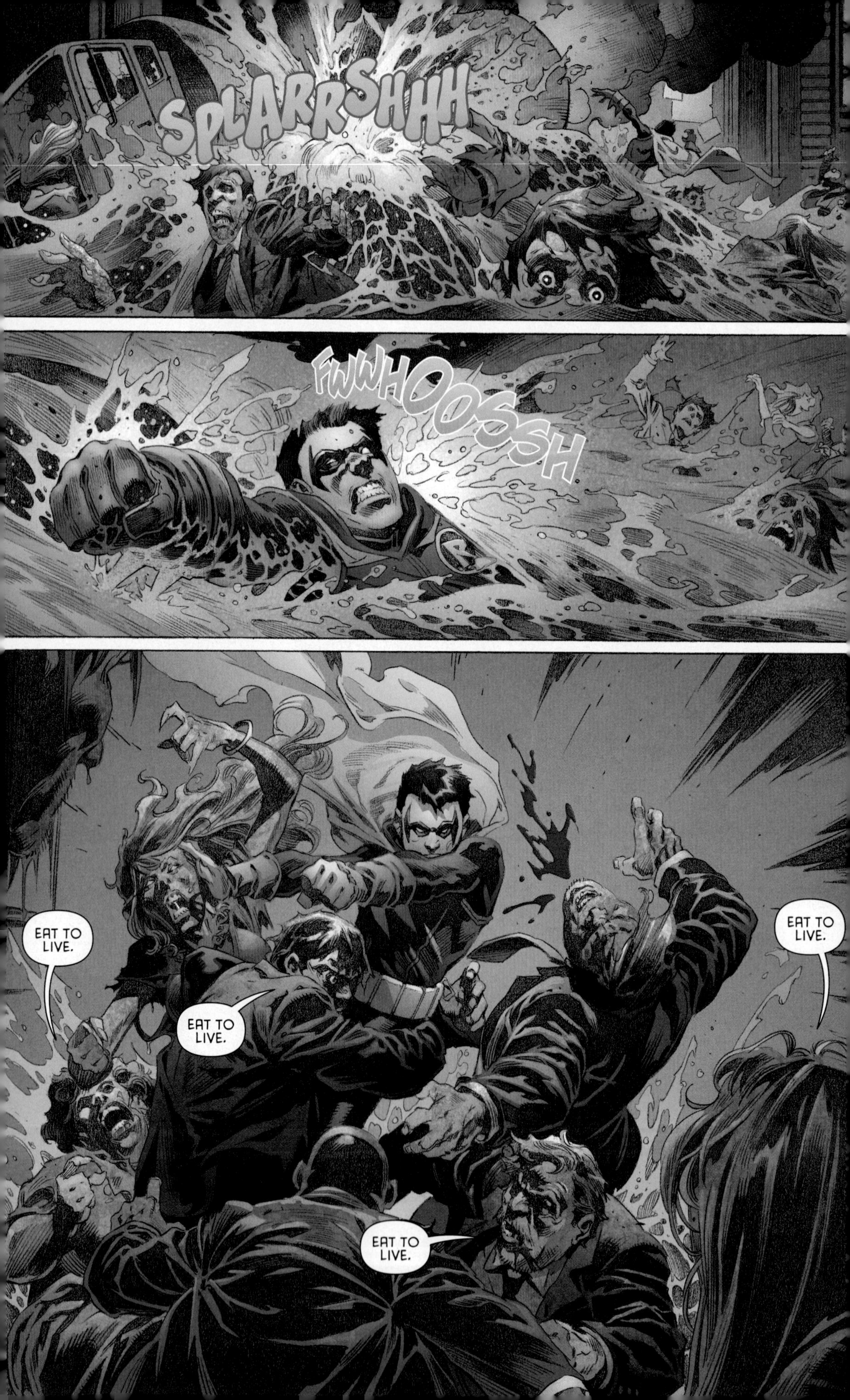
SPLARRSHHH
FWWHOOSSSH
EAT TO LIVE.
EAT TO LIVE.
EAT TO LIVE.
EAT TO LIVE.

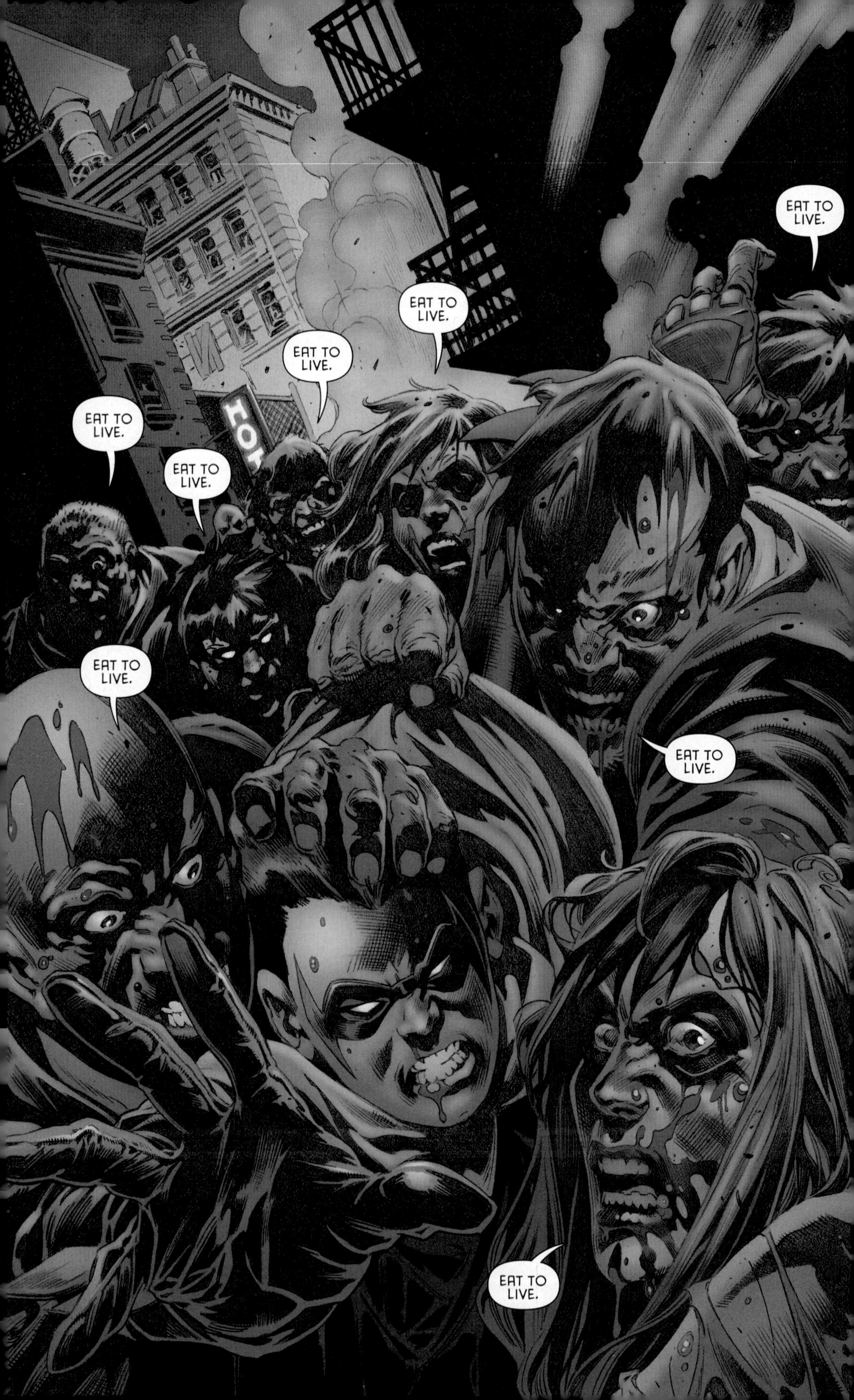
EAT TO LIVE.
EAT TO LIVE.
EAT TO LIVE.
EAT TO LIVE.
EAT TO LIVE.
EAT TO LIVE.
EAT TO LIVE.
EAT TO LIVE.

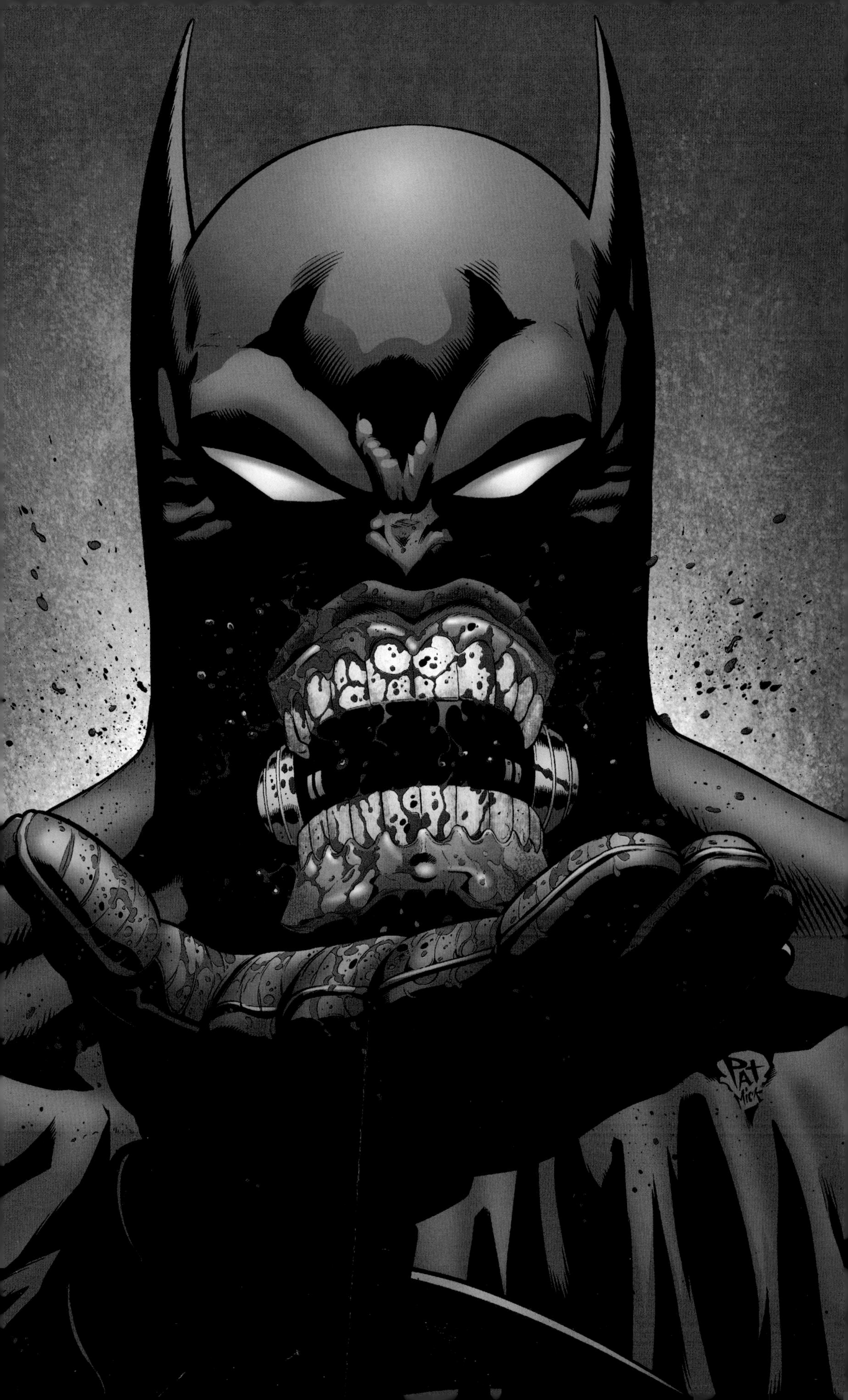
Pat
Mick

## DEVOURED

**PETER J. TOMASI** writer **PATRICK GLEASON & TOMAS GIORELLO** pencillers **MICK GRAY** inker
cover by **GLEASON, GRAY & KALISZ**

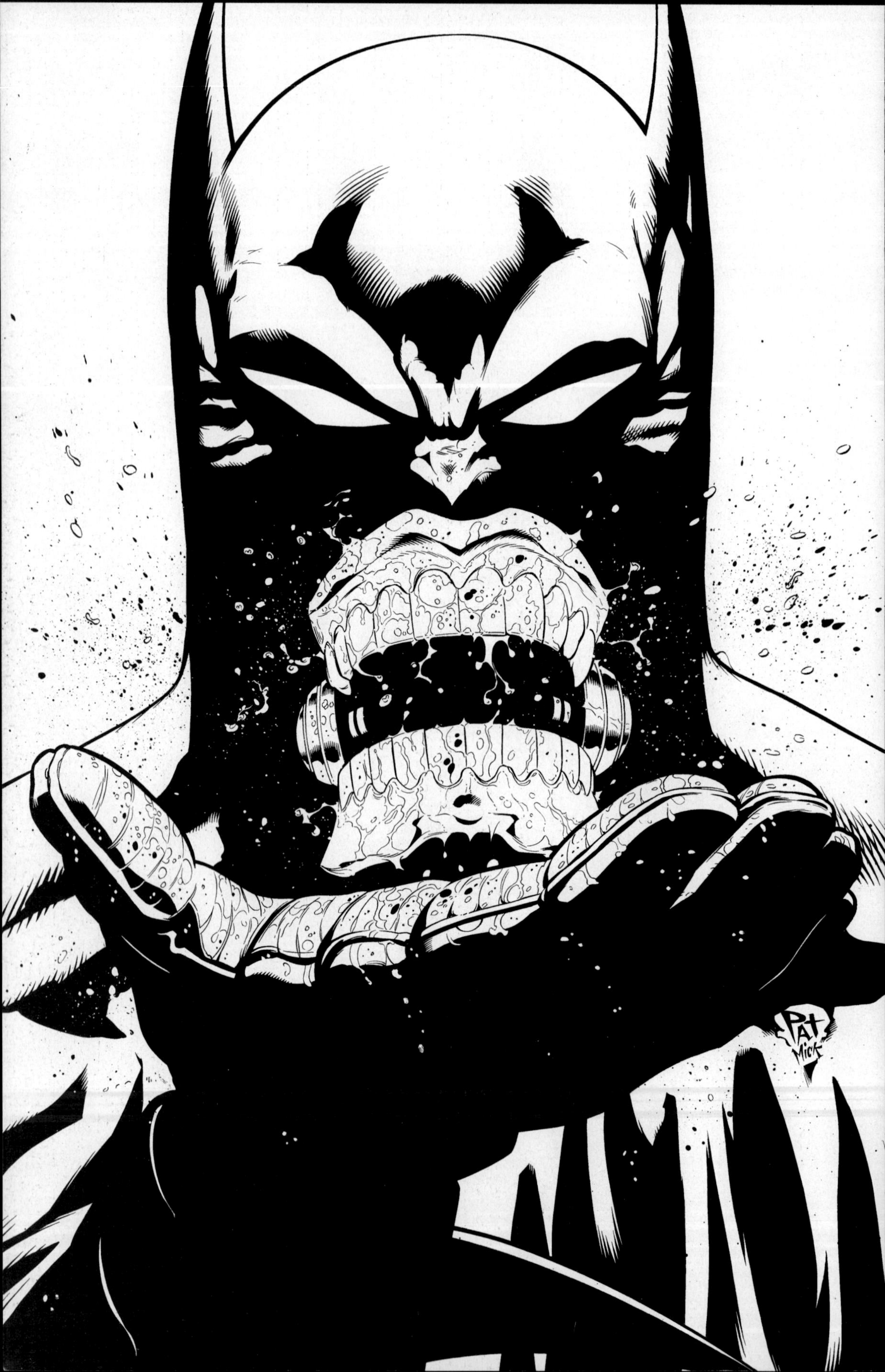
PAT
MICK

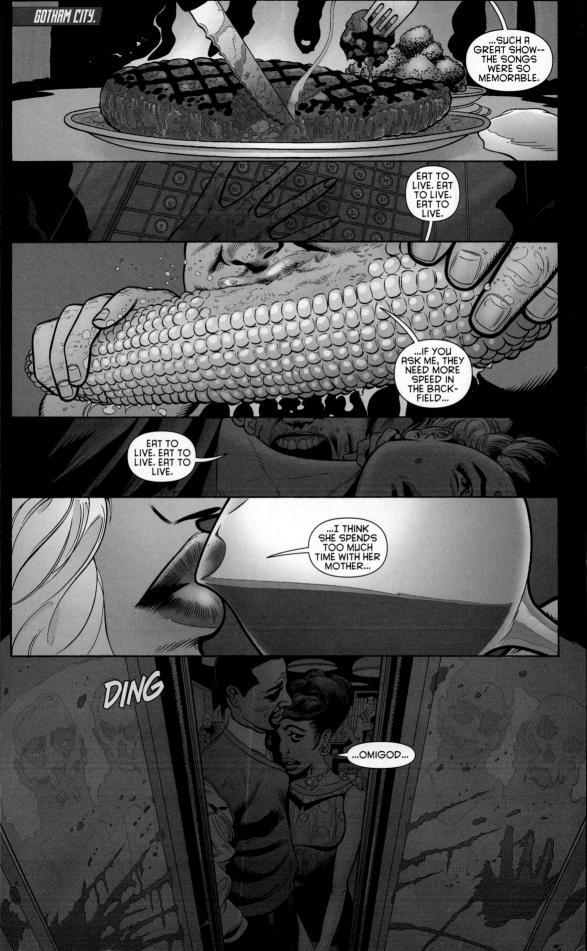

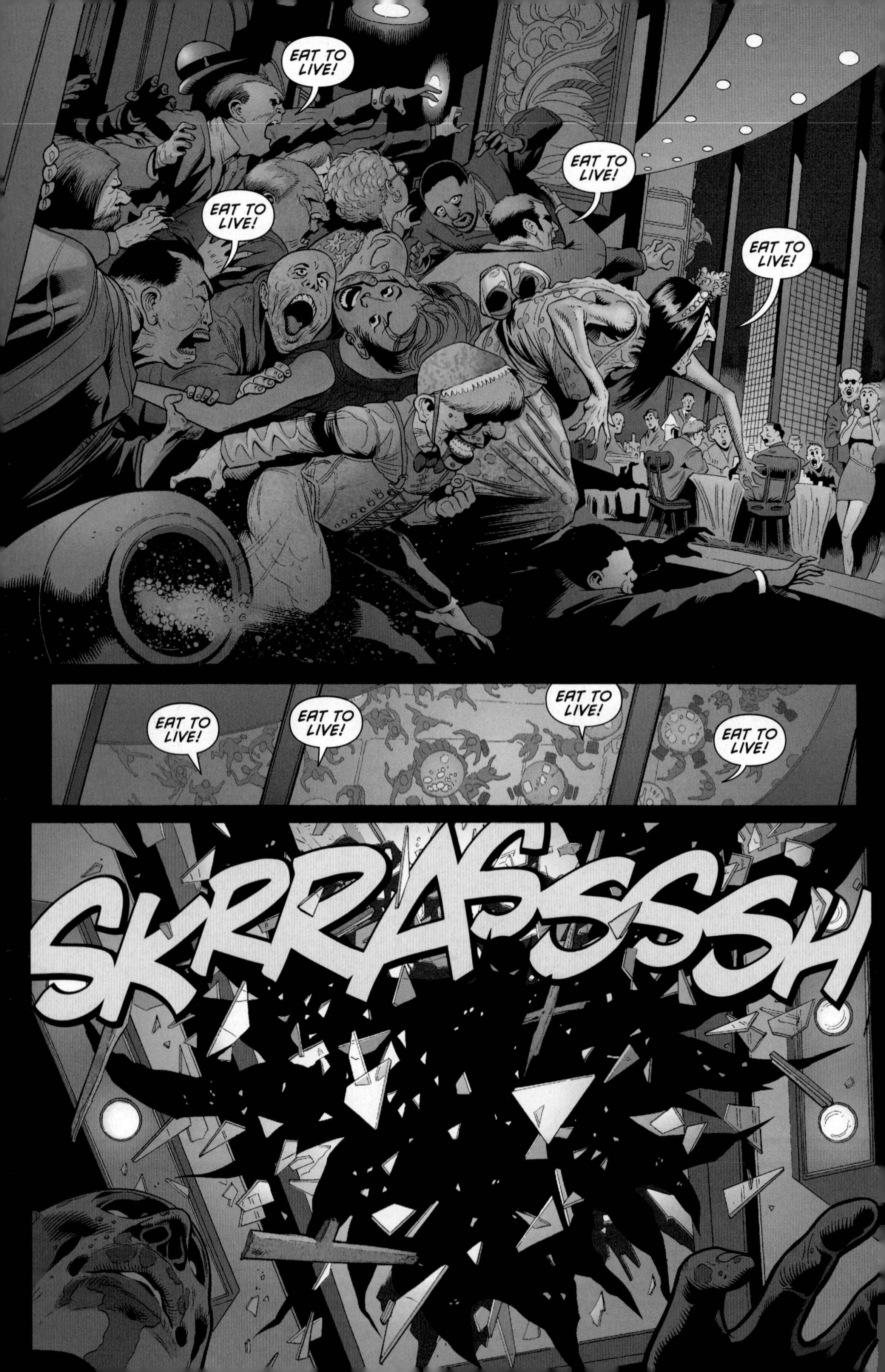
EAT TO LIVE!
EAT TO LIVE!
EAT TO LIVE!
EAT TO LIVE!
EAT TO LIVE!
EAT TO LIVE!
EAT TO LIVE!
EAT TO LIVE!
SKRRASSSSH

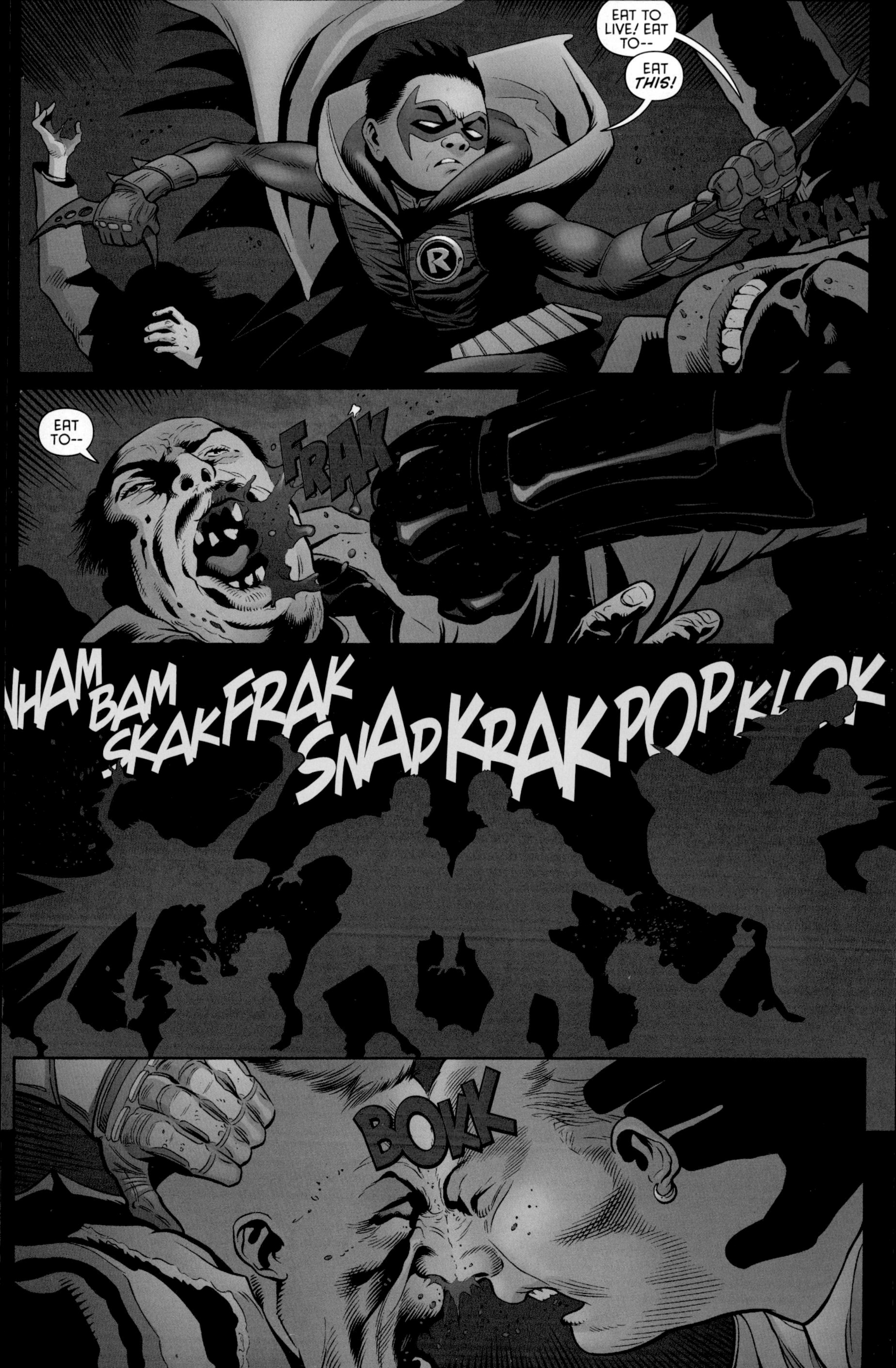
EAT TO LIVE! EAT TO--
EAT THIS!
SKRAK
EAT TO--
FRAK
BAM
SKAK
FRAK
SNAP
KRAK
POP
BOKK

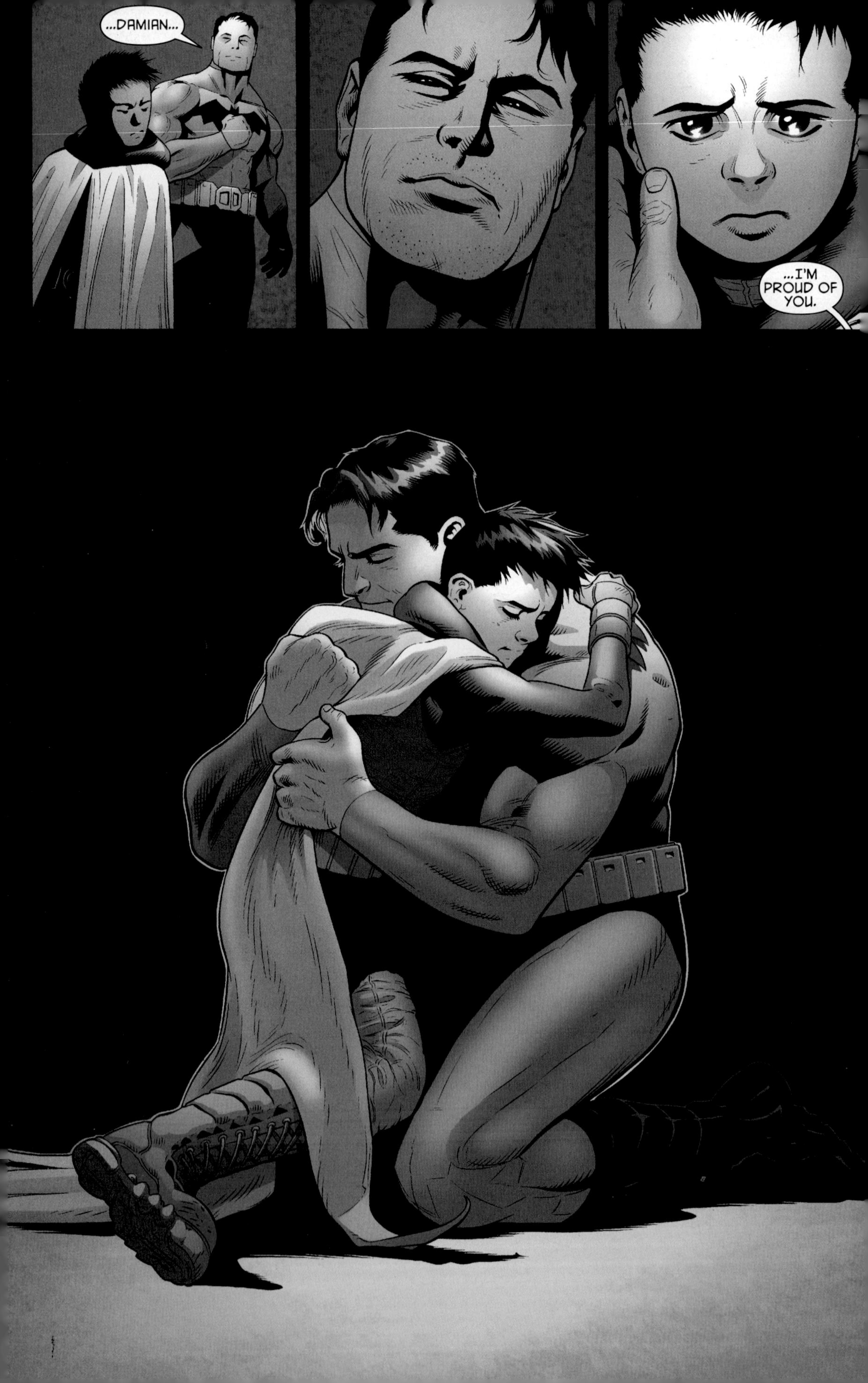
...DAMIAN...
...I'M PROUD OF YOU.

# BATMAN AND ROBIN ZERO

*PAGE 4*
panel 1
What we're seeing is DAMIAN'S 9 MONTH OLD INFANT FACE inside the artificial womb, its special seal now open at this moment, the amniotic fluid completely drained. You know how some kids have a lot of hair when they're born, well, that's Damian, a nice mop of black hair on his itty-bitty head.

**BANNER CAP:**   Before...

**BANNER CAP:**   Before...

**ELEC:**   Amniotic fluid draining...

**ELEC:**   Incubator womb unlocked.

**ELEC:**   Nine-month term cycle complete.

**ELEC:**   Infant weight six pounds, ten ounces.

panel 2
Cose on TALIA from just behind Damian as she reaches her hands towards him. Beautiful and exotic, we can't tell what she's feeling just yet about her child.

**TALIA:**   Come, my little one...

panel 3
Pull back so we see we're in the hi-tech lab on Talia's island. Check BATMAN 665 for ref, but I'd say you have a lot of latitude since it's the New 52. Make it your own. Angle on Talia, in her skintight jumpsuit, holding Damian as 2 NURSE-MAID ASSISTANTS trail her, ready to do what she needs at a moment's notice, including breast feeding. If you can add some background elements such as other small pods with other body parts being cloned in all different sizes and stages, from infant to adult. No full bodies.

**TALIA:**   ...show me you have the strength...

panel 4
Same day, as we see Talia having walked through double doors that are still swinging, into a small pool area where she is taking the first step down into the water with Damian in her arms while her Nurse-maidens are taking positions at the edge of the pool. Also, the pool isn't for fun, there's no aesthetic sensibility to its construction. It's simple and utilitarian. Also a note, whenever you want, have League of Assassin dudes stationed around the place, standing like Buckingham Palace guards ready for anything.

**TALIA:**   ...and willpower...

*PAGE 5*

panel 1
I'm seeing a riff of the famous NIRVANA ALBUM cover here, only Damian is the infant
doing the swimming/floating and of course there's no money in the crystal clear water. Match
the angle and positioning of the baby on the album cover, but tweak it a bit so we don't get
nonsense from Legal. Also, as mentioned earlier, Damian has a bit more hair than the average
infant and it's jet black too. Google Water Babies for great ref.

**TALIA:**    ...to do what is necessary.

panel 2
Angle on Talia, still not showing any emotion yet, holding her hands out towards Damian
paddling away, as one of the Nursemaids standing at the pool's edge, seems a bit worried by
the baby's exertion in the water. The other Nursemaid looks nervous, giving one of those
sidelong glances that say "are you crazy, keep your yap shut".

**TALIA:**   Let me see the steel in your eyes.

**MAID 1:**   Miss Talia, you're placing the baby at great risk with this nonsense.

panel 3
Angle on Talia as she suddenly whips a small blade from her hand without even looking at
the Nursemaid. Have a speed trail right to the Nursemaid, whose head is tilted back and now
holding the knife buried in her throat.

**TALIA:**   Never tell a mother how to raise her child.

**SFX:**    shunk

panel 4
Angle on Damian paddling away on top of the now lightly reddish water, passing the Nurse-
maid lying dead at the edge of the pool, her lifeless eyes wide, almost as if they're staring at
him, blood from her neck running into the water. A literal 'Death's Head' already present in his
first moments of life.

**TALIA:**   Bring me another Nursemaid. He will need another breast to suckle.

panel 5
Angle on Talia as she lifts Damian under both arms from the light reddish water as it runs off
his infant body. A subtle baptism of blood (well, maybe it's not that subtle, but what the hell).
Also, we see for the first time the love and joy in Talia's features as she's accepted and
connected to her child.

**TALIA:**   Welcome to our world, Damian.

PAGE 6
panel 1
Another day. Angle on Damian, now a 3-year-old, and Talia, as they practice with wooden swords on the balcony. She's dressed in another of her skin tight jumpsuits while Damian has a little karate uniform on and is wielding a size-appropriate wooden sword.

**DAMIAN:**  Mama, tell me another story about Alexander the Great.

**TALIA:**  Of course, my son.

**TALIA:**  Once there was a horse called Buccephalas...a wild black stallion that was given to Alexander's father, King Philip, as a gift that no one dared ride, and one day —

**SFX:**  klak

panel 2
Angle close on Damian as he suddenly lowers his sword and stares at Talia as she taps the bottom of his sword to prompt him back into action. Remember, even at 3 years old, Damian is a precocious child.

**DAMIAN:**  Who is my father, Mama?

**TALIA:**  A man that lives very far away — now keep your sword up — what have I said about lowering your defenses?

**DAMIAN:**  How come you never tell me stories about him or show me pictures?

panel 3
Angle as mother and son continue sparring.

**TALIA:**  Because I choose not to at this time, my darling boy.

**DAMIAN:**  Is he a king too?

**TALIA:**  I suppose in a way he is.

panel 4
Angle close on Damian and Talia sparring. The purity of his curiosity obvious.

**DAMIAN:**  Can I meet him?

**TALIA:**  When you earn the right to, yes.

**DAMIAN:**  How?

*PAGE 7*
panel 1
Angle as Talia simply knocks Damian's wooden sword from his hand.

**TALIA:** By not losing your focus! No easy wins in life, Damian. Everything worth having is hard fought.

**TALIA:** Today's your birthday my love, and when you best me in a duel on your special day, that is when you will be ready to meet your father.

**TALIA:** Then — and only then — will I tell you his —

panel 2
A HOLO of NETZ is on a hi-tech console. Talia and Damian lower their swords.

**ELEC:** Miss Talia, as you requested, I have Otto Netz on a satellite link.

**TALIA:** Is it a secure line?

**ELEC:** Yes.

panel 3
Damian sees his mother talk to the HOLO of Netz. Between Damian and Talia is her bed and we can see a small ornate trunk at the foot of it.

**TALIA:** ...I grow weary of excuses, Netz. Make sure the Meta-Bomb program stays on schedule.

**ELEC:** I endeavor to make your dreams a reality.

**TALIA:** As well you should...

**TALIA:** ...but any further disruptions and you will find yourself expendable. Understood?

panel 4
Damian opens an ornate trunk at the foot of Talia's bed. He's placed his sword on her bed.

**NETZ:** You have my word there will be no further complications.

panel 5
Damian sees mementos of Talia's night spent with Bruce years ago: 2 champagne glasses, an empty bottle of Dom Perignon, and Batman's cowl poking out from underneath it all.

**TALIA(off):** I'll have more than your word, Netz, I'll have your head.

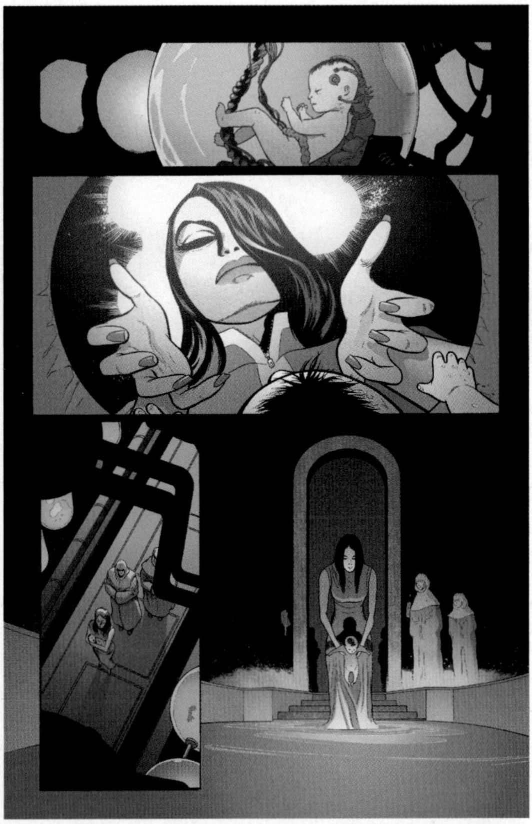
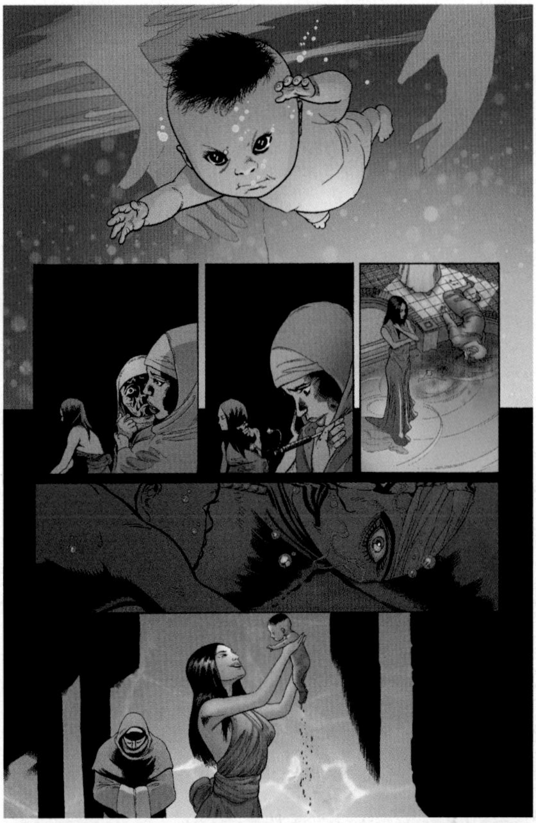
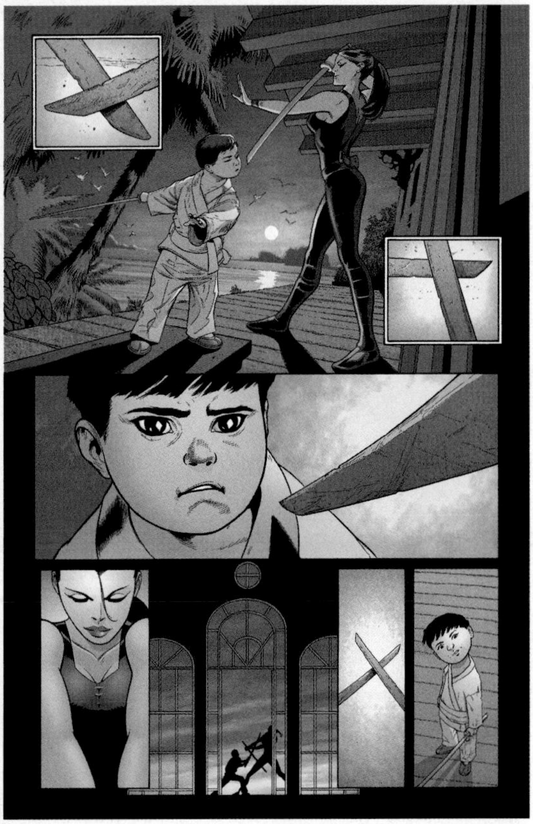
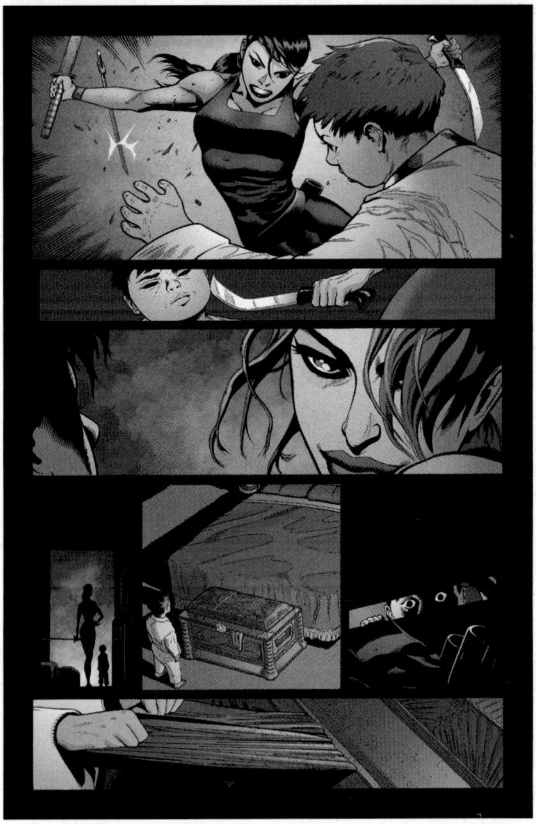

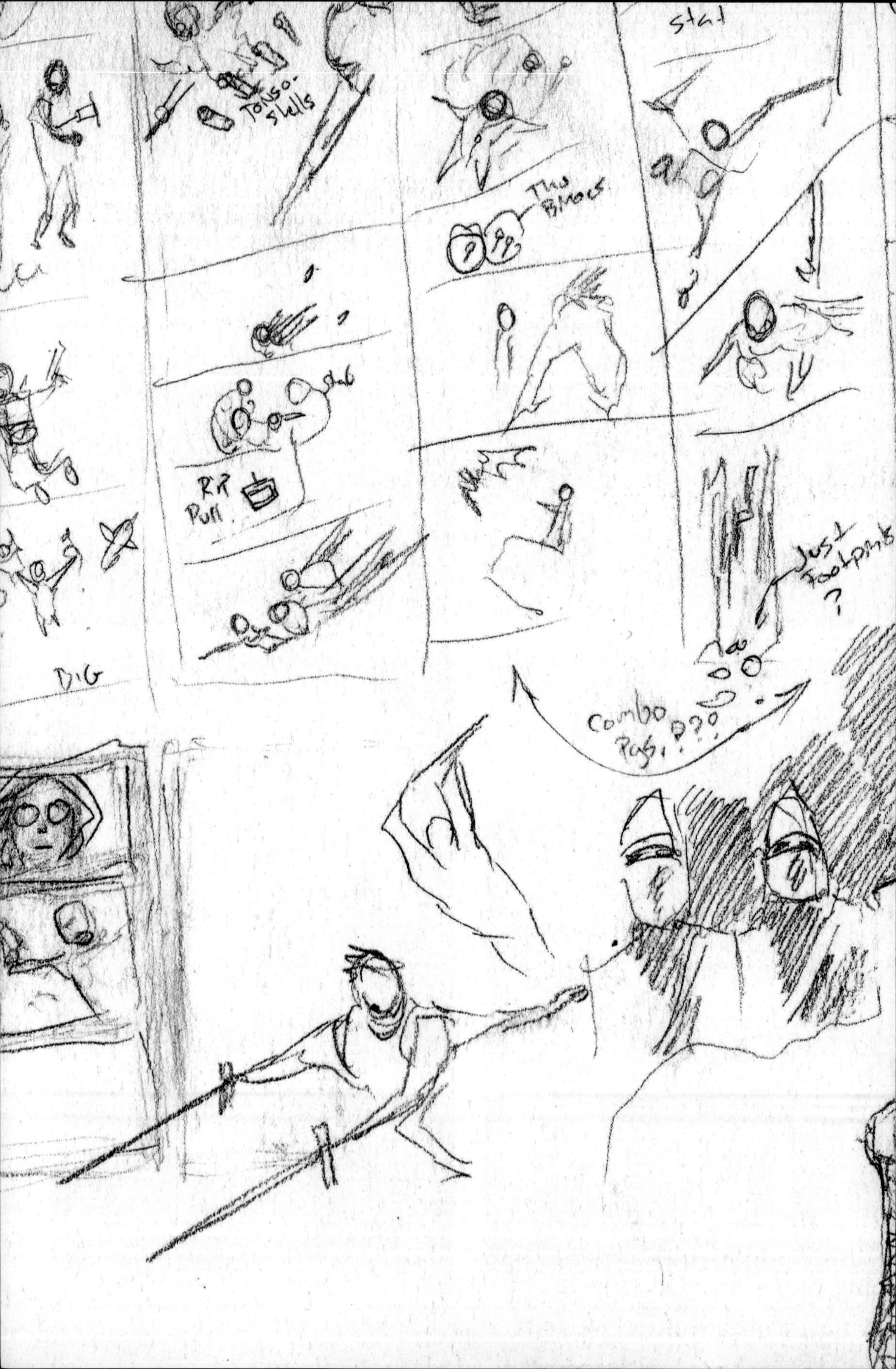
Torso-shells
RR Pull
DiG
Just footprint ?
Combo Pgs. ???

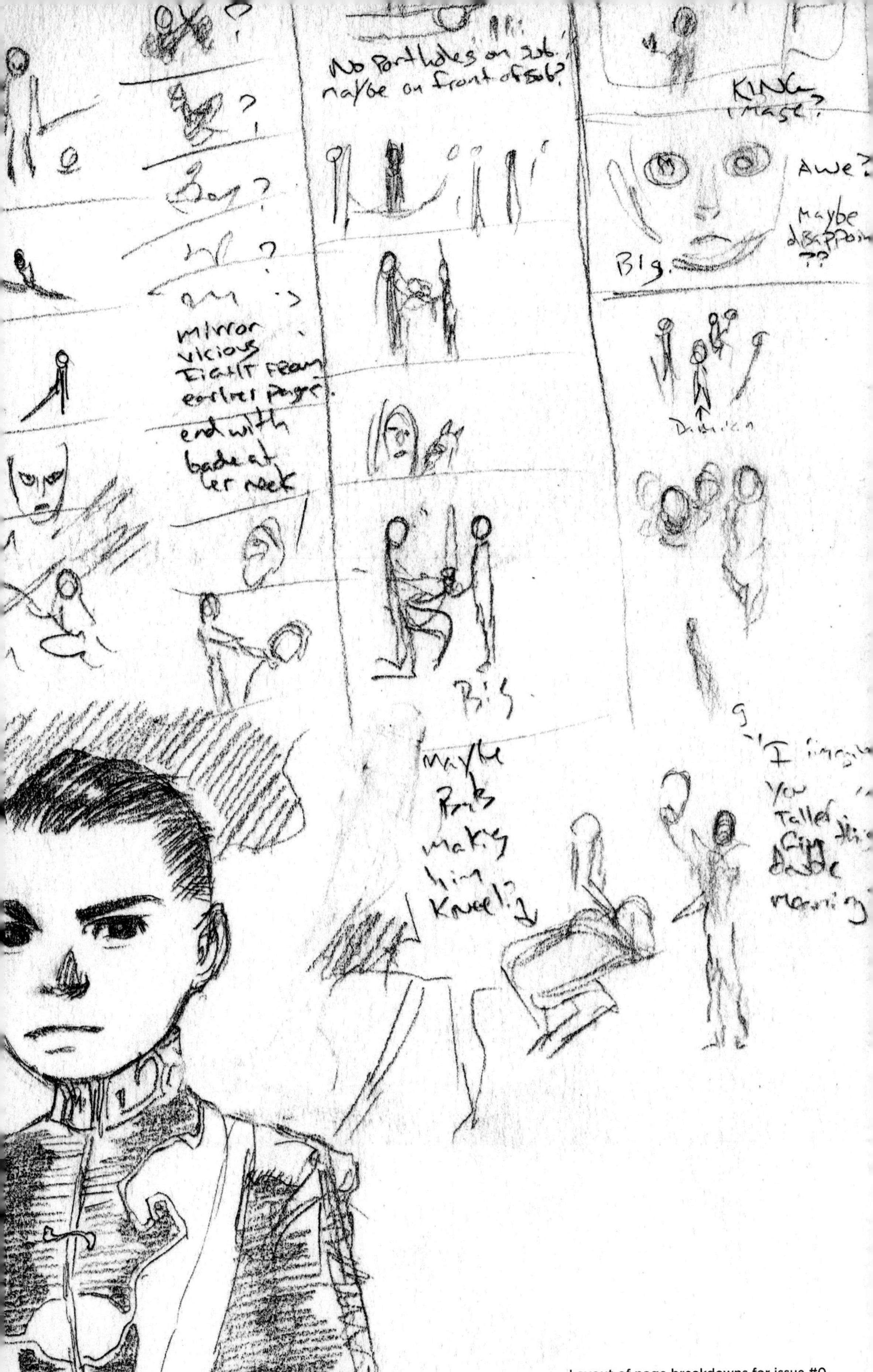


Layout of page breakdowns for issue #0

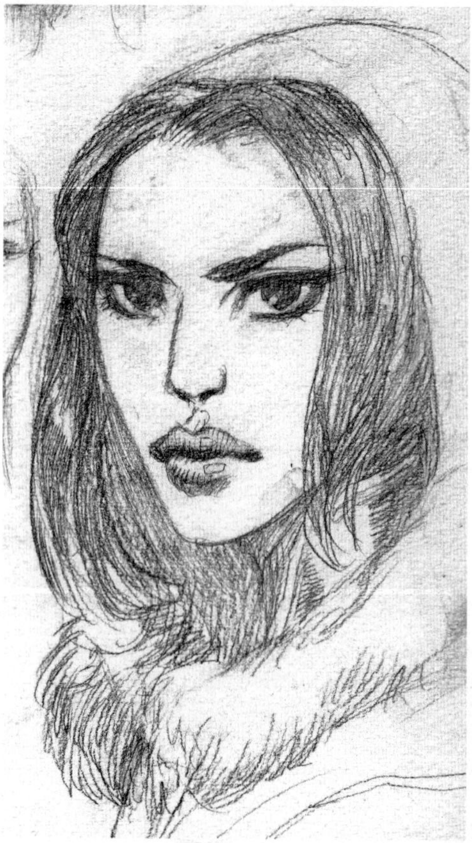

Character studies of Talia and Damian

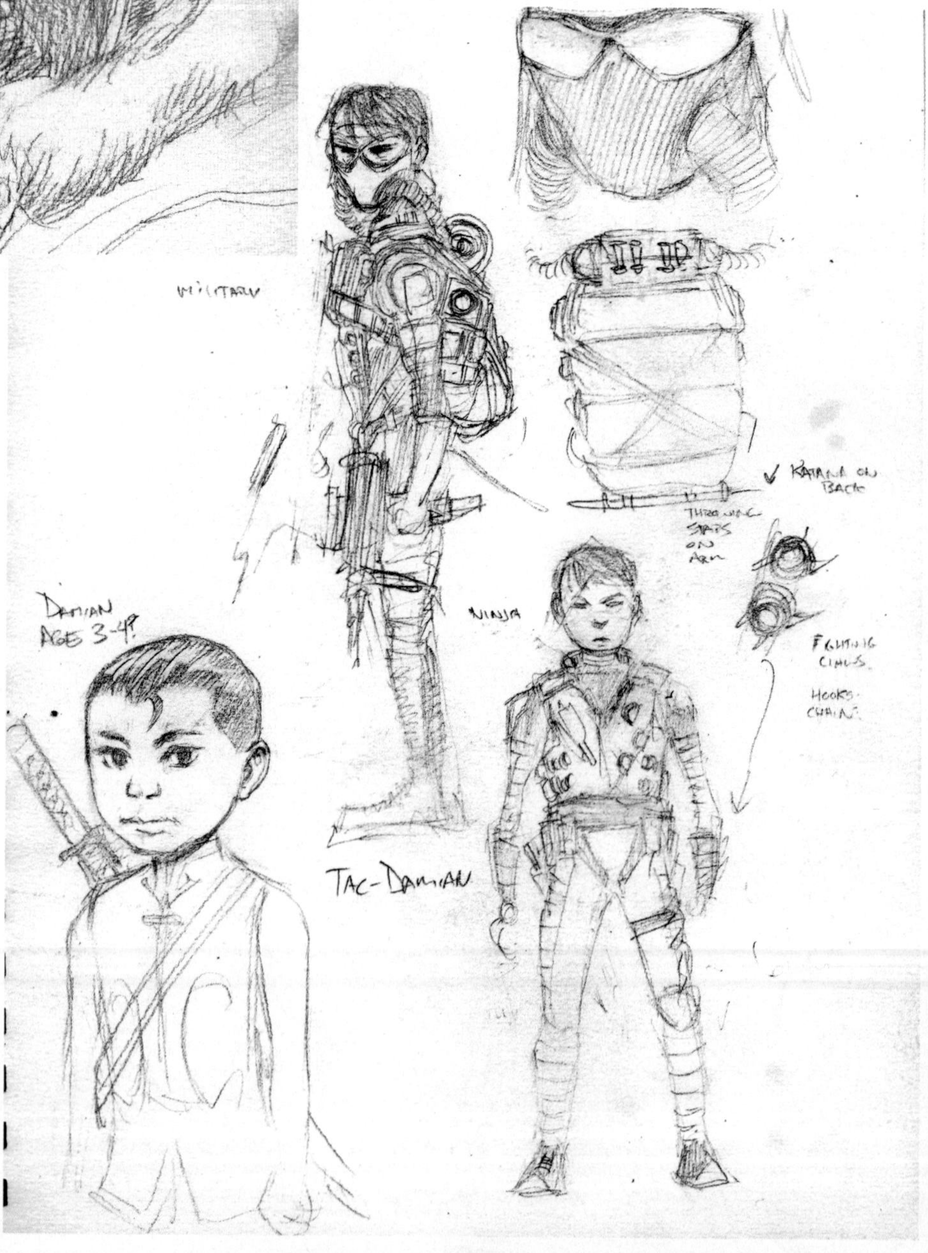
MILITARY
KATANA ON BACK
NINJA
DAMIAN AGE 3-4?
TAC-DAMIAN

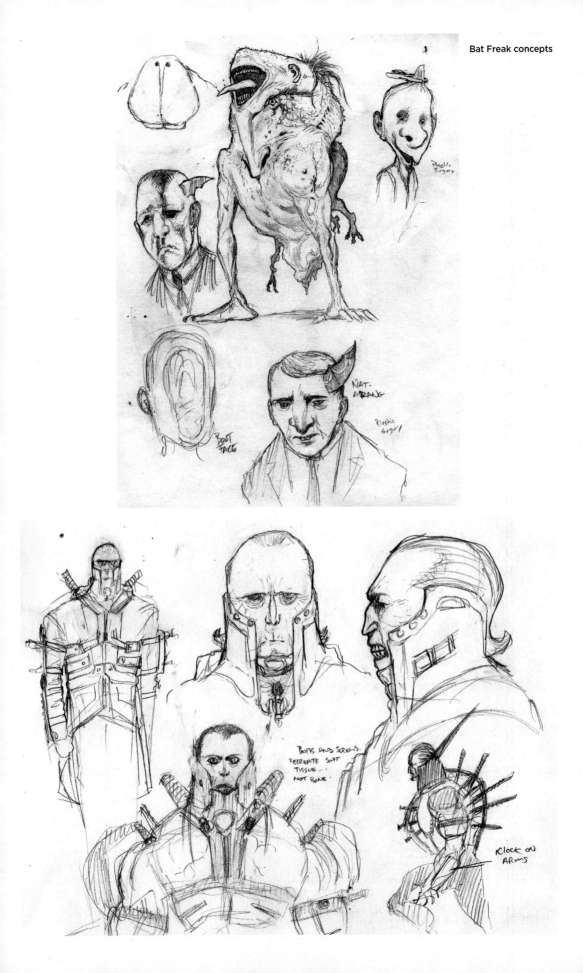

BAT-FREAKS; ALL BUT SMUSH WILL WEAR BACKPACK, THE BRANDING GUNS AND WHATEVER

BAT HEAD

WEARS HAT TO COVER HIS HEAD.

BOOT FACE —

JASON STATHAM + DOUG MAHNKE'S LOVE CHILD.

BLACK LEATHER JACKET, WITH ORANGE FLAME DETAILING UP SLEAVE.

SMU
WILL M
A BIG, DA
"QUASIMO
ARMS W
COME OF
BACK. HIS
A MAGG
HE CAN
REAR J

TY SLINGS.
AN BE WORN ON THESE.

Tura Piccol

DC WILDSTORM
PENCILLER
TITLE
INKER
PAGE#
ISSUE #
MONTH
INTERIORS

SCALLOP.

PRETTY GIRL
MARRED BY PIERCINGS.
SHE HAS AN INTENSE,
CRAZY LOOK IN HER EYES
TATOO'S UP HER ARMS
AS WELL.

HANG MAN.

WAS LEFT FOR THE COPS
HANGING UPSIDE DOWN
BY BATMAN. ONLY, THEY
NEVER SHOWED UP. HE
SURVIVED FOR WEEKS
BY DRINKING FROM A
NEARBY DRAIN + EATING
AN OCCASIONAL RAT.

BE WEARING
LOAK LIKE
UERS BODY AND
FIGHTS IT WILL
NG DOWN HIS
ARE FUSED INTO
TAIL, WHICH
HER AROUND OR
IGHT LIKE A MONSTER

HIS SKIN GREW OVER THE WIR
AND NOW IS PERMINENTLY EMBED

Pencils from issue #0

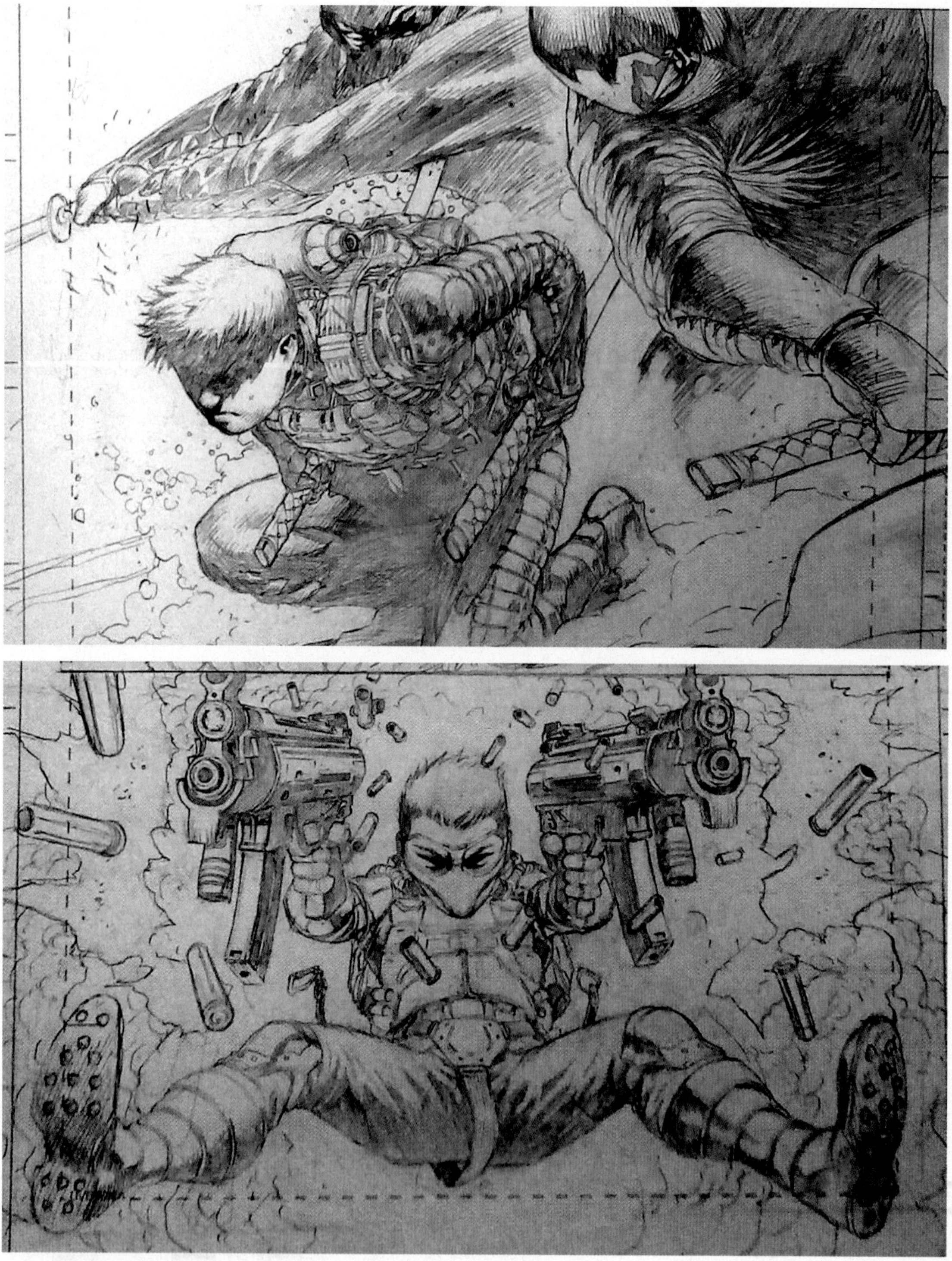

Pencils and inks from issue #12

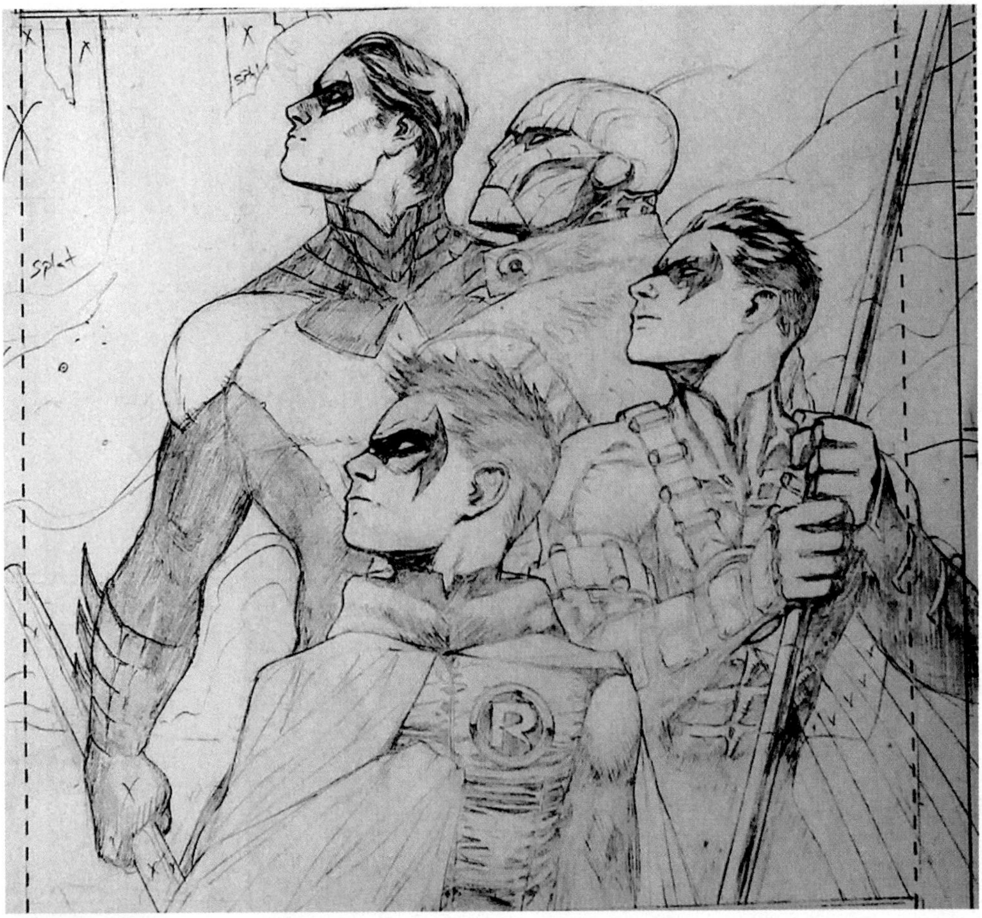

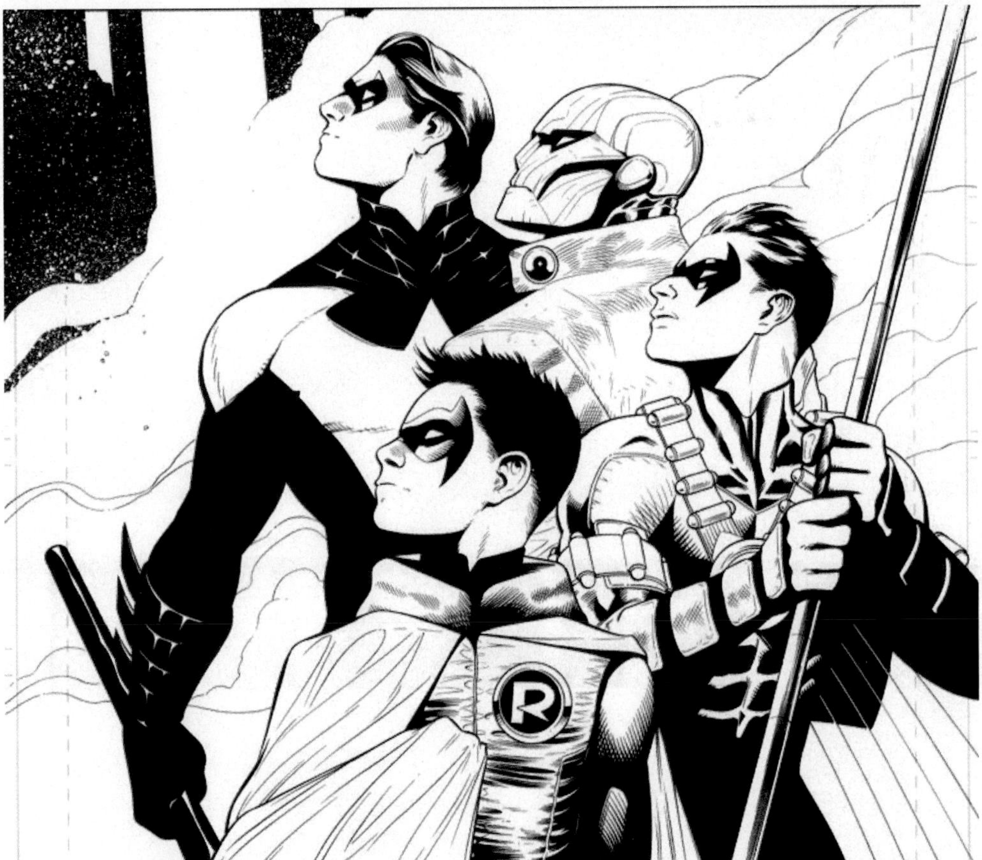

Pencils from issue #13

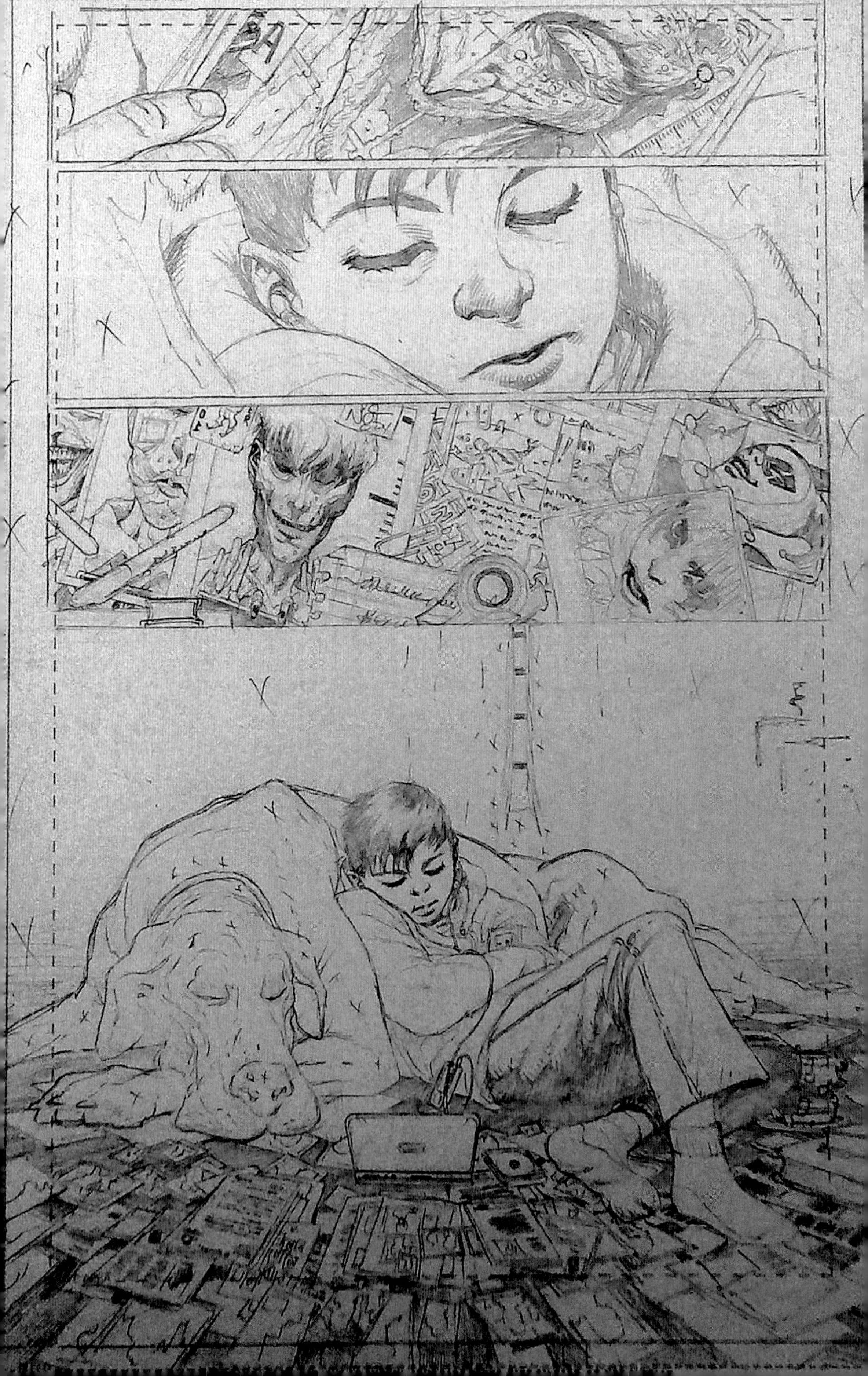

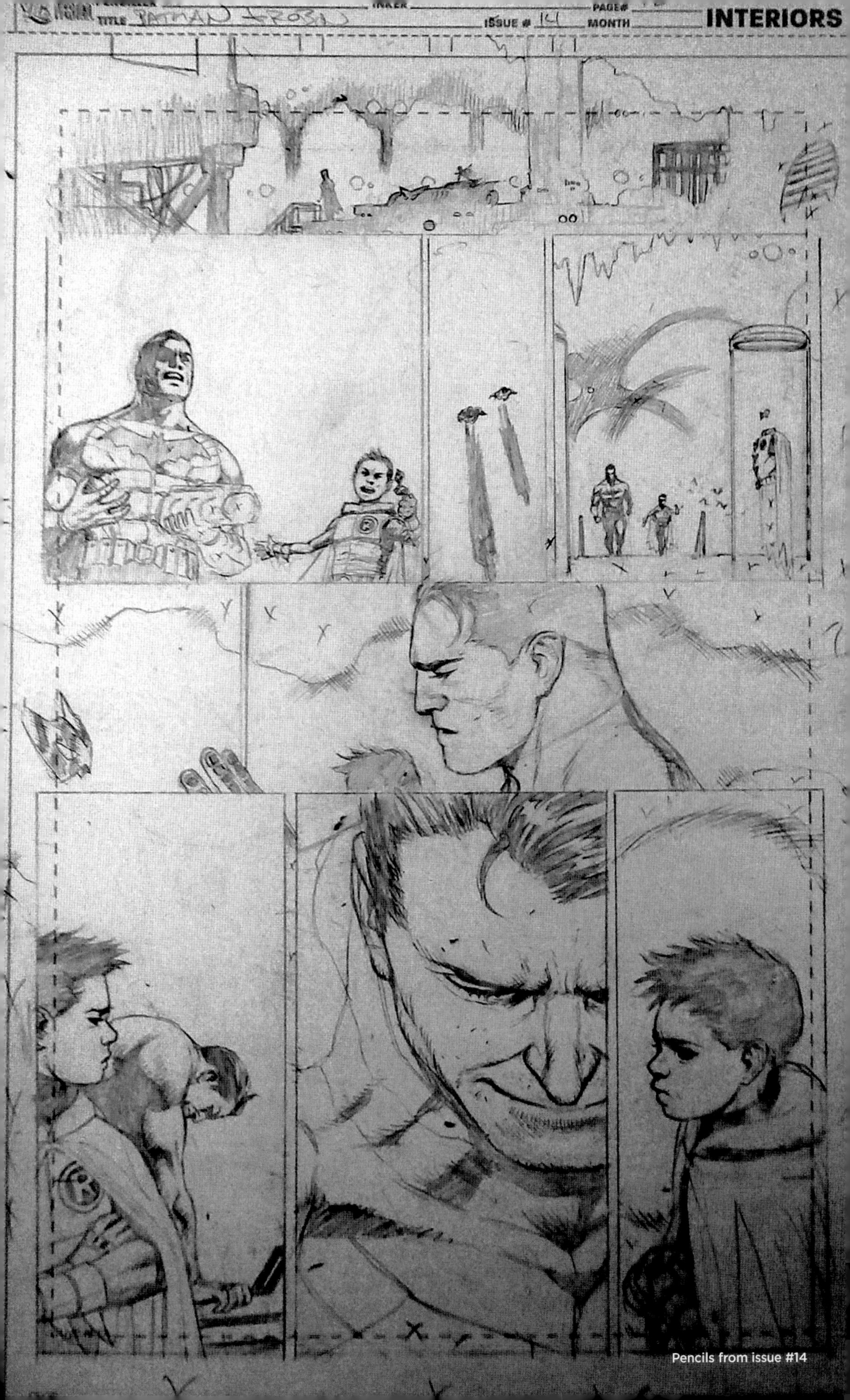
TITLE
ISSUE # 14
PAGE#
MONTH

Pencils from issue #14

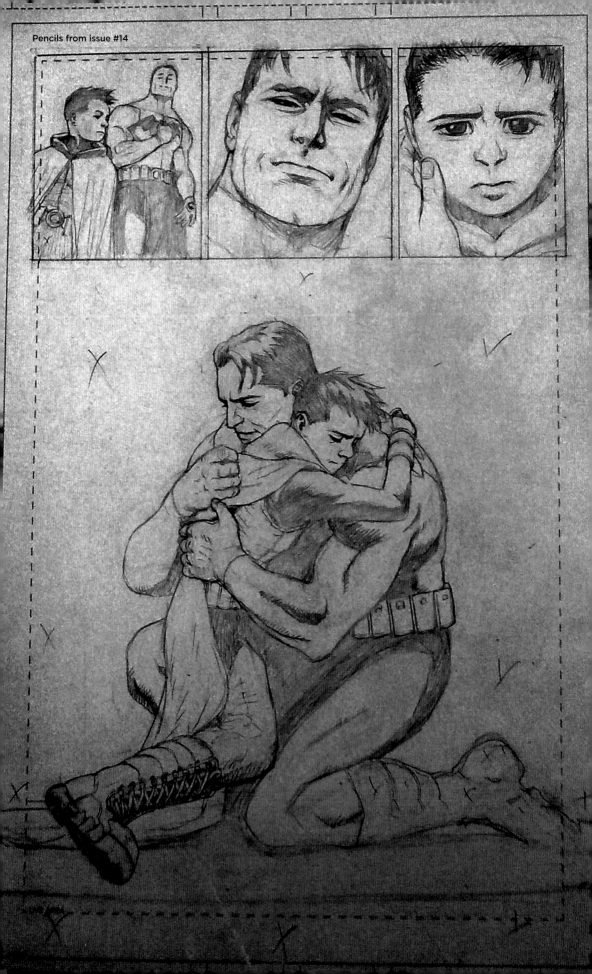

Pencils from issue #14

Pencils from issue #13

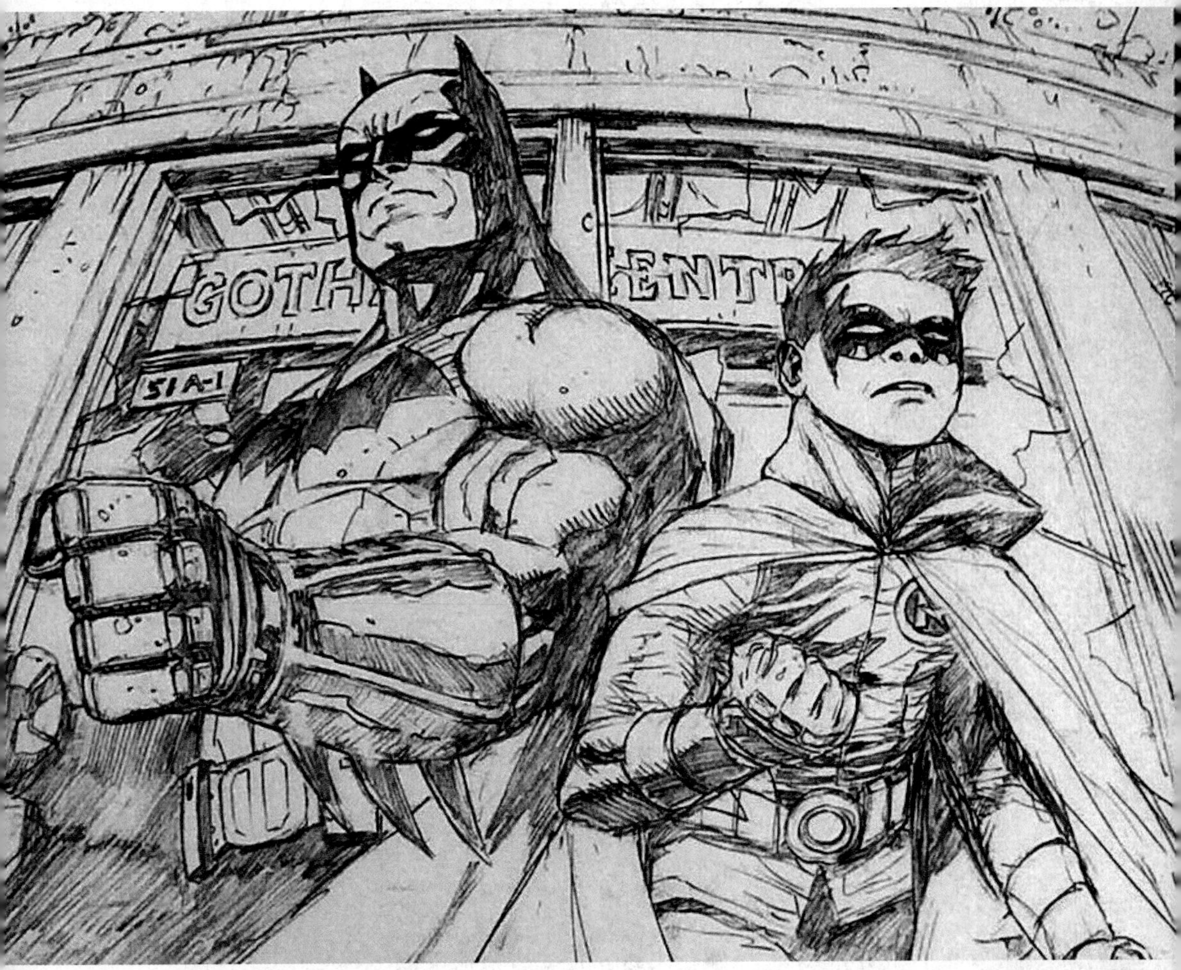

GOTH
ENTR
51A-1

# GRANT MORRISON

## BATMAN & ROBIN VOL. 1: BATMAN REBORN with FRANK QUITELY & PHILIP TAN

VOL. 2:
BATMAN VS. ROBIN

VOL. 3: BATMAN &
ROBIN MUST DIE!

DARK KNIGHT VS.
WHITE KNIGHT